Praise for *Sharkey*

"Nothing says 'vaudeville' so much as a trained seal act. If the reason why is not self-evident to you, Gary Bohan's incisive new book will put you right, for it's not just a biography of showbiz's most famous sea lion, but a portrait of an entire family of successful animal trainers, the Hulings, and their delightful doings over the decades, from the days of tented circuses and vaudeville, to the time of *The Ed Sullivan Show*. While everyone from Milton Berle to Kitty Carlisle cherished memories of appearing on bills with Sharkey, Bohan's portrait of the old-school business universe overall and the place of animal acts within it, is the real attraction here. A valuable look at a neglected lane in entertainment history."

— Trav S.D., author of *No Applause—Just Throw Money: The Book That Made Vaudeville Famous*

"Vaudeville—a lost world—where animals performed on equal terms with humans, none more so than the intelligent seals Charlie and Sharkey. Their remarkable stories, and those of their ingenious human trainers, bookend the peak and decline of vaudeville. Along the way they encounter numerous celebrities and dramatic events around the world."

— Bill Egan, author of *Florence Mills: Harlem Jazz Queen*

"What an absolute joy to read this book! With Gary Bohan's words, I felt like I was transported to the 1940s and '50s with a front row seat to the sensational Sharkey! The story about Sharkey in the Harvard dorm room had me rolling! Through the years, one thing has clearly remained unchanged; the ability of sea lions to capture the hearts of trainers and audiences."

— Jennifer Rant, longtime professional senior sea lion trainer

"A beautifully written and impeccably researched tale of a bygone era when a fantastically trained seal—with his own unique sense of humor—traveled the country, stole the show on Broadway, appeared in movies and on television, and grabbed worldwide headlines. Bohan's book takes you on a journey through twentieth century history as a performing seal and his pals and dedicated trainers negotiate the Depression, two World Wars, new forms of entertainment, and changing fads, all the while capturing the hearts of those who witnessed them in action."

— Karen Berelowitz, Producer and Studio Manager at Blauweiss Media and coauthor of *The Story of Historic Kingston: Featuring 950 Images and Connections to the Catskills & New York City*

Sharkey

Sharkey

WHEN SEA LIONS WERE STARS OF SHOW BUSINESS
(1907–1958)

Gary Bohan Jr.

excelsior editions

AN IMPRINT OF STATE UNIVERSITY OF NEW YORK PRESS

Cover photo of Sharkey used with permission from the Embassy Theatre Foundation.

Published by State University of New York Press, Albany

© 2022 Gary Bohan Jr.

All rights reserved

Printed in the United States of America

No part of this book may be used or reproduced in any manner whatsoever without written permission. No part of this book may be stored in a retrieval system or transmitted in any form or by any means including electronic, electrostatic, magnetic tape, mechanical, photocopying, recording, or otherwise without the prior permission in writing of the publisher.

Excelsior Editions is an imprint of State University of New York Press

For information, contact State University of New York Press, Albany, NY
www.sunypress.edu

Library of Congress Cataloging-in-Publication Data

Name: Bohan, Gary, Jr., author.
Title: Sharkey : when sea lions were stars of show business (1907–1958) / Gary Bohan Jr.
Description: Albany : Excelsior Editions, 2022. | Includes bibliographical references and index.
Identifiers: LCCN 2021023968 | ISBN 9781438487120 (pbk. : alk. paper) | ISBN 9781438487137 (ebook)
Subjects: LCSH: Sharkey (Sea lion) | Huling, Mark, 1883–1951. | Sea lions—Training—United States—History—20th century. | Animals in the performing arts—United States—History—20th century. | Human-animal relationships in the performing arts—United States—History—20th century.
Classification: LCC GV1831.S4 B65 2022 | DDC 791.80973—dc23
LC record available at https://lccn.loc.gov/2021023968

10 9 8 7 6 5 4 3 2 1

In memory of my brother Darren

Contents

	Preface	ix
1	The Huling Brothers	1
2	Huling's Barn	23
3	Seal College	39
4	Sharkey Goes Broadway	57
5	Higher and Higher	77
6	Dry Act, Wet Act	99
7	Sharkey Goes Hollywood	119
8	Movie Palaces and Nightclubs	133
9	Sharkey Meets the President	153
10	A Postwar America	167
11	Sharkey Goes Television	187
12	Vaudeville Revival	203

13	The Show Must Go On	225
14	The End of an Era	241
15	Bygone Days	257

Epilogue	263
Acknowledgments	265
Notes and Sources	267
Index	301

Preface

"Sharkey? Do you know who Sharkey is? Well, at any rate he is well worth knowing."[1] Those words opened a *New York Post* review of a 1940 Broadway play, and those words still ring true today. The review reported on the Broadway debut of Sharkey, a seal, the amphibious kind with flippers, which are actually a species of sea lion.

My great-grandfather Mark Huling trained Sharkey. Mark trained many seals over his lifetime; Sharkey was his favorite. Add to that, my grandfather Lew Bohan was Mark's son-in-law and one of his assistants. So my family history is chock-full of trained seals.

But in my childhood mind, growing up in the 1970s, seal training was nothing more than this odd thing my relatives had done. Though even as a kid, I figured they must have been pretty good at it, having been told they had appeared on *The Ed Sullivan Show*. Yet when something so extraordinary is so close to home, it can go more unnoticed than perhaps it deserves to. Sharkey and Mark died before I was born, and my grandfather Lew died when I was young. My father rarely reminisced about his father and grandfather having worked with Sharkey and the other seals. And the couple of conversations that did happen were matter-of-fact, void of any talk about Sharkey being famous.

Jumping to 2015, now in my fifties, I was contacted by Matthew Billy, a New York City journalist looking to do a story on Sharkey. Many years had passed since I had thought about Sharkey, and I had no idea why a journalist would have any interest in him. Matthew's podcast, *Between the Liner Notes*, focuses on "music, why it is the way it is and how it got to be that way."[2] As a musician myself, it sounded intriguing. But what possible relationship could a seal have to music history? In any event, I told him he needed to talk to my father, not me. He did so without going into any specifics. Three months later, Matthew released a podcast episode titled "Why Won't They Let Sharkey on the Radio?"

The podcast chronicled a 1941 music royalty dispute. Radio stations across the country refused to sign a licensing agreement with the American Society of Composers, Authors, and Publishers (ASCAP) in response to ASCAP's demand for higher radio airplay royalties. As a result, essentially all popular music of its day disappeared off the air. And who do you suppose got caught up in it all? Sharkey, of course. ASCAP prevented Sharkey from performing his newly mastered music feature on the radio, a popular Irish-American melody. The incident made headlines nationwide. As it turned out, the dispute and its aftermath shaped popular music for a generation and beyond, and Sharkey had been part of the story. Seventy-five years later, no one in our family had any idea.

I learned more about Sharkey and my great-grandfather by listening to that forty-minute podcast than I had previously learned my entire life. I began asking questions. Why and how does one start training seals? And how does one end up on *The Ed Sullivan Show*?

There must be a story.

Gary Bohan Jr.
April 2021

Chapter 1

The Huling Brothers

Never Before, Never Again

Sharkey was minutes away from making history. He had made it to Broadway: opening night at the Shubert Theater. Only the raising of a curtain separated him from his destiny.

In the wings was his trainer, Mark Huling. The fifty-six-year-old, short-statured trainer (not overly short, just "below average" short) beamed with pride. And with good reason. Less than two years prior, he was a retired seal trainer and owner of a nightclub in Upstate New York. He had since sold his club, returned to seal training, and presented seals at the New York World's Fair. Now he was in the heart of the most celebrated theater district in the world to watch his young animal prodigy, Sharkey, take the stage.

Stardom lay ahead, for on this early spring night, sandwiched between the start of World War II and the attack on Pearl Harbor, Shubert patrons witnessed the unprecedented inclusion of a trained seal in a Broadway musical comedy. Glowing notices about Sharkey would appear the next morning in practically every newspaper in New York City, putting him on the fast track to becoming the world's most famous seal. For the next seventeen years, Sharkey appeared with the biggest names in show business, names like Bob Hope, Ella Fitzgerald, and the Three Stooges. He entertained the president of the United States, shared the bill with sports legends like

Jackie Robinson, performed with soloists from the Metropolitan Opera, and headlined the country's most prestigious theaters.

That a trained seal could be part of pop culture for so long resulted from circumstances never seen before, and never to be seen again. First, society was both old-fashioned enough to enjoy his skills and modern enough to spread his fame; television, in particular, provided exposure previously unattainable, minus the overexposure trappings of today's digital world. Second, Sharkey was unusually intelligent, with exceptional physical ability and a gifted stage presence. Third, he received his instruction from a world-renowned seal trainer, Mark Huling.

For decades, Mark and two of his brothers had developed a seal-training tradition that set them apart, for not only did they teach seals feats others couldn't achieve; more importantly, they taught seals feats others couldn't even imagine. Put aside for a moment the image of a seal with a beach ball on its nose. Imagine instead, seals that tap dance, sing with an orchestra, ride horses, and perform sketch comedy routines. Such is a glimpse into the world of Huling seals.

Though Mark was initially eclipsed by his two brothers' greater rise to fame, and though tragedy had seemingly cut his seal-training career short, fate would ultimately prove otherwise, eventually leaving him with a legacy unsurpassed in the annals of seal training, led by the unlikely arrival of Sharkey.

And so it began in 1940 on an early spring evening on Broadway. The Huling brothers' collective seal wisdom now set the table for Sharkey, who stood in the wings of the Shubert, poised to make history. His performance that night would ignite a remarkable career-long chain of events. But also necessary were the chain of events leading to his Broadway debut. So before we raise the opening curtain on Sharkey, the story really begins with Mark and his two seal-training brothers, and their foray into show business.

We Didn't Know Any Better

For twenty-three-year-old Mark Huling, his day trip to Buffalo began like many others, with a three-mile horse-and-carriage ride from the family farm to a ferry dock. Joined by his brothers Frank and Ray, they took their half-mile ferry across the Niagara River on a small barge, pulled by a tugboat. Once ashore, they headed toward Buffalo, ten miles away, the eighth largest city in the country. The young men were in search of work—never mind the economic woes of that year's Panic of 1907.

En route, they visited a family acquaintance, where they encountered the welcoming barks of a bunch of seals. The explanation was simple: the family friend was Captain Thomas Webb, the first bona fide seal trainer in the United States.[1]

"Seal" in this case means "sea lion." Sea lions are more social, more physically mobile on land, and better suited for training. At the time, the animal exhibition world often used the terms *seal* and *sea lion* interchangeably, as will be done here.

Webb, originally from Buffalo, had been given a set of seals fifteen years prior by a man dabbling in the nouveau realm of seal training. Webb pioneered a host of training techniques and then crisscrossed the country with his groundbreaking seal act, presenting at theaters, fairs, and with leading circuses. He had also traveled abroad, performing before royalty, and established himself as North America's premier seal trainer before settling back near Buffalo, in Tonawanda, where he set up a shop, "Captain Webb's Educated Seals and Sea Lions."

Webb offered jobs to the three Huling brothers that day. In fairytale fashion, they accepted. And just like that, they became assistant seal trainers. Years later, when asked why, Mark said, "We were so very young, we didn't know any better."[2]

Goodbye Farm, Hello Show Business

Frank Huling took to seal training with unusual prowess. At thirty-one, he was the oldest of the three brothers. A self-described rolling stone, he had previously held several jobs, making little money or headway at any, all of which changed when he began working with seals. "I could see great possibilities in the animals and was determined to see what I could do with them," he said.[3]

Within a year, Frank was appointed manager of Webb's operation.[4] Shortly after, Frank and his brother Mark went on their first big trip. With seals and props, they left for Berlin, Germany, performing at Circus Busch with Harry Houdini.

Ray Huling made his first trip abroad months later. An agent contacted Captain Webb looking to send acts to Venezuela, assuring him "there was a wad in it," stating the Venezuelan government had made the request.⁵ Thirty-three performers set sail from Manhattan in a whirl of excitement, including Ray and Webb's seals, jugglers, trapeze artists, acrobats, other circus types, and a promoter fronting $4,000 of his own money. They played a Caracas bullring that filled with spectators, save for the fact that "duels in three prominent families kept the highest priced boxes available. . . . The occupants to be, however, had paid in advance, and so there was no loss except the loss of life."

After eighteen days of sold-out performances, absent any pay from the Venezuelan government, word came that "the bubonic plague was also playing Caracas." Authorities told the performers they could either leave town within two hours or stay for a six-month quarantine. Neither option included being paid. They left town.

The troupe traveled twenty miles to La Guaíra. They tried to board a steamship but were denied when the captain heard they had left a plague-infected district. And so they trudged to nearby Macuto, waited a week for a boat, and set sail for Barbados. But on the way, an outbreak of yellow fever hit Barbados, forcing the troupe to debark early for Trinidad. Within hours, the bubonic plague hit Trinidad, quarantining them from further travel. After the quarantine, cash reserves were insufficient to get home. The promoter thought it best to do shows in Trinidad to raise the needed money, so he arranged for a large circus tent, which arrived two weeks later, just in time for an eight-day tropical rainstorm. The promoter at last capitulated. "I can lose no more because I have no more money left to lose."

After the storm, the troupe did four shows, which yielded a sizable profit, though not enough to make it home. Ray and a few others kicked in the rest from their own wallets. The weary lot boarded a ship and was greeted eight days later by the Statue of Liberty. Ray traveled 400 more miles to Tonawanda, hopped a ferry, and headed to the family farm. For the twenty-two-year-old seal trainer, sleeping in his own bed must have never felt better.

No sooner did Ray return home than his brother Mark was having difficulties of his own. Captain Webb sent him 150 miles south of Tonawanda to perform at a summer fair. Mark awoke one morning to find a seal had escaped. News raced across town. One paper termed the fugitive a "savage beast." Citizens panicked. Many stayed indoors fearing attack. Mark searched the city in vain. Authorities placed a bloodhound on the trail that nosed his way to a clump of woods about a mile from the city and found the seal—asleep, safe, and unharmed.[6]

Ray suffered a similar fate while supervising Webb's quarters. A prized seal dove into the backyard creek and swam into the nearby Erie Canal. A motorboat company came to the rescue, but the seal evaded the pursuing boats for quite some time before being retaken. The news made front-page headlines: "Exciting Chase for Sea Lion, Escaped from Training Quarters by Climbing through Window, Up and Down the Canal, Hundreds of Spectators Saw Swimming Exhibition the Likes of which Had Never Been Seen Before."[7]

Indeed, Mark and Ray both attended the School of Hard Knocks. They journeyed near and far, presenting seals in novelty shows that ran continuously from noon until night, at times in obscure dives, some just a tiny stage and a few rows of bench seating. Harpo Marx, recalling his early years as a traveling entertainer during this same period, wrote, "If you should ever hear an old-time vaudevillian talk about 'the wonderful, golden days of one-night stands,' buy him another drink, but don't believe a word he's saying."[8]

Postcard of Mark rehearsing with a seal band, ca. 1910. Courtesy of Luc Sante.

But while shady stage managers, vermin-infested motel rooms, rowdy crowds, and the like may have made life less than wonderful, opportunities were plentiful. An ever-growing middle class spurred unprecedented demand for family amusement. Silent movies and radio were still in their infancy, leaving live entertainment to fill the void. In the words of one performer, "People were starving for stimulus!"[9] Later asked how he honed his craft during his formative years, Mark said, "By dint of hard work and perseverance."[10]

Frank, meanwhile, stayed in Europe. So popular was his seal act that he attained celebrity. He kept a letter received from Mademoiselle Mangen, the French president of the Society for the Protection of Animals, who wrote, "I have much pleasure in announcing that owing to the way you present and treat your animals, your act is really a treat to watch. I have never seen animals better trained than those, and they seem to have a great affection for you."[11]

"That's one of the points I insist on, kindness," Frank said. "They have a keen brain but they seem to be all the while using it to kind of take a rise out of you, but if you treat them kindly, you can get along with them all right."[12] Frank was more than getting along with them. He taught the seals to play billiards, jump rope, and discharge firearms. "There is scarcely any work these beasts cannot be trained to do," he said, adding that his standout performer "hasn't reached his limit. It is only a question of inventing something new. . . . When you realize they can do juggling tricks impossible for men, you can form an idea of how many other things they can do." Frank and the seals bonded. "They grow very attached to you," he noted. Upon returning a seal to the ocean on the hunch he desired to go back to his native haunts, the seal swam until a speck on the horizon, only to later return and reunite with his trainer. Another time, Frank recalled joining up with one of his seals after a long absence. "When he caught sight of me, he nearly died of joy."[13] Kindness, respect, imagination, bonding: They were the pillars of Frank's training philosophy, which he would impart to his brothers.

Back home, Frank's brothers Mark and Ray continued to assist Captain Webb, who had a long history of enlisting young locals, green in the area of animal training, to be his assistants, serendipitously turning Tonawanda into the seal-training capital of the world. Tonawanda's four training quarters—Webb's, two others run by prior Webb assistants, and another run by three nephews of Webb—supplied over two-thirds of all performing seals worldwide, about seventy-five new trainees a year. Trainers practiced with seals on their front lawns, though most locals no longer bothered to watch, having seen it so often.

Frank returned from Europe, having been gone two years. His seal-training skills now rivaled if not exceeded those of Captain Webb. For the next two years, Webb and Frank toured with the Forepaugh & Sells Brothers Circus, the third largest circus in the country, exceeded only by the Ringling Brothers Circus and the Barnum & Bailey Circus; all three of which were owned by the Ringling family, and all three of which toured separately.

Webb and Frank were Forepaugh & Sells Brothers's highest-paid act. During the 1911 season, each earned $250 a week, about $6,000 a week in today's dollars.[14] But the Ringlings subsequently dropped Forepaugh & Sells Brothers and focused on their namesake circus, "Ringling Brothers, World's Greatest Shows."

Four locomotives and eighty-six railcars strong, when Ringling Brothers rolled into town, factories closed, schools let out, and masses flocked to see the circus joyfully parade through city streets. Spectacular shows followed, presented in a tented enclave awash with a ground cover of sawdust, and concessions of buttered popcorn and pink lemonade. Traveling rail circuses were the pop mega-events of their day, none bigger than the circus established twenty-eight years earlier by Al, Otto, Alf, Charles, and John Ringling.

Following the disbandment of Forepaugh & Sells Brothers, the Ringlings offered Frank a contract to be a star attraction in the upcoming season with "Ringling Brothers, World's Greatest Shows."

It was the break of a lifetime.

Ringling Brothers

Helped by a loan from their father, the Huling brothers bought out Captain Webb. Frank and Mark immediately went to work for Ringling Brothers, who promoted the seals with the usual circus fanfare: "The most remarkable examples of animal education ever. Vastly more accomplished in their performances than any human circus actor that ever breathed. Trained seal acts of the past should not be thought of in connection with these new ones."[15]

Ringling Brothers's 1912 season opened at the Chicago Coliseum. Two seal troupes performed on platforms between the three rings. Frank presented on one, Mark presented on the other. *Variety* wrote, "The Huling animals pulled a hit [and] made their exit to big applause."[16] After Chicago, the circus stopped at 150 cities, performing under the Ringling Brothers big top, a tent capable of accommodating 12,000 spectators, the largest piece of canvas ever raised.

During the winter break, the three Hulings moved to Atlantic City. The seaside vacation spot awoke next spring, brimming with tourists and honky-tonk attractions. Ray stayed and worked a seal act opposite a Punch and Judy show at the Million Dollar Pier.

Frank and Mark returned to Ringling Brothers, which again opened in Chicago. Al Ringling was ringmaster, a ballet spectacle reenacted Joan of Arc at the Coronation of Charles VII, and sixteen larger-than-life circus acts put on a presentation. All of society came out opening night. "Nothing but congratulations can be bestowed on the Messrs. Ringling for the show that has just made its bow to the Windy City," a critic reported. He wrote of the Huling seals, "The animals gave a marvelous performance, and were highly appreciated."[17]

After season's end, the brothers sought work, customary for circus performers during the off months. Frank toured Europe; Mark and Ray worked theaters across the United States. The Hulings were back next spring with Ringling Brothers, which started again at the Chicago Coliseum before going under canvas. That same year, the three brothers looked to set up a home base for their seals. They decided on Kingston, New York.[18]

Located in the Hudson Valley, ninety miles north of Manhattan, Kingston had already served as the headquarters for a popular traveling circus and would serve as the headquarters for the Huling seal training facility for years to come. Much like Webb's facility in Tonawanda, the Huling property had one key attribute—access to water for the seals, needed to regularly recharge their water tanks. The Huling's lot was next to the Esopus Creek. They erected a two-story wooden building for the animals. The first seals arrived October 1914.

∽

Frank Huling soon found more fame. Wirth Brothers, owners of the oldest and largest circus in Australia, had seen Frank performing at the Blackpool Tower Circus in England and offered him a contract. On September 15,

1915, Frank and six seals set sail from the west coast. Thirty-two days later, they arrived in Melbourne.

Wirth Brothers' sensation that year was to be family member May Wirth, renowned for doing forward and backward somersaults on a galloping horse. Her return to Australia followed four years abroad, where she had been a top draw with Barnum & Bailey.

But much to everyone's surprise, most notably poor May, it was another equestrian rider and his comrades who received the highest praise. Night after night, Frank's star seal, Mascot, juggled while riding a pony. Another seal walked a tightrope while balancing a table lamp atop a pole on his nose. The court jester seal induced laughter with his humanlike gestures and bubbly personality. Others whipped around rubber balls to one another, resulting in newspaper accounts of speed and accuracy that read more like reviews of the Harlem Globetrotters.

Frank supervised with stoic perfect posture; his slender five-foot-nine frame housed in a regal captain's uniform. For the music finale, three seals played horns, a fourth played cymbals attached to his flippers, and a fifth pounded time with a mallet, his body draped over a bass drum marked Huling's Sea Lion Band. "The fifth makes the bass drum resound through the arena with reverberations no human would dare to provoke," Frank said. "I believe the sound of the drum appeals to him, and he seems to take great pleasure in it."[19]

A Melbourne journalist wrote, "Nothing in Wirth's Circus programme this year has so caught popular interest as the wonderful performances of Captain Huling's seals. They simply eclipse all anticipation of what might be expected." The circus next crossed the Bass Strait to Tasmania, where a critic wrote of the seals, "One can hardly believe that anything has been more amazing."[20]

Onward the act went. Newspapers declared the seals "the most wonderful act ever in New Zealand." Postcards made it to market, one showing Mascot riding a pony, another showing the tight-roping seal. Returning to Australia, beset and delayed by rough seas, the circus played for eight weeks at the grand opening of the Sydney Hippodrome. Critics professed the seals "The Sensation of Sydney."[21]

The circus toured Australia for months more. Accolades followed the seals wherever they went. The most imaginative praise, by far, came from a high-ranking government official who said, "If I told Queensland people what I saw those seals do, they would call me the biggest liar since Ananias."[22] (Ananias, according to apostles of Jesus, died suddenly after lying to the Holy Spirit.)

Frank stayed in Australia. He fell in love; they married. The newlyweds had a postshow wedding reception on the Sydney Hippodrome stage. During the show, his wife sat in a VIP box. "The bride like all brides was the subject of general admiration," reported the *Sydney Daily Telegraph*. "The clowns of course had a good deal to say about weddings and married life. . . . The seals themselves seemed to realize the importance of the occasion and by their acting signified the appreciation of their master's choice." Another paper predicted that the wedding couple "will live happily ever after—unless Mrs. Huling demands the glossy coat belonging to one of the seals."[23]

Not forgotten is May Wirth, today considered the greatest circus bareback horse rider of all time. At age seventy-five, long after her career was over, Wirth spoke of the seals upstaging her that year in Australia. She chuckled, "And oh, that got my nanny goat."[24]

~

Frank Huling in Otago, New Zealand, 1915. Courtesy of the *Otago Witness*.

Frank Huling in Sydney, Australia, 1916. National Library of Australia. nla.obj-393104284.

Back in the United States, Frank's brother Ray was busy innovating. Instead of presenting a troupe of seals, as was typical, he presented a single seal; a seal comedian. Among the seal's gags was using the latest in technological marvels by ordering food over a telephone. He also got laughs by repeatedly blowing out a match with which Ray was trying to light his pipe, and by doing a ventriloquist bit. Ray's solo comic seal was an instant success (a concept later used by Ray's brother Mark in his training of Sharkey), and so Ray set his sights on vaudeville.

Vaudeville was in its prime. It had blossomed in the late 1800s as a means of entertaining the bourgeoning post–Civil War middle class. Shows were "polite and non-vulgar," consisting of singers, dancers, comedians, jugglers, novelties, and the like. Programs often included about eight acts, each running about fifteen minutes. Contemporary vaudeville expert Trav S.D. writes, "Vaudeville utterly dominated American popular culture during its formative years."[25]

B. F. Keith established a franchise of vaudeville theaters and sent acts from one theater to the next, providing a steady stream of talent to cities and towns. The successful business model bred other circuits, most notably, Orpheum. If you played the Keith circuit, you were playing the "Keith time"; if you played the Orpheum circuit, it was the "Orpheum time." The Keith and Orpheum Theaters in major cities were the envy of every vaudevillian. The pay was better, the crowds were bigger, and the tickets were reserved seating. Equally important, it was only two shows a day, versus smaller theaters, which staged three or four shows a day, if not more. To use a vaudeville expression still popular today, playing two-a-day Keith and Orpheum Theaters in major cities was the "big time." Everything else was "small time."

Ray and his clown seal made it to the big time. "Rarely does it occur that a member of the animal kingdom, whose principal function in life has been principally to supply downy wrap to the most fastidious, rise to the coveted position of vaudeville star, yet such exists in Huling's Clown Seal. He possesses a pronounced sense of humor [and] he combines comedy and dexterity in a manner that has elicited the most eulogistic praise from the critics of the larger cities," a journalist wrote.[26]

Soon after, the United States entered World War I. Frank returned from Australia and went back to Ringling Brothers. The three Huling brothers, Frank, Mark, and Ray, registered for the draft, but at ages forty-one, thirty-four, and thirty-two, none received the call to serve. Then came the flu pandemic of 1918. The deadly strain of influenza killed tens of millions, significantly more than the number killed in World War I. The government shut down public gatherings. Frank and Mark had a shortened season with Ringling Brothers. Ray and his clown seal made few theater appearances. The better news that year came in November, when Germany signed an armistice agreement ending the war.

Four months later, the Ringling family joined their two amusement assets on a trial basis, in part due to US government control of railroads during and right after the war, which, in 1918, limited the number of locomotives expected to be made available the next year to the family, only enough for one circus.

On March 29, 1919, the Ringlings' trial production debuted at Madison Square Garden in what must have been an awkward reunion of sorts for the Huling seals and May Wirth, both of whom were featured acts. Little could they know the experiment that began that day would last almost a hundred years before taking its final bow; an ensemble that went by the name "Ringling Brothers and Barnum & Bailey Combined Shows, The Greatest Show on Earth."

Asleep in the Deep

Ask anyone who knows anything about vaudeville to name its most famous venue and you will invariably get the same response: The Palace Theater in Midtown Manhattan. It was Keith's flagship, the most desired vaudeville booking in the country. Acts included the Marx Brothers, Ethel Waters, Al Jolson, and every other big timer from the era. Eight acts a week, 400 acts a year—room enough for just a sliver of the tens of thousands of traveling performers during the height of vaudeville.

On April 16, 1923, the Palace Theater presented "a delightful mixture of class and comedy" intended to "please the most jaded vaudeville palate." A seal act opened, which *Variety* said, "went as big as any show starter that has played the Palace in ages. The animal is perfectly trained and directed by a superior showman in Ray G. Huling."[27]

That animal was Charlie.

Named after Charles Ringling, Charlie arrived in the early 1920s with abilities surpassing Ray's original clown seal. He started in a Ringling Brothers seal troupe, then went solo and became the era's most famous trained seal. If not for the arrival of Sharkey a generation later, he would have been the greatest ever. Although a skilled juggler and a gifted comedian, it was two other talents that brought Charlie his most recognition: his ability to sing and dance.

Charlie did an "Indian war dance" in costume, sounding war whoops. He also did the Charleston and the shimmy, a popular ragtime dance. And he was a tap dancer, made possible by specially constructed hard-sole shoes that fit over his front flippers. His *piece de resistance*, however, was a Hawaiian hula dance.

Palace Theater patrons watched as Ray approached Charlie with the setup. "Now, I want you to do a little dance for me."[28]

The orchestra broke into an up-tempo number. Charlie whirled into a 360 spin. His body undulated with the music in a flurry of rapid-fire posterior shakes, each accentuated by the grass skirt wrapped around his waist. The music pulsed. Flippers flew in every direction, leaving and returning to the floor like a finely tuned four-cylinder engine. The orchestra segued into snake-charmer music, the tempo increasing, the melody rising in pitch and intensity. Charlie stayed in perfect rhythm: shaking, turning, and flapping, never missing a beat.

An orchestral ritardando provided the cue for Charlie's dramatic closing move. As the music slowed, he lay on his belly, chin to the floor, and gazed forward. Using his front flippers for support, he lifted his torso and back flippers, approximating a headstand. Gravity reversed the direction of his grass skirt, which fashionably draped over his head, providing a curtsy effect. Ray joined his partner and took a bow as the orchestra brass hit a triumphant *ta-da!*

∼

As for singing, it was Charlie who came up with the idea. "To tell the truth," Ray said, "I had no idea of teaching Charlie to sing. He was smart enough to think up new sounds himself, just to win my attention—and a few extra fish."[29]

Although his natural barks were in the tenor range, Charlie chose a bass register for singing. Over the course of two years, he learned notes and memorized melodies. His breakout moment came when a friend of Ray's accompanied him on cello.

"I was absolutely astounded to hear him try to pitch his notes in tune with those of the cello," Ray said.[30]

Charlie not only matched notes, he sang harmony. Working with his cellist tutor, he learned everything from folk tunes to opera. He took a particular liking to an old ballad called "Asleep in the Deep," a song, curiously enough, about those who have drowned at sea. Ray commissioned an orchestral arrangement to feature Charlie in duet with a cellist. A review from the *Chicago Tribune* lends insight into an actual performance.

> Charlie takes his cue like a veteran, and when the introductory notes die away in the orchestra pit, he lets the song roll out. The deep resonant strains of an accompanying cello serve but to enrich Charlie's basso tones. "*Loudly the bell in the old tower rings, telling the sailor the warning it brings*," booms Charlie, the

seal: he appears to feel the weight of the warning and when he passes the dread news along, "*Sailor beware; sailor take care!*" he puts his heart into it, and shakes his flippers solemnly at the astonished audience. "*Danger is near thee, beware—*" Charlie's voice drops down and down, and when the final "*Beware!*" comes rolling from his thunderous vocal cords he holds the note until the bow completes its journey across the low C string on the cello. He then takes a bow with all the aplomb of an operatic favorite, and eats a fish with the wink of an eye.[31]

Charlie bedazzled critics. Ray cheerily fielded their questions. Asked to comment on Charlie singing "Asleep in the Deep" in duet with a cellist, accompanied by an orchestra, in front of a theater audience, Ray replied, "I've heard it sung worse."[32]

∽

Charlie's song and dance skills landed him a gig in Manhattan at the 5,000-seat Keith Hippodrome, then the largest indoor theater in existence, described by the *New York Times* as "a sort of eighth wonder of the world."[33] Contemporary vaudeville expert Trav S.D. considers it "the most fabulous theater ever built in the United States."[34] The one-week extravaganza brought together Charlie, the Hippodrome Corps de Ballet, a dance troupe from Paris, and Florence Mills, a singer and dancer who epitomized the 1920s Harlem Renaissance. She had recently headlined the Palace, a first for a black entertainer.

Florence Mills was a trailblazer for African American entertainers, a woman who broke free from the era's negative racial stereotypes embedded in blackface minstrelsy and the menial black roles often found in silent films, such as domestic servants. Enabled by the vaudeville stage, Mills sang and danced with grace and dignity. She was a revered celebrity who charmed audiences with her effervescent presence. She entertained racially mixed crowds and starred in the first all-black revue to command top Broadway prices. A newspaper at the time called her "an ambassador of good will from the blacks to the whites."[35] Vaudeville was "the first major American institution to offer serious opportunity for advancement no matter a person's race," serving as "an agent of assimilation."[36] Championing the way was Florence Mills.

For her week at the Hippodrome, Mills did a spot with tap dancer Bill "Bojangles" Robinson, the highest-paid black entertainer of his day, billed as "The Dark Cloud of Joy." Mills and Robinson joined in a dance finale, backed by an all-star, all-black hot jazz band directed by African American Broadway composer Will Vodery.

Florence Mills on the same stage with Bill Robinson, backed by an all-black orchestra, performing in the biggest indoor theater in the world, was a defining moment in the development of American show business. And there as witness to history was Charlie, a trained seal, whose act directly preceded Mills and Robinson. The show received national accolades. *Billboard* praised Charlie for his singing and tap dancing.[37]

But it is a photo that provided the show's most enduring legacy. Florence Mills posed with a fellow dance star, though it wasn't with Bill Robinson. Florence and Charlie posed on the Hippodrome stage: Florence in costume, doing a dance step; Charlie next to her, upside down, wearing a hat, doing his closing dance move. A captioned picture ran coast to coast: "Regardless of shape or size, the girls are all teaching the men the latest in dancing, the Charleston, and Miss Florence Mills of the Hippodrome, New York, who claims to be the originator of the dance, has as her latest pupil, Charlie, the most light-footed of tame seals."[38]

The photo has resurfaced in recent scholarly books, including *Black Heroes* and *Black Women in America*. A full-page image of Florence and Charlie can be found in the deluxe hardcover 2014 publication, *The Complete Encyclopedia of African American History*.

Unlucky Thirteen

In 1926, Frank Huling retired, regarded as among the world's foremost authorities on sea lions. Ray Huling and Charlie toured, with Charlie now regarded as the most celebrated sea lion in show business.

Meanwhile, Mark Huling, in the shadows of his brothers, though no slouch, "known as the 'seal king' in circus channels," trained one seal after another for Ringling Brothers and for others as far away as Japan. He also sent a troupe to the world's fair in Philadelphia to celebrate the country's 150th birthday. Press raved about Neptune, who "had learned feats of balancing and judgment which scientists cannot account for," and Pico, who was "adept at juggling anything."[39]

Florence Mills and Charlie at the New York Hippodrome. Bettmann Archive via Getty Images.

In 1927, Ringling Brothers opened per usual at Madison Square Garden. Mark presented five troupes, twenty seals in all. *Variety* singled out "Huling's champ seal," a newcomer named Major. "With its tail resting on the side of a special saddle the sea lion did his tricks on the back of a circling horse. A novelty, perhaps the best yet, thought out for such animals."[40] Major rode the horse while balancing on his nose a torch flaming at both ends, with long knives perched atop the torch. He also dressed the part, sporting a rhinestone-studded collar.

Mark went to London during the next off season to perform with the Bertram W. Mills Circus at Olympia, the most prestigious circus in England.

The Huling Brothers | 17

Along tagged Charlie. Although Ray was Charlie's main trainer, Mark had worked up a bit with Charlie playing "America (My Country, 'Tis of Thee)." The song often served as a de facto national anthem before the 1931 adoption of "The Star-Spangled Banner." Circus agents in London papered the city with colorful lithographed posters, advertising the upcoming five-week spectacle: "Charlie the Musical Sea-Lion Presented by Captain Huling, and Twenty Other Sensational Novelties."[41] Charlie was to play Britain's national anthem, "God Save the Queen," a melody of rather convenient choice, it being identical to "My Country, 'Tis of Thee."

Opening night drew thousands to the indoor arena. Attending dignitaries likely included proprietor Bertram Mills, joined by his right-hand men, the Earl of Lonsdale and Lord Daresbury. A concert band opened with a rousing version of John Philip Sousa's military march, "The Liberty Bell," better known today as the TV theme song from *Monty Python's Flying Circus*. Acts performed in a center ring—acrobats, stilt walkers, a human cannonball, trapezists, and others—many from Ringling Brothers, including famed woman tiger trainer, Mabel Stark.[42]

When it came time for Charlie, the concert band played a lively selection to set up the act. Mark and Charlie entered the ring. In the middle were tin horns mounted on a horizontal frame. Nearby was a music stand with sheet music. The band finished to respectful applause.

The circus barker addressed the audience. His stately voice reverberated over the arena loudspeakers. He paused between phrases; each pause elongated for effect.

"My Lords . . . ladies . . . and gentlemen."

The crowd hushed.

The barker proceeded with measured drama.

"Introducing the most wonderful achievement in sea lion training. (*Pause*) The sea lion (*pause*) will actually play the national anthem (*pause*) without any mechanical aid."

Charlie positioned himself near the horns. Mark belted out his instructions. "Blow on there. Hard. Real hard."

Charlie blew into the horns. He played the first four notes of the tune, then let loose a gargantuan *Burrrrp!* that echoed through the air with grotesque hilarity.

Gales of laughter filled the arena. Charlie gave a smug look. Mark acted the stooge. The two played off each other like the seasoned pros they were. All the while, the crowd kept howling.

Charlie refocused on the horns. Mark commanded with amplified vigor. "Real hard this time. Blow it right in there."

Charlie blew into the horns. Again, the first four notes. Again, a belch. Again, the crowd in hysterics.

Mark acted in frustration and moved the music stand closer. "Go on now. Blow on there, harder. *Real* hard."

Charlie played the first four notes and spewed another enormous belch. The crowd laughed even louder.

Acting at his wits' end, Mark outfitted Charlie with a pair of comically oversized glasses and gave another pep talk. "Come on now. Louder. Real hard. *Real* hard. Blow it right in there."

With glasses in place and the music stand properly situated, Charlie played the first half of the melody to perfection. The crowd gave a round of applause. Charlie flawlessly played the remaining melody. The crowd gave an even bigger round of applause. Then the finale: Charlie replayed the melody at blinding speed, over twice as fast, each note receiving a

Mark, Charlie, and Charlie's adoring fans; London. Bertram W. Mills Circus at Olympia press photo from the author's collection.

crisp, staccato attack. The crowd listened in awe to his virtuosic rendition of "God Save the Queen."[43]

Mark later explained two ways of blowing a note, by the mouth and by the nose. "Inasmuch as a seal puts his mouth around a horn when he blows by the former method, for fast choruses we teach him merely to exhale through his nose as it is much swifter."[44]

∼

Returning from London, Mark and several seals went straight to Florida. Biographer Richard Thomas, in his book *John Ringling, Circus Magnate and Art Patron*, reported on the happenings.

> John Ringling decided that Mark Huling and his trained seals, a popular act of his circus, would be a profitable attraction on his St. Armand's Key, across the causeway from Sarasota, that winter. He had a building erected in which they were to live and present their act and made arrangements for a supply of a certain type of fish they were supposed to like. The act moved into the building but the seals refused to eat the fish provided. John then wired a fish company to send out a boat immediately to catch a more expensive variety it was believed the seals could not resist. But when the fish arrived, they were also spurned. As his seals were unhappy at St. Armand's and as he was afraid they would die of their self-imposed starvation, Huling packed up the troupe and returned, as quickly as possible, to Kingston, New York, his winter home.[45]

John Ringling docked Mark $500 ($7,500 in today's dollars) from his first paycheck the next circus season. Ringling said the building on St. Armand's Key had cost him twice that, and Mark's "refusal to put on a show there had caused him to lose that amount," so he was charging him half. Mark finished his contracted season with Ringling Brothers, then gave his notice.[46]

Ringling became embroiled in a dispute the next year with Madison Square Garden, refusing to accept their demand to preempt the circus on Friday nights for boxing matches, which were wildly popular at the time.

The Garden responded by awarding their subsequent circus contract to Ringling's archrival, the Sells-Floto Circus.

For 1929, Sells-Floto signed cowboy movie star Tom Mix, known for his silent Westerns, idol to millions of boys. They also signed Mark, advertising Major as "Huling's trained horse-riding seal, a remarkable example of training unequalled in the world."[47] America at the time was enjoying an unprecedented wave of prosperity that hit fever pitch. Sells-Floto rode the wave and, according to circus historian Fred Pfening III, "enjoyed what was probably the most profitable season in American circus history."[48]

John Ringling, not to be outdone, bought out Sells-Floto and four other circuses that September, reclaiming the helm as the undisputed giant of the industry. (The move proved to be a disastrous one that nearly bankrupted him later.) Not since 1907 when the Ringlings had bought Barnum & Bailey had there been such a blockbuster circus deal. Given that Sells-Floto was still on the road, Mark, ironically, was back on the Ringling payroll. He returned to Kingston after the Sells-Floto season, arriving a week before the stock market crash.

Two days after Black Tuesday, Mark was back with the seals, raising money at a local VFW Halloween costume benefit ball. With that, the eagerly awaited off-season arrived. Little did Mark realize the tragedy that lay seven weeks ahead.

It happened on December 13. The culprit was a kerosene stove heater that caught fire. Flames jumped to clothes hung underneath an interior stairway. Before long, smoke was billowing from the two-story wooden structure. Wiltwyck Hose Company No. 1 received an alarm. The Huling seal quarters was ablaze.

The fire chief dispatched a central pumper.

Firemen raced to the scene. Off in the distance, a soft burning glow infused the late afternoon December sky.

Flames spread to the second floor with frightening speed. Thick smoke rolled through the building. Inside were fifteen seals. Many dove into the large seal tank and stayed underwater to escape the toxic fumes. But as they came up for air, they suffocated.

Firemen arrived and extinguished the flames. They tried to rescue the scared seals from the tank, but the seals remained submerged except to surface for gulps of lethal air.

In a haze of pea-soup smoke, firemen scoured the building for other seals. They found one unconscious in his stall and then found another and a third, scattered about. Firemen dragged the three seals outside. Bystanders gathered, their stomachs knotted and hearts sunken. According to one eyewitness, "The seals appeared almost human in their dumb appeals for aid from their trainer, Mark Huling, whom those able to gasp, seemed to recognize."[49] An emergency crew from Central Hudson Gas & Electric Corporation used a Pulmotor (a forerunner of the modern-day ventilator) to resuscitate the three seals. Onlookers described their actions as heroic.

Two of the three resuscitated seals survived. The third died later that evening. The twelve seals in the water tank all died.

Mark's teenage daughter, Marjorie, would forever refer to the horrific calamity as Unlucky Thirteen: that thirteen seals would die in a fire on Friday the thirteenth.[50]

News of the event hit the front page of the *Daily Freeman*. Another local paper called it "one of the most disastrous fires to break out in Kingston in some time." A story ran nationally in *Billboard*.[51]

Mark called the loss of his seals "a staggering blow." After recovering from the shock, his initial reaction was to start afresh with new seals and rebuilt training quarters. He soon had second thoughts. Perhaps he was road-weary from circus life; perhaps he wanted to spend more time with his wife and fifteen-year-old daughter; or perhaps the thought of losing another troupe of seals was too much to bear. Whatever the reason, at age forty-six, after having played the big time, after having given a command performance before England's King George V and Queen Mary, and after having worked twenty years for Ringling Brothers, Mark came to his dispirited decision: "I decided to quit show business entirely."[52]

Chapter 2

Huling's Barn

Three-two Beer

Over the next several years, Mark would repeatedly reinvent himself, pursuing a number of careers in Kingston while his brother Ray stayed in show business, servicing an ever-dwindling vaudeville market. Their brother Frank, meanwhile, took ill and kept a low profile.

Within months after the seal-quarters fire, Mark built a miniature golf course. The affordable pastime soared in popularity right after the stock market crash, a craze that historians call "The Madness of 1930."[1] Fifteen thousand courses were built in the US during the first half of the year. Thousands more surfaced that summer and fall. "Everybody is baffled by the wildfire spread of the miniature golf phenomenon, it confronts the eye everywhere," wrote a reporter from *Modern Mechanics and Inventions*, a phenomenon he termed "The 1930 Gold Rush."[2]

Huling's Miniature Golf Garden opened that August on the same plot where the former seal building once stood. Mark integrated a grove of trees so patrons could golf in the shade. He promised "real pleasure" and said the course was "artistically designed." Ads boasted, "It's Classy, No Knowledge of Game Necessary."[3] Among the features was a clown that blinked its eyes when a hole was made and stuck out its tongue when it was missed.

Mark opened a second facility that fall in nearby New Paltz. He named the indoor course Huling's Tropical Golf Gardens. It had lush greenery and palm trees. "One could imagine he was stepping out of his car at Palm Beach," a local said.[4] The two courses rated among the finest in the state. Record-low scores made front-page news. The ladies of Kingston challenged the ladies of New Paltz in match play for the minigolf championship of Ulster County. New Paltz High School competed in minigolf contests against Kingston High School.

By 1932, the miniature golf craze had fizzled. Mark kept his courses open but expanded his Kingston operation to include a daring carnival ride called an Acroplane—a mechanical contraption with a double-swivel base, an electric motor, and a real aircraft propeller. Brave souls crawled into a cockpit that climbed, dove, and looped in all directions using controls that mimicked a real airplane. Even with the stock market sinking to Depression-era lows that summer, Mark's carnival ride flourished.

"The airplane at Huling Amusement Park has been going for some months now and its popularity seems to grow by the day," wrote the *Daily Freeman*. "You get tossed around plenty if you wiggle the stick much and feel as lost as a bedbug in a wrinkled blanket."[5]

In 1933, Mark closed his minigolf courses and amusement park and set his sights on starting a new business, one that involved selling beer during Prohibition. Bootlegging was an activity for which the area held a dubious distinction. Two years prior, one of the biggest raids of its day had occurred in Kingston. Federal agents long suspected a Kingston brewery of illicitly making and distributing beer, but couldn't figure out how. At last, they busted two warehouses a half-mile away from the brewery and confiscated thousands of barrels of beer. A subsequent brewery raid uncovered hidden stashes of brewing equipment, cash, and weapons. The smuggling technique? A notorious gangster named Jack "Legs" Diamond had paid local plumbers to run a two-and-a-half-inch rubber hose through city sewer lines, allowing secretly pumped beer to flow from the brewery to remote warehouses for kegging and distribution.[6]

Mark, on the other hand, legally sold beer during Prohibition. By 1933, the movement to repeal Prohibition was gaining support from newly elected President Franklin D. Roosevelt right on down the line. Although Prohibition didn't end until that December, the prohibition on selling beer ended eight months earlier.

On April 7, 1933, a bill went into effect whereby Washington lawmakers reclassified beer up to 3.2 percent alcohol by weight (4 by volume) as nonintoxicating, making it legal, even during Prohibition. The legislative sleight-of-hand allowed for the sale of "three-two beer" while the constitutional repeal of Prohibition worked its way through the process. President Roosevelt signed the bill into law, famously quipping: "I think this would be a good time for a beer." Beer connoisseurs now celebrate April 7 as National Beer Day.

Mark refurbished his former seal quarters into a nightclub. True to his farming roots, he designed the interior to have the look of a barn. The club opened on the Fourth of July, less than three months after beer was legalized. Two old-fashioned lamps lit the outside entrance. A tall roadside wooden sign next to the building read "Huling's Barn."

Opening night attracted an overflow crowd. Swarms jammed into a front room that had a hand-crafted mahogany bar and dining tables. A pianist hammered out Tin Pan Alley melodies on a stage that barely fit its red-varnished upright. In the back of the building was a ballroom. On its walls hung rustic scythes, farm wagon wheels, harness horse collars, ox yokes, and barn lamps. Lining two sides of the room were open barn stalls, each with table seating packed with customers. A hayloft formed a canopy for the stage, from which came the scintillating sounds of the Silver Rhythm Kings. The ballroom floor was made from the area's finest maple, its fresh surface teeming with a stampede of happy dancers. Most newsworthy of all, after thirteen years of temperance, available on draught was an unending supply of Pabst Blue Ribbon.[7]

Death of Vaudeville

In the years leading up to the fire, Ray Huling's standout seal, Charlie, rose to stardom after hitting the big time. Vaudeville, however, was in decline. Silent movies had surpassed it in popularity. Once mere incidental novelties that accompanied patrons exiting vaudeville shows, silent movies had become feature-length, star-studded productions. Vaudeville suffered. The numbers tell the tale. When the Hulings broke into show business, there were 5,000 vaudeville theaters. But by the time Charlie first played the Palace in 1923, less than 1,000 remained. Three years later, 100 remained, only a dozen of which were two-a-day, big-time theaters.

Vaudeville now mostly served the lesser role of providing a live entertainment prologue before the showing of a feature-length silent film.

Countless movie theater palaces sprang up during the 1920s; many former vaudeville shrines became movie houses.

If vaudeville was dying, Charlie never got the memo. He started 1926 in Canada doing the Orpheum circuit. In March, he did a week at the Los Angeles Orpheum, which had opened just three weeks earlier, where he shared the all-vaudeville, reserved seating, two-a-day bill with super-diva Nora Bayes and showbiz immortal Jack Benny.

Variety was critical of the LA Orpheum's all-vaudeville format, writing, "Just how bookers or executives figure it out is beyond conjecture." In reviewing the show, the magazine wrote of Charlie, "This seal seams to possess more intelligence than some of those that book straight vaudeville. It gauged its audience for laughs and applause which is more than many a booker can do."[8] The next month, upending their long-standing format, *Variety* moved the coverage of silent films ahead of vaudeville in its front pages.

Charlie followed with more Orpheum time, ending at their flagship, the Palace Theater in Chicago, another of the few remaining all-vaude, reserved seating, two-a-day theaters. There, he worked with Smith and Dale, archetypes of the two-man comedy act, a duo that lasted seventy years, a show business record to this day.

Charlie played the biggest theaters. He headlined, something practically unthinkable for an animal act. He returned to the Palace in New York, meriting a key spot on the bill. He honed his act to where he could go solo. "Without the usual trainer in evidence," a reporter observed, "the seal appears on stage unaccompanied, carrying on and off his props and going through his routine of tricks."[9]

In October 1929, two months before the seal-quarters fire, Charlie shared a stage bill with silent-film actress Leatrice Joy, George Burns, and Gracie Allen. That week, Charlie and Leatrice did a radio broadcast to promote the show. Charlie sang. Excluded from the broadcast were Burns and Allen. (Seven days later, the now-historic Burns and Allen short film *Lambchops* hit movie theaters, their first of many films, propelling the comedy duo on the path to cinema, radio, and ultimately television legendry.) Charlie's touring schedule spared him from the tragic fire. He was on his way to the Palace Theater in Chicago for a week of Christmas shows, working again with Bill "Bojangles" Robinson.

Ray Huling and Charlie returned home that winter. After assessing the fire-damaged quarters that now left Charlie homeless, Ray decided to build Charlie his own private home elsewhere in Kingston. The interior had a pool (tiled in black with white trim), a sun parlor, and a marble slab floor; the exterior had a private beach and a wrought-iron fence.[10] Charlie also had his own butler, a former Huling seal-handler assistant from their days with Ringling Brothers. Ray summed up his philosophy: "Take care of thy seal and thy seal will take care of thee."[11]

Ray and Charlie continued playing the big time, including repeat stints at the Palace in Manhattan, one of just four remaining all-vaudeville, two-a-day theaters. They also performed at Europe's top variety theaters. But opportunities for work were fast shrinking. Vaudeville was now competing against an undefeatable foe: movies with synchronized sound. Talkies were all the rage.

Returning from overseas, Charlie again played the Palace in Manhattan, the last big-time theater to survive. Soon after, it too dropped its two-a-day policy, becoming a four-a-day vaude-film grind house like other small-time theaters. Months later, it dropped stage acts altogether and went all film.

Ray and Charlie preparing for their stage entrance. Press photo by A. N. Mirzaoff from the author's collection.

Author and vaudeville lover Sarah Addington wrote of hundreds attending a wake, herself included. "The rites were held at the Palace Theater; the corpse was Vaudeville, being shown for the last time in the last two-a-day, reserved-seat, non-film vaudeville house in America. . . . The two-a-day is gone, and another ghost walks the American scene. Gentlemen, your hats, while we speak of the dead."[12]

An Offer I Couldn't Refuse

Ray and Charlie played what was left of tattered vaudeville circuits. They worked the biggest theaters that still presented variety acts ahead of movies, places like the Palace in Chicago and the Roxy in Manhattan. They appeared at events for famous politicians and worked at nightclubs after Prohibition. They also went to Hollywood.

Sid Grauman booked them for a stage show at his Chinese Theater, already featuring its tradition of celebs leaving handprints and footprints in the concrete forecourt. Sid paired the stage show debut with the world-premiere screening of *I'm No Angel*, starring Mae West in her most successful film. One reporter called it "the most elaborate first night opening in the history of the theatre, with almost 30,000 people gathered around the boulevard trying to get a glimpse of the many stars."[13] Attendees included Mae West, Charlie Chaplin, and W. C. Fields, who caused a stir by arriving on a horse-drawn wagon loaded with barrels of beer. Hollywood's most celebrated critic, Louella Parsons, wrote, "A highlight was Ray Huling and his trained seal, whose incredible antics kept the audience amazed and amused by turns."[14]

Charlie returned to Manhattan, regarded as "one of the highest paid animal performers in the world. He performs before the elite of the New York social world at exclusive parties as well as banquets and civic functions. . . . Once he came out before a gathering of hard-boiled bankers who for hours wrestled with problems of great magnitude. A few capers by Charlie and he had them rolling in aisles."[15]

Ray and Charlie then crossed the ocean aboard the newly christened SS *Normandie* luxury liner, the biggest passenger ship of its day. Arriving abroad, they played the London Palladium, sharing the bill with showbiz superstar Gracie Fields. Theater work followed in Scotland, France, and Germany. Ray considered the trip a career highpoint.

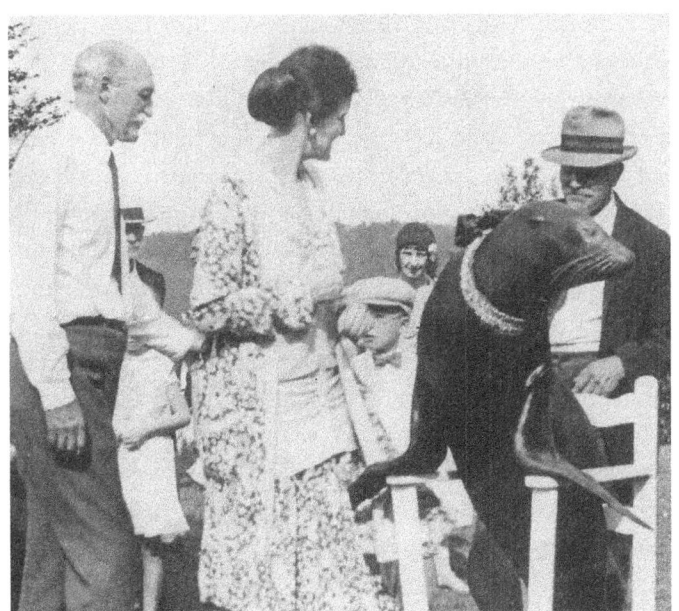

Governor and Mrs. Gifford Pinchot are joined by Charlie at their Grey Towers estate in Milford, Pennsylvania. Acme Newspictures. Press photo from the author's collection.

Back in Kingston, New York, Huling's Barn became the area's top nightspot. Mark hired first-rate dance bands and obtained all-night liquor licenses. He held fashion shows, dance contests, and beauty pageants. He staged variety shows. He hosted banquets, receptions, and proms. Business thrived, seemingly immune to the Great Depression.

While Mark was tending to his club and Ray was in Europe, their brother Frank died following a long illness. He was fifty-nine. Ray returned from Europe four months later. Retirement plans soon materialized. Ray and Charlie worked the summer of 1937 in Cleveland at the Great Lakes Exposition, then did a seven-city farewell tour that ended at the Los Angeles Orpheum.

Charlie took ill shortly after. Ray brought him to the New York Aquarium, the oldest operating aquarium in the country, where they agreed to monitor and treat the aging sea lion. "He's more than just a pet," Ray said. "I wanted him to be in some place like this where I could come in and see him every three or four days."[16] After Charlie recovered, Ray decided that Charlie should spend his remaining days there, receiving needed medical care. A syndicated theater critic couldn't resist:

> This is a news flash from the Aquarium, which hasn't yielded a fresh, piscatorial item in quite a little while. It is about Charlie, the Aquarium's newest tenant who moved in a couple of weeks ago and is now occupying the star dressing tank. He is getting along swimmingly, according to the attendants. . . . Charlie is as talented and as weary a sea lion as ever plowed through the brine. . . . For eighteen years, Charlie trod the boards under Huling's aegis, a headliner wherever he went. . . . Charlie, the sea lion, now frisks about with two sea lions named Frisco and Cally, who will get over it. They are frankly awestruck by their recent roommate, for Charlie wears his glamour on his furry sleeve.[17]

After a stretch of improved health, Charlie died. The reported cause was old age and a bronchial ailment, although absent daily companionship from his trainer, the Associated Press wrote, "aquarium officials said he died of a broken heart."[18]

Ray retrieved Charlie's remains and gave him a last resting place at his home. The *Daily Freeman* published an obituary that read, in part, "There has been many a human whose death has not caused as much regret."[19] Ray arranged for a stone monument that stands in Charlie's honor to this day, engraved with Charlie's name and date of death, April 14, 1938.

For the first time in thirty years, there were no Huling seals and none on the horizon. But though the days of Huling seals seemed gone forever, destiny soon laid other plans. A month or so after Charlie's death, Mark received the proverbial offer he couldn't refuse. Someone was eager to buy his club. Mark had refused many offers over the years, but this latest one was, in his own words, "especially lucrative."

"I couldn't resist the fantastic profit," he added. "With a pocketful of money, and for the first time in my life, idle moments for reminiscence, it is only natural that my thoughts again turned to seals. It was only a matter of a short time before the idea took material form."[20]

Mark planned a new building next to his nightclub, a place where he could train the many seals he hoped would soon arrive. He also enjoyed one last novelty as owner of Huling's Barn.

Mark hired "Hanyan the Hypnotist, King of the Ice."[21] Hanyan staged a much-ballyhooed stunt whereby he hypnotized his assistant and buried her alive outside the club in an ice-filled casket under six feet of earth without food or water—or so the story went. Five hundred viewed the burial. Periscopes allowed for a look at the frozen subterranean assistant, for a nominal fee, of course. Crowds came out nightly for morbid viewings. After seven days, Hanyan dug her up. Bystanders bunched around the lifeless assistant. The hypnotist noted with feigned concern her swollen face and parched lips. She suddenly perked up. Hanyan gave a dramatic sigh. Lo and behold, she was alive and well.

With that, Mark retired from nightclub ownership and focused on his latest dream, the creation of a one-of-a-kind facility, a place where he imagined seals under his tutelage at the largest seal-training institute ever to grace the world.

Jungleland Here We Come

And so, at age fifty-five, after having been a farmer, a seal trainer, a miniature golf and amusement park proprietor, and a nightclub owner, Mark embarked on his most ambitious endeavor to date. The climate was less than favorable. Vaudeville circuits big and small were gone. Metropolitan movie palaces still paired stage presentations with film screenings, but those were tough gigs to get. And circuses, once the heart and soul of mass culture, were now a mere appendage, badly beaten down by the Depression. Only two railroad circuses remained—Ringling Brothers and Cole Brothers—down from thirty-two during the peak circus season of 1911. Mark nonetheless set out to reestablish himself.

Returning to Ringling Brothers was not an option. When Mark left, they replaced him with the Tiebor family, colleagues from Tonawanda who stayed with Ringling Brothers into the 1950s. (The Hulings and Tiebors presented seals for Ringling Brothers for over forty-five years.) Ringling Brothers still indirectly provided the crucial break, courtesy of their star attraction that year, Frank Buck.

Buck trekked into jungles and collected live wild animals of all sizes for circuses and zoos. In a time prior to tranquilizer darts, he devised snares to catch animals safely and humanely, never intentionally hurting or killing any, of which he took great pride. His techniques earned him the nickname: Frank "Bring 'Em Back Alive" Buck.

Buck wrote best-selling books, starred in hit movies, and rivaled the popularity of sports heroes and Hollywood celebrities. He was also planning a jungle-themed amusement park for the upcoming New York World's Fair, to this day the second-largest fair in US history, exceeded only by St. Louis in 1904. His Jungleland attraction was to have thousands of animal species: rare birds, exotic reptiles, elephants, monkeys, camels, and—trained seals.

Buck went looking for a seal man. He soon caught wind of a Ringling Brothers alumnus making waves about reentering the business. Sure enough, Mark landed the contract—not a bad start for a fifty-five-year-old animal trainer looking to make a comeback.

I Supply the World with Sea Lions

Mark's seal-training facility was well under construction. He was booked for the World's Fair. Everything was falling into place except for one thing: he had no seals. The solution seemed easy. He would contact his old friend, Captain George McGuire.

Headquartered in Santa Barbara, California, McGuire had forever been catching sea lions, providing them to aquariums, zoos, and seal trainers throughout the US, Europe, and Australia. He ran a virtual monopoly operation. So prolific were his abilities, the slogan on his stationery read, "I Supply the World with Sea Lions."

Regulations then only required a readily obtainable state permit. That changed with the 1972 federal Marine Mammal Protection Act, which would have undoubtedly put a damper on McGuire's freewheeling operation were it in effect. Yet it is hard to imagine a better marine mammal steward than Captain George McGuire.

McGuire developed special nets and techniques that didn't harm the animals, versus the horrific approach used by his predecessors of clubbing them unconscious, hoping most would awaken onshore. Though his role was paid supplier, he often bonded with the seals he netted. He named one El Capitan, saying he was the most intelligent, good-natured seal he had ever seen, admitting he had serious doubts about being able to part with him.

Business boomed. McGuire developed an unusually keen eye for finding the best specimens. Every seal came with a money-back guarantee, though returns were few. Trainers valued his judgment; McGuire knew precisely the kind of animal they desired and thought nothing of throwing back catches that didn't meet his standards.

McGuire had supplied the Hulings going back to their early days, so you can imagine Mark's disappointment when reports surfaced of McGuire's recent retirement. Mark contacted him anyway, explaining his pressing needs for the World's Fair.

Exactly how Mark pleaded his case is unknown, but whatever he said worked. At age eighty-five, Captain McGuire agreed to round him up six male seals.

McGuire was a cheerful sort; slim and fit, with sparkly eyes and a broad mustache that complemented his full head of gray hair. He wore a youthful look and had a playful demeanor that belied his age. "One of these days I'll be getting old," he joked.[22]

Outfitted in a captain's hat, jacket, and tie, and a matching button-down vest, McGuire projected an air commensurate with his vast accrual of ocean wisdom.

Captain George McGuire at age eighty-five. © Santa Cruz Island Foundation.

Huling's Barn | 33

McGuire reenlisted his assistants, Danny Pico and Al Newton, former cowboys turned fishermen. Much ado surrounded the fact that their great-grandfathers had opposed one another during the Mexican-American War. (Danny's great-grandfather was Pío Pico, California's last governor under Mexican rule; Al's great-grandfather served under US General John Fremont.) But Danny and Al got along just fine and worked well together. Crew in place, McGuire boarded his most recent purchase, a sea-hardened, forty-foot motorboat that went by the name *Pelican*.

McGuire and his two assistants departed Santa Barbara and ventured into the Pacific. They traveled twenty-eight miles before reaching the island of Santa Cruz, where they anchored in Fry's Harbor. Scattered about the rocky cove were thousands of California sea lions. The team hauled out a 200-pound, three-mesh net. Unraveled, it measured 150-feet long by 25-feet deep. The bottom was weighted; the top had corks for floatation.

Danny and Al fastened one end of the net to rock outcroppings. They then stretched the behemoth fabric across the mouth of the cove and fastened the other end to a strong stand of kelp. After that, they tossed a specially built trap into the water. The open-slatted wooden crate was four-feet long, two-feet wide, and two-feet deep. They next lowered a rowboat dinghy and climbed in. The crate floated nearby.[23]

In the expanse of the cove, a mass of sea lions unknowingly auditioned for a career in show business. For six, the proceedings would forever change their lives. McGuire evaluated his many prospects. Barkers were best. Snoozers had their place, but for maximum trainability, McGuire insisted on barkers. He was convinced they were smarter. Other claimed metrics of intelligence were the width between a seal's eyes and the shape of a seal's nose. Smart ones supposedly had peaked noses. Young sea lions, one- or two-years old, were preferred. With an average twenty-year life span in captivity, that allowed for a long career. McGuire singled out a sea lion and called on his trusted assistants stationed in the rowboat dinghy.

Danny heaved on the oars. "A fine way for honest cowpunchers to make a living, Al."[24]

The rowboat lurched. Al caught his balance and grabbed a lasso. "Cowpunchers? We're seal-punchers, Danny."

The boat sliced through the cove; paddles slurping through water and oarlocks clunking with rhythmic purpose. Danny steered the seal toward the mesh; the seal dove for safety.

When the animal surfaced for air, Danny drove him into the netting. Now enmeshed and none too pleased with his unsolicited pending career change, the seal flailed and thrashed. The captive eventually gave up and calmed down. Then came an aquatic rodeo.

Al twirled his lasso and let it fly. The noose landed around the seal's neck. Al roped him in. The seal lunged and nipped one of Al's fingertips, adding to his collection of bites from prior missions.

Al stoically grimaced as he threaded his rope between the slats of the nearby floating crate. After he manhandled the seal inside the crate, he clamped the crate closed and lashed it to the dinghy.

Captive in tow, Danny rowed back to the *Pelican*. Al stood guard and triumphantly goaded his catch. "Go ahead and bark, baby. The captain loves a good barker."

Minutes later, the dinghy and *Pelican* bobbed side by side. Danny and Al hoisted the loaded crate onto the main boat. Captain McGuire at

Danny Pico mans the oars while Al Newton lassos a seal. © Santa Cruz Island Foundation.

once transferred the seal into a wire cage. "Seals are curious animals," the captain later explained, "so we put them in wire cages. They can see what's going on, so they're philosophic about it."

The process repeated until McGuire had six top prospects. The *Pelican* then voyaged back to the mainland. Up on deck, the captain cooled the seals with a good hose-down, spraying them with quiet pride, like a master gardener watering his prized flower beds.

The crew disembarked onto Stearns Wharf, a busy commercial wooden pier that extended 2,000 feet into the ocean. After crating their noisy cargo into sturdier confines, they proceeded to the Santa Barbara train station, just off the wharf. The transportation hub bustled with activity. An expressman checked the seals into their travel accommodations. The captain instructed him to keep them regularly hosed down.

Soon after, a Southern Pacific express train departed toward New York; onboard were six male seals, tagged to Mark Huling.[25]

The Runt

Three thousand miles later, Mark uncrated his cargo. But excitement soon turned to frustration. Captain McGuire, of all people, had seemingly sold him short. Mark later lamented, "There arrived one day a shipment of six young seals, of which one in particular was such a little runt. He was so small, I considered him worthless because small seals seldom come through the rigors of captivity, or grow sufficiently in stature to make an impressive showing." Mark would often recall his disappointment with the captain that day, saying, "It threatened to become the cause of the breaking up of a friendship of many years standing."[26]

But now was not the time to dwell on this. The captain's apparent lapse in judgment was something Mark would reconcile later.

First was getting the seals to eat. They were used to catching their own fish and initially turned their noses up at the dead ones offered by a trainer. (McGuire provided no food for their long journey, ensuring that they arrived plenty hungry. According to the captain, they could go for a month without food.) Mark tied a piece of string to a pole. On the other end of the string, he attached a piece of fresh fish, which he dangled before his newly arrived guests, acting more fisherman than seal trainer. The seals observed with languid interest. The hunger strike lasted days. Mark kept at it, knowing they would eventually succumb.

Snap! Music to Mark's ears, the sound of the first seal snapping up the choice morsel suspended from the long pole held in his outstretched hands. The tasty treats quickly became a desired commodity among the mob. They graduated to snatching long tosses directly in their mouths, caught with the ease of a baseball player shagging down a routine fly ball. Mark soon became a preferred customer at the local market, shopping for six seals. Each ate about fifteen pounds of fresh fish daily: butterfish, herring, sardines, and other soft-boned fish.

Focus next turned to taming the seal's bite, which, according to Mark, was "more vicious than that of a mad dog." Mark wore homemade metal pants, articulated at the hips, knees, and ankles, and took steps that bore the look of the Tin Man as the seals hacked at his armored exterior. "The only way to show them you're immune is to let them nip," Mark said. Even the runt dented his pants. "That boy could really dish it out." In time, they stopped. Mark explained: "Being smart mammals they soon get wise that biting the boss is tougher than opening up a can of sardines and eventually they lose their appetite for human fare."[27]

Ground rules established, the seals were tame and friendly. Mark worked with his five choice seals. The sixth, the runt, perched in the corner, envying the attention his comrades were receiving. It wasn't until Mark fell ill with a cold that things changed.

Mark was blowing his nose with regularity when he "felt something nudge his hand and a blast of air hit him" accompanied by a loud honk.[28] The runt seal had snuck up and copied him. Without hesitation, the seal blew his nose into Mark's hankie and delivered a flurry of comical, exaggerated snorts, then gazed up with an impish look, as if to ask, "*Now* will you give me a shot?"

Mark later recalled that "This little fellow began to draw attention to himself by his unusual and intelligent antics, and before a month had passed, he had so thoroughly established himself in my admiration, I decided to give him a try."[29]

Once in the pool, the chocolate-brown seal raced through the water. He darted back and forth, then submerged. A moment later, he leapt high in the air. He swam in graceful downward and upward arcs. If this was anything like the show Captain McGuire had seen, there could be little doubt why the pint-sized animal had made the cut. The seal ended his impromptu exhibition by disappearing underwater, instantaneously reappearing on the wooden floor next to the pool, as if out of thin air.

"The way he swam reminded me of a shark," Mark said.[30]

The little runt soon had a name: Sharkey.

Chapter 3

Seal College

Seal Training 101

Vaudeville and circus popularity had both declined, so Mark sought other work beyond the upcoming World's Fair. Radio was now a big deal and provided one such opportunity. Mark would soon receive another opportunity—one especially earmarked for Sharkey and one that Mark couldn't have imagined in a million years.

But first was the task of training his new seal arrivals. Asked how to train a seal, Mark said, "By the smallest degrees, you contrive to make the pupil understand what you want him to do. Gradually he understands what is desired of him. The point is that he is exceedingly anxious to learn, impelled powerfully by the love that lies in a seal's heart. And the trick of my trade is to appeal to that love."

"What does a seal love?" the interviewer asked.

"Fish," Mark replied.

Mark clarified that balancing does not come naturally for a seal, though he did note certain physical advantages, explaining, "The seal has capacities for nose balancing due to native agility and exceeding flexibility of neck. The animal's setup supplies a radius of motion of the snout unequaled in either the animal or vegetable kingdom."[1]

First was getting a seal to balance a ball. Mark gently placed a wooden paddle (slightly bigger than a Ping-Pong paddle) on the seal's nose. That accustomed the seal to feel nose pressure. When the seal accepted the paddle pressure, he received a piece of fish. Over time, Mark moved the paddle upward so that the seal had to position his nose vertically to receive his prize. Eventually, a leather ball substituted for the paddle, one with a laced glove stitched into the top. Mark slipped his fingers into the glove and held the ball firmly on the seal's nose. In due course, Mark steadied the ball with just one finger and walked around. The seal followed him, trying to keep the ball on his nose. Mark lifted his finger to see if the seal could freely balance the ball. Success earned extra recompense. After much patience and effort from both trainer and animal, the seal independently balanced the ball on his nose.

Mark also taught the seals to clap. He tickled a seal's tummy until the seal involuntarily smacked its flippers together. Fish rewards reinforced behavior. The seal ultimately connected clapping with reward and clapped at the waving of a stick or raising of a hand.

Sharkey took it a step farther. He clapped after another seal did a trick. When people laughed, he did it even more.

It soon became obvious that Sharkey knew how to get laughs. He also knew he knew how to get laughs. He had timing. He had presence. And he had an uncanny knack for doing the absurd. In the eyes of Mark, Sharkey was a natural-born comedian. And to those inclined to dismiss such a claim as mere puffery or hyperbole, Sharkey would prove them wrong time and again.

∼

Mark met with Walter Jennier, one of Mark's former assistants from his days with Ringling Brothers. Jennier had studied under Mark in the 1920s. A newspaper account described them as close friends.[2] Jennier was now among the country's top seal trainers. Mark offered him an associate partnership position; Jennier accepted.

Mark also hired two assistants. Much like when the Huling brothers started thirty years earlier with Captain Webb, neither knew what might be in store. Both were in their mid-twenties; one was Billy Roe; the other was Lew Bohunicki.

Billy was a longtime Kingston resident who lived less than a mile from the seal-training quarters. He was of medium height and slender build, with thick coiffed black hair; a man whose five o'clock shadow customarily arrived sometime before noon. Billy had been a waiter the past five years, likely working for Mark at Huling's Barn.

Lew, originally from Schenectady, was midsized with prematurely depleted hair. He worked as an upright bass player in a dance band that often played at Huling's Barn, and had married Mark's daughter, Marjorie, the year before. Lew took on the surname Bohan as his seal training stage name. For everything else, he remained Bohunicki.

Mark made sure his new assistants treated the animals with respect and kindness. He forbade harshness of any kind directed toward the seals. Even a dirty glance was prohibited. The animals received every courtesy. Billy and Lew addressed each seal as *sir*.

Billy and Lew helped with chores like meal preparation. They also helped with training and learned the basics of presenting an act by studying Mark's every move, seeking nuances that might provide insight into the secrets of his craft. (It was Lew who noticed that Mark adjusted a seal's pedestal chair whenever he began an interaction, barely picking it up, then resetting it an inch or two away as he called over the seal. Lew adopted the technique as his own. Years would pass before he realized the quirk was an inconsequential habit of which Mark was unaware.[3])

Billy and Lew gained the needed skills. Between them and Walter Jennier, Mark had the staff needed to meet what he hoped would be an increasing workload. The World's Fair was to open in less than four months. With plenty to do and little time to do it, everyone kept busy.

∽

Mark and the seals bonded. On this point, some contend that the notion of a seal bonding with a trainer is anthropomorphism, assigning a human trait to an animal. Rewards, say some, merely create the illusion of a bond. Take away rewards and you no longer have a seal friend. Mark thought differently, stating, "Rewards come into it, of course, but I don't use rewards as much as people suppose."[4]

Fish rewards were even less important during advanced training. "This helps a lot, although it is really not necessary," Mark explained. "This custom, an institution in seal performances, seems to make a hit with audiences and also with the seal who was coaxed into doing his stunts by this method in early training."[5]

Mark convinced himself that seals were the smartest of animals. "I've just about got to believe it," he said. "Talk to 'most any seal-goofy chap and he'll swear it's a fact. It's my personal opinion that if a trainer doesn't make his head work that way he might as well put the pedestals, tubs, and teeter boards in the storehouse and go to farming."[6] What's more, Mark convinced the seals themselves that they were the smartest of animals, noting that once a seal "gets bitten with the 'I am a mental prodigy' idea, he will learn as many as a hundred tricks if you don't stop him."[7]

Mark was conversational with the animals. He spoke to them in plain language without the slightest condescension. The seals responded well to his respectful tone, and, at some level, seemed to understand him. "They detect almost exactly what type a mood a trainer is in," Mark said, "and their eyes are as easily read as those of a human being." So adept were the seals at detecting Mark's moods, he needed to be constantly upbeat when training, for if he was "upset about something, the seals feel it immediately and it is almost impossible to do anything with them." Mark sized up the personality and talents of each, which varied greatly. Patience and good judgment were the keys to success, so thought Mark, who once told a reporter he was "the most patient man living."[8]

Such was the daily training atmosphere that began in the morning with Mark making the rounds. He greeted each seal with a wide smile and a hand-flipper shake: "How are *you* today?"[9]

Grand Opening

Mark came up with a name for his new venture, a concept the press would find irresistible and a hook that would last the entire run of the operation. Henceforth, the facility would be known as Seal College. He painted billboard-sized signage atop the building facade with the words "Seal College" extra bold and triple-sized.

VISIT THE WORLD'S
LARGEST
SEAL COLLEGE
A UNIQUE INSTITUTION
WHERE SEALS
ARE TRAINED AND EXHIBITED

Seal College was listed in a New York vacation brochure. Ads for the World's Fair said it was among the state's leading attractions.[10] The Kingston Hotel and Restaurant Men's Association called it their "very latest asset from a sightseeing standpoint."[11] It hardly seemed to matter that it hadn't yet opened to the public. But that soon changed.

On Sunday, March 5, 1939, at three o'clock, Seal College opened its doors. Inside the building, on the left, was a reception room. A hallway led to an indoor expanse, two stories high, with a domed roof. Into view came a fifteen-by-thirty-foot concrete pool, six-feet deep, surrounded by a wooden floor. One seal perched on a seven-foot-high diving platform next to the pool, overseeing the proceedings as if he were king. Another lounged in a poolside bathtub. Yet another splashed in the pool. Others waddled nearby as if they owned the place.

Adjacent to the pool was a stage performance area. Behind that was a classroom, where seals received group instruction. Next to that was a smaller room for private tutoring, with an assortment of gadgets and paraphernalia stored on the walls. In the back of the building was a kitchen—its fish-stench manifest—equipped with a chest freezer, an industrial sink, and an area for meal preparation. Next to that was a dormitory with resting pools and benches for the seals to eat, relax, and sleep. The building also had a workshop where props were fabricated. A visit to the faculty room rounded out the tour. The coal stove in the middle served as the primary building heat source. Adventurous types went outside to the building crawl space. Underneath the kitchen were pumps that drew from and discharged untreated water into the adjacent Esopus Creek, replenishing the indoor pools on a continual basis. Total building construction cost, in today's dollars, was about $275,000.[12]

Ceremonies proceeded with all the pomp one might expect at the opening of the world's largest seal-training facility in the relatively commonplace city of Kingston, population 28,000, its claim to history as New York's first capital before being burned to the ground by the British. An emcee presented Mark and Walter to the 350 gatherers. Alderman-at-large John Schwenk delivered a speech: "It gives me great pleasure to preside at this occasion, because it marks the beginning of added fame for Kingston and Ulster County."[13]

Graduation Day

Seal College presented its first shows two weeks later. Mark added bleachers overlooking the pool and stage area. Bleachers had always been part of the plan; having seals perform before an audience was an important part of their syllabus. Two full houses witnessed the seals in their World's Fair preview.

Mark also provided a free show for orphans. The mayor of Kingston called on volunteers to provide transportation. Citizens used their own cars to bring 150 children to Seal College from four local institutions. The children were charmed, as were the teachers and chaperones, one of whom "considered the show as much educational as entertaining in that it taught what can be accomplished by kindness or coaxing rather than driving the animals in training."[14]

Two weeks later, in honor of the seals having completed their rudimentary coursework, Mark held a graduation ceremony. Another full house assembled at Seal College. Media outlets attended, including a national newsreel crew from Fox Movietone News.

As Mark gave his opening remarks, a nearby seal darted his neck and snuggled up to Mark's face, displaying nonstop affection. With unintended comedy, Mark dodged the seal's playful lunges as he unevenly delivered his prepared statement: "Now we find that the training of these seals is a much more difficult problem than bringing up children. It requires at least three years of constant training to bring them into a state of perfection. And we find that owing to their timid natures, that the utmost kindness has to be practiced at all times."[15]

Mark brought out four graduation candidates—Jumbo, Rocket, Teddy, and Sharkey—and put them through their paces. Then came the graduation ceremony. The newsreel crew focused their lights on the podium. Mark situated himself near the microphone. The cameraman gripped his hand-crank and began grinding away.

Before the crowd stood the Class of 1939; eight seals, each in a cap and gown: Jumbo, Rocket, Teddy, Sharkey, Alf, Pal, and Walter Jennier's two veteran seals, Buddy and Neptune. Mark delivered a commencement address. After that was the presentation of diplomas. Each seal approached Mark, accepted his parchment, and returned to his stand. That is, until it came time for Sharkey.

For Sharkey—class clown, class jock, and valedictorian—it was but another chance to steal the spotlight. After receiving his diploma, he instead headed toward the pool. Mark's mantra for subduing whatever tomfoolery the comic seal might have in store was to repeat "Take it easy, Sharkey" in a gentle singsong manner. But no amount of "take it easy" cajoling could stop the class clown on his graduation day.

Sharkey shuffled poolside. Then, with every mischievous bone in his body, he plunged into the water—cap, gown, diploma, and all.

"Astonishment struck everyone present including the cameraman who forgot to keep grinding," Mark later recalled. "A moment later, at my command, Sharkey was out of the pool and back to his original position, but by this time, the audience was convulsed with laughter. Sharkey's gown now clung to him, dripping and bedraggled. His once crisp diploma, which was still proudly clutched in his mouth, had become a soggy wad of paper, and his mortarboard, which he had somehow managed to retain, was cocked jauntily over one eye!"[16]

Fox Movietone News released their newsreel the following Thursday. That same day, in Missouri, Walter Jennier and Buddy kicked off a seven-

Mark watching a graduate clutch his diploma; Seal College, Kingston, New York. Photo by Alfred Eriss.

month tour with Russell Brothers Circus. "Star Sea Lion of Circus Is a College Graduate," read a headline. "Buddy is a graduate cum laude of the world's only sea lion college."[17]

New York World's Fair

Days later, on April 30, 1939, the New York World's Fair opened, coinciding with the 150th anniversary of George Washington's inauguration. The opening ceremony aired on TV, the first regularly scheduled commercial broadcast in television history, seen on about 200 sets scattered about the metropolitan area. Over 200,000 attended. Speakers included President Franklin D. Roosevelt and Albert Einstein.

The fair promised a glimpse at "The World of Tomorrow." Fanciful displays highlighted emerging technologies like color photos, FM radio, fax machines, fluorescent lights, and nylon pantyhose. Futuristic novelties included Elektro, a seven-foot robot who smoked cigarettes and swept a house clean. General Motors sponsored Futurama, a motorized diorama housed in a 35,000-square-foot pavilion, the largest-scale model ever built. Hundreds of slot cars traveling on utopian elevated highways moved to and from realistic-looking model villages and cities, while spectators traversed the exhibit seated in chair cars on a guided track.

Frank Buck's Jungleland was in the World's Fair amusement zone. Buck designed his attraction in the style of a Malaysian village. Face-painted natives in traditional garb played indigenous drums in a hut above the admission archway. Displayed throughout Jungleland, on a grand scale, were wild animals, birds, and reptiles, with an oval track for elephant and camel rides. Also inside was a man-made, moated, eighty-foot-high massif called Monkey Mountain, crawling with 600 monkeys. Next to that was Sea Lion Pool, patrolled by graduates of Seal College. Behind that was a re-created Malaysian jungle camp, with a restaurant serving Malaysian food. Visitors also lined up four times daily at the Jungleland indoor arena to watch lions, tigers, and college-educated seals in a presentation called the *Wild Animal Show*.

The World's Fair continued into the summer. Mark's assistants worked the fair, while Mark stayed at Seal College and worked with new recruits. He bought additional seals from Captain McGuire for $100, trained them, then sold them for upward of $3,500, if not more. Though rail-traveling circuses were all but extinct, truck-traveling circuses remained popular. Requests for college-educated seals poured in from circuses the world over.

Mark also worked with Jumbo and Sharkey. He withheld them from the World's Fair so they could receive extra advanced training. At 400 pounds, Jumbo looked his name. Mark took a page out of the circus playbook and marketed him as the "World's Largest Trained Seal." Stories about Seal College ran that summer in *Life* magazine and *Popular Science*.[18] Both featured Jumbo, who was soon garnering bookings at fancy prices, everything from local clubs to big-city engagements.[19] Sharkey meanwhile mastered tricks that usually took weeks of training in just a few days' time. He learned some on his first try. "Sharkey's early training came along remarkably fast," Mark said. "By the end of six months, he was far advanced beyond the other pupils at Seal College. By this time, his exceptional talents and possibilities had become apparent and the shaping of a new act was in progress."[20]

Sharkey had talent; Sharkey had confidence; Sharkey had charisma. Mark spoke highly of his many seals over the years, but reserved one superlative just for Sharkey: brilliant.

Sharkey at Woodstock

Everyone has heard of Woodstock, the 1969 music festival that defined an era. Many also know it didn't take place in Woodstock, the quaint town in Upstate New York (known as a haven for artists, musicians, and writers from which the festival derived its name), but rather, it took place at a nearby farm in Bethel, NY. Less known is that Woodstock and Seal College were only ten miles apart. And it so happened that Woodstock is where Sharkey was discovered.

Since 1932, the Woodstock library has held a summer fair, a fun-filled family event that continues to this day. At their 1939 fair, Mark stopped by with Jumbo. "With the assistance of Jumbo," a local story began, "all previous records in attendance and finance were broken."[21] Sharkey also tagged along in what was his very first show outside of Seal College. Mark had nurtured him like a sports coach with a young top draft pick, waiting for the right moment to let him shine. At last, Sharkey's moment had come. One local reporter wrote, "Round after round of applause greeted his every move."[22]

Woodstock resident and playwright Gladys Hurlbut was among those in attendance. The *New York Herald Tribune* would later memorialize her reaction to Sharkey that day: "Right then and there she realized he was no ordinary amphibian, but a consummate clown with the soul and technique of a great artist. Everything he did bristled with distinction and personality. Sooner or later she was going to do something to further his performance career."[23]

That time came sooner rather than later.

Within two weeks, a Broadway producer hired Hurlbut to write the book for a musical comedy. She soon hit on the idea of adding Sharkey as a cast member. Mark received word of her plan. The concept was unlike anything any of his seals had ever done. On the other hand, Sharkey was the most advanced pupil he had ever had. And it wasn't as if Mark had contacted Hurlbut; she had contacted him. Mark, as was later noted, "assured her that the plan was practical."[24]

The yet-to-be-named play was the latest from the best songwriting team in the business, Richard Rodgers and Lorenz Hart, who had assembled an all-star lineup. Hollywood movie star Vera Zorina was lead actress. Dwight Deere Wiman, a veteran of over forty Broadway shows, was producer. And Joshua Logan, a brilliant young talent, was director. Rodgers and Hart had used the same team for *I Married an Angel*, a recent hit show on Broadway. Hart was to write the book, but that never materialized. Logan took over the book-writing responsibilities but got busy and ran into personal problems. That's when the producer involved Logan's good friend, Woodstock resident Gladys Hurlbut.

Rodgers and Hart were superstars who were coming up with one hit show after the next; they had recently made the cover of *Time* and had recently written tunes like "My Funny Valentine," "The Lady Is a Tramp," and "My Romance." One historian describes their output during this stretch as "the most remarkable run of shows and songs ever produced by a single songwriting team."[25]

For Mark Huling, Gladys Hurlbut's offer must have sounded too good to be true. Perhaps so. But there was no denying that she was writing the book for the next Rodgers and Hart musical and had every intention of using Sharkey. That Rodgers and Hart were unaware of her plan to add a trained seal to their show was a detail she would tend to later.

Radio Days

Four weeks after the Woodstock Library Fair, to the day, Mark and Jumbo did a radio show in Manhattan. It was not a first, however, for a Huling-trained seal. Radio had come of age in the 1920s, yet another emerging entertainment medium along with silent films and the phonograph that began competing with vaudeville. A 1921 headline prophetically proclaimed: "Radiophone Cuts into Show Business: Vaudeville Exchanges First to Realize That Their Value Diminished by Wireless Appearances."[26]

In 1924, WJZ (now WABC) broadcast the Ringling Brothers menagerie (a radio first) on location from Madison Square Garden. The seal introductions went well until "some unthinking individual passed their cage with a bucket of fish just as [Frank] Huling was trying to get one to confine his outbursts to the microphone. That was what caused the pandemonium you probably heard."[27]

Ray Huling and Charlie made their radio debut three years later on a two-year-old station owned by the Edison Electric Illuminating Company of Boston, a station known by the corresponding call letters, WEEI. Charlie went on a children's show hosted by "Big Brother" Bob Emery, a fixture on the Boston media scene for the next forty years.

Kneeling on one knee, Bob held a carbon button microphone, roughly the size and shape of a coconut, and directed it toward Charlie, who was dressed in his calling-card hula skirt.

Ray set up a routine. "You see it's like this. I got a big yarp-yarp-atoire and you'd be surprised, but Boston folks seem to like my yarp-yarp-yarp-hula best. Yaarp, gulp! No, I ain't gotta cold. It's this grass step-in that's making me sneeze. It tickles. Har har. Listen!"[28]

Charlie whooshed his skirt Waikiki-wiggle-style and yowled a Hawaiian lullaby into the microphone. He then neighed like a horse, meowed like a cat, and bleated like a lamb. He also buzzed like a bee and did bird calls. Reports of the novel transmission hit newsstands from New York to Texas, and received press in *Radio Digest*.[29]

About that time, the newly formed National Broadcasting Company (NBC), a division of the Radio Corporation of America (RCA), began broadcasting coast-to-coast, something unthinkable in years past. NBC set up two radio networks, one labeled Red for commercial programming, the

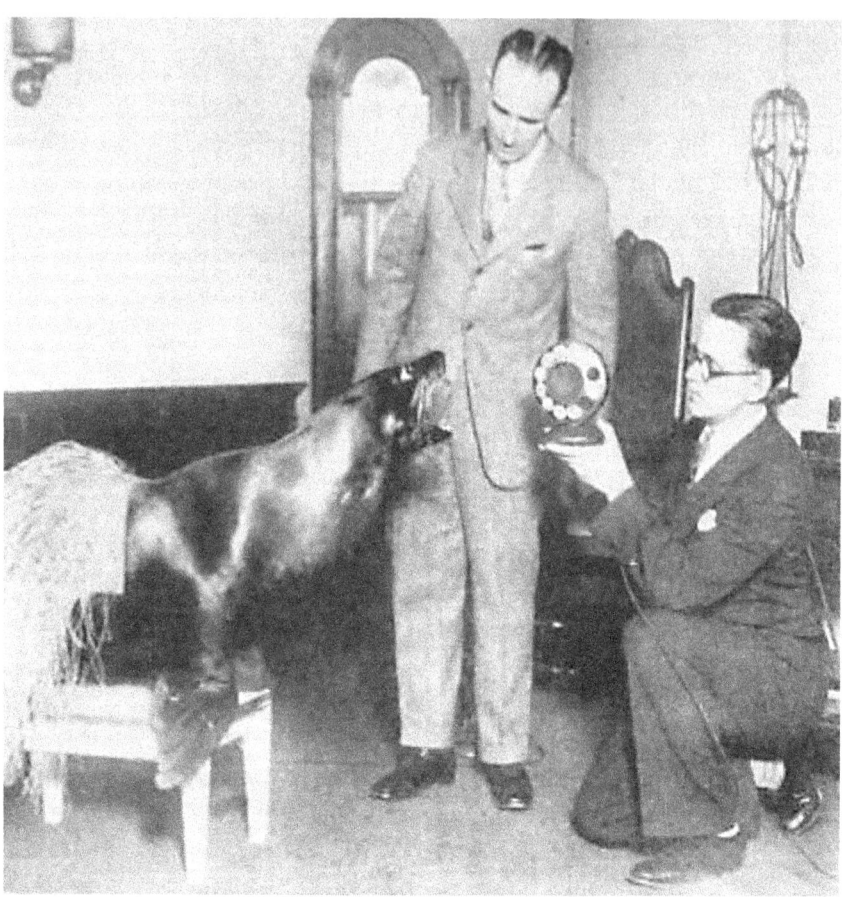

WEEI broadcast—Ray watches as Charlie vocalizes for host Bob Emery. Retrieved from *The Online Books Page*.

other labeled Blue for educational programming. In addition, RCA acquired the recently combined Keith and Orpheum theater chains and formed the Radio-Keith-Orpheum (RKO) Corporation. The blockbuster deal provided RKO with control of both radio and theater markets across the country.

In 1929, NBC and RKO collaborated to produce a weekly vaudeville radio show called the *Radio-Keith-Orpheum Hour*. It broadcast on Tuesday nights at 11:00 p.m., from New York City's first radio station—a station that had become the NBC Red Network flagship on its way to becoming the most storied radio station in history, known then as WEAF, later renamed

WNBC. Network broadcasting was such a fresh concept that East Coast theater managers installed radio receivers in their main halls, lounge areas, and smoking rooms so patrons would stay after regularly scheduled theater programming to listen to the *Radio-Keith-Orpheum Hour*. Charlie was in Manhattan playing engagements at the Palace and Hippodrome and was booked almost immediately onto the new radio show. On Tuesday, March 5, 1929, he was to headline the show's seventh airing.

Ray and Charlie proceeded to Fifth Avenue and Fifty-Fifth Street. Before them stood a new fifteen-story office building of unassuming block limestone exterior. Once inside, they rode the elevator to the thirteenth floor. Awaiting them was NBC headquarters.

They maneuvered through a labyrinth of the most superbly engineered sound studios in the world. The one-year-old complex had seven studios, each on floating springs for sound isolation, each with a thick-windowed control booth that had a console equipped with multi-microphone inputs, channel crossfaders, and other forward-looking features that would become the template for modern-day sound studios. The air-handling system for the seven tightly sealed studios rivaled the biggest in the world, exceeded only by those found in South African underground diamond mines.

The *Radio-Keith-Orpheum Hour* broadcast from the largest studio. Its two-story open floor plan measured 2,000 square feet. Art Deco chandeliers hung from the ceiling, each with clusters of massive cylindrical fixtures. Floor-to-ceiling draperies hugged the walls. A slightly raised, minimally adorned stage ran the width of the room.

As the appointed time neared, orchestra members moseyed into position. All were dressed in black suits, white shirts, and black bow ties. All were white males.

Charlie also moseyed into the studio. He brought with him an unmistakable presence, for in no time flat, it became obvious that NBC's state-of-the-art air handling system was no match for his odor, described by one eyewitness as "a distinctly fishy smell."[30]

Ray gently fended off curious bystanders. Charlie insisted on having his own personal space. "He will not permit anyone to touch him just before it is time to go on for an act," Ray said. "He has a real artistic disposition. After his act is over, he is willing to get acquainted with folk."[31] Ray intermittently washed the temperamental artist's face with a dripping sponge and treated him to a hunk of fish.

The show that night included big timers Harry Fox (of foxtrot fame) and vocalists Van and Schenck, the era's "highest salaried song team."[32] Also on the bill was Gilda Gray, an attractive theater and film star known for her flashy dancing and exotic hula outfits. Branded the Hula-Hula Girl, she had popularized the shimmy, a suggestive frenetic dance embraced by the liberated women of the 1920s flapper era, a dance deemed so sexually provocative in conservative circles, many dance halls banned it. Charlie happened to do a pretty good shimmy himself, bringing together the unusual, yet oddly logical, pairing of artists. During the broadcast, emcee Joe Laurie Jr. brought out Gilda and Charlie. Gilda took to the stage in an atypically modest dress and feathered hat. Charlie came out in a grass hula skirt. The orchestra reeled into a dance tune. Charlie and Gilda shimmied in unison. By one observation, Charlie "waggled with true Gilda Gray sinuosity."[33] Charlie also did two vocal numbers. The orchestra played as he crooned his tenor and baritone melodies.

Ninety miles north in Kingston, New York, residents crouched around radios dialed to AM 660, listening to their hometown hero. Reception was crystal clear.[34] Elsewhere, from coast to coast, people tuned to their nearest NBC Red Network radio station. Like magic, Charlie's vocal musings entered their living rooms from afar. National broadcasting was here to stay.

According to the *Daily News*, "Ray Huling's trained seal ran away with the ether vaudeville show."[35] After the show, Charlie and Gilda posed for a press shot that ran in papers nationwide. "Gilda Gray and her seal coat," quipped Gilda, offering a title for the photograph.[36]

Charlie then obediently followed Ray onto the building elevator. Once outside in the brisk midnight air, the trainer and his celebrity seal crowded into the backseat of a waiting taxicab, which is something you don't see every day, not even in New York City.

~

Flashing forward ten years to 1939, radio was in its prime, having surpassed magazines in total annual advertising revenues. Radio was now the undisputed king of home entertainment, a crown it would wear unchallenged for the next decade.

On August 16, 1939, Mark and Jumbo visited NBC headquarters in the studios of WEAF, relocated to the recently built seventy-story RCA

Building at 30 Rockefeller Center, a broadcast industry mecca known at the time as Radio City.

Jumbo went on a show called *Celebrity Program*. George Jessel emceed, a role he provided both on and off the air. So frequent was he the master of ceremonies at political and luminary banquets, FDR nicknamed him "Toastmaster General of the United States."

Jessel's guests that night were Mrs. Theodore Roosevelt Jr., vaudeville star Frank Crumit, Hollywood actor Peter Lorre, and Jumbo. Though Jumbo had yet to complete his graduate coursework in music, he could play a passable version of "My Country, 'Tis of Thee" on tin horns. Mark bragged on-air that Jumbo could do most anything, including dance, sing, and act. Jessel dismissed the idea as an obvious exaggeration. Minutes later, as Jessel was running down a song, Jumbo blurted a flurry of unwelcome noises, bringing the show to an abrupt halt.

The discomforted host jeered, "I suppose that's singing."

Mark heckled back, "No, I forgot to tell you that Jumbo's a critic, too."[37]

There would be no trash talking of any Seal College graduates. Not as long as Mark Huling or Jumbo had anything to say about it.

Peace Pipe

A week after Jumbo's radio broadcast, Mark conducted shows at the Ulster County Fair and Farmer's Field Day, held at Forsyth Park, about a mile from Seal College. Advance publicity assured the arrival of his two best seals, Jumbo and "Sharkey the Comedian."[38]

Six thousand people attended the fair, the largest such event ever held in the city. Spectators lined up outside a tent marked Seal College. Shows were twenty-five cents for adults, ten cents for children, and free for a handful of youths who managed an old familiar trick, lying on the ground and peeking underneath the tent, in this case, in plain view of a nearby absentminded booth attendant.

The *Daily Freeman* wrote that Seal College was "chief among the entertainment attractions."[39] That same day, the *Freeman* front-page banner headline read: "Berlin Source Says Danger of War Is Over."[40] A more unprophetic headline there has never been. Less than a week later, Germany invaded Poland; two days later, Britain and France declared war on Germany. And so began World War II.

That fall, the 1939–1940 New York World's Fair concluded its first of two years. Seal College graduates returned from Jungleland. Walter Jennier returned shortly after with his two veteran seals, Buddy and Neptune, following their circus season with Russell Brothers. Seal College was again flush with seals.

Mark introduced postgraduate curriculum by using a teaching method that relied on jealousy, for he had long concluded that the only thing that made a seal more miserable than not being able to show off was watching another seal show off. Mark engendered a healthy spirit of jealous competition. The resultant popularity contests inspired students to new heights. Outcomes were usually successful, if not always predictable, as was the case that fall.

On the syllabus was smoking. Mark gave Neptune a wooden, full bent pipe; a smoking instrument of a style customarily associated with the most distinguished of socialites. The veteran seal was a quick study and embraced his new skill with profound delight. "When Neptune learned to inhale," Mark said, "he became as unbearable as a 15-year-old boy with his first stogie and an audience of 12-year-olds."[41]

Indeed, Neptune strutted the halls of Seal College, blowing smoke in the faces of the other seals. Every now and again, to showboat even more, he reared back and ejected a sooty belch. Expulsions of such magnitude, Mark likened them to a huffing steam engine.

"To correct his behavior," Mark said, "we decided to teach one of the freshmen sea lions how to smoke, thinking that the sight would make Neptune so crestfallen he wouldn't enjoy showing off any more."

Enter Pal, a freshman, who in Mark's words, "picked up smoking like a potential marijuana addict."[42]

As good luck would have it, Pal accidently blew a smoke ring in front of his comrades. Neptune, clearly outdone, promptly ceased showing off. He even sulked and pouted.

Mark gloated. "He's cured."[43] Or so he thought.

Mark tried the routine at Seal College, before a crowd. He let Pal do the smoking. Neptune observed from the side, jealous and sullen, until at last, he lumbered onto the stage, barking in a fit of righteousness.

Mark took the pipe from Pal and gave it to Neptune. With great importance, Neptune puffed clouds of smoke.

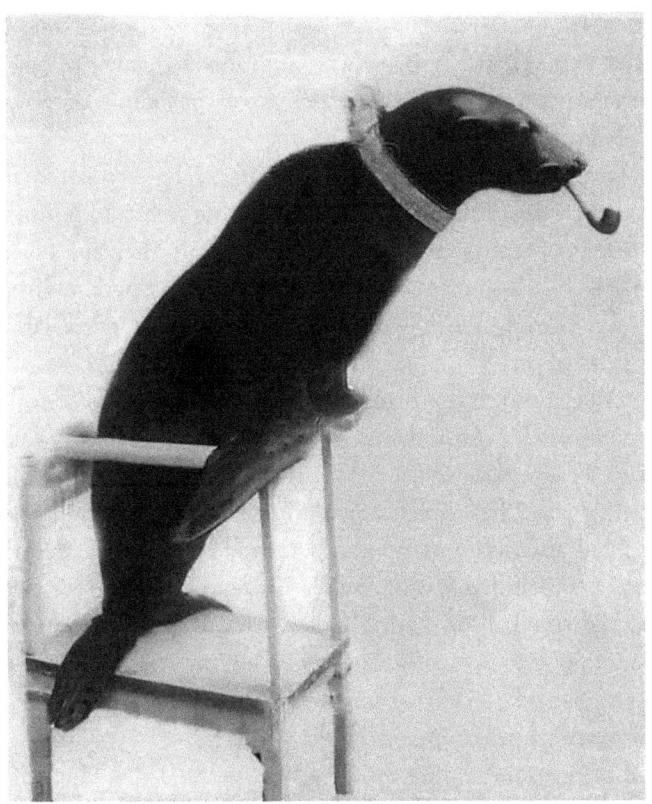

Huling-trained seal enjoying a smoke. Press photo from the author's collection.

Pal watched until he could watch no longer. He chomped through the seat of Mark's tuxedo trousers and yanked out his shirttail. Mark retook the pipe from Neptune and returned it to Pal, who happily resumed smoking as Mark scurried in search of wardrobe.

Suffice to say, there are things that happened at Seal College that didn't happen anywhere else.

~

Sharkey meanwhile rapidly matured. Mark did whatever he could to put him in front of a crowd. Sharkey performed for Brownies, Boy Scouts, and at a private party on somebody's lawn. It fell far short of the two years' experience Mark preferred before a seal worked a theater, but there was no time for that. Sharkey's Broadway audition was fast approaching and you could count on one hand the number of shows he had given outside of Seal College.

Ninety miles south, a New York City press release spoke of an upcoming musical comedy: "The Rodgers-Hart-Hurlbut vehicle for Zorina which is yet untitled will probably be completed about the end of November and rehearsals will begin as soon as the finished script is delivered."[44] As it turned out, complications would delay the start of rehearsals until the following February.

Seal College stayed on a roll. In December, Jumbo went to New York City and performed a musical number, heard over the CBS radio network. In January, *Popular Mechanics* did a feature story on Seal College. That same month, Jumbo headlined a local Shriners show to benefit a Kingston orphanage. He also received bookings for extended engagements in New York, Detroit, and Indianapolis. Walter Jennier agreed to tour with Jumbo so Mark could stay behind with Sharkey, who, come February, was poised to meet and potentially work with some of the biggest names in show business. On Saturday, February 3, 1940, Mark and Jumbo did one last local show before Jumbo left on his lucrative tour.

Mark now set his sights on Broadway and Gladys Hurlbut's curious proposition. Would his exceptionally talented but largely unproven seal rise to the occasion and meet its call?

It would be one heck of a wild ride before they found out.

Chapter 4

Sharkey Goes Broadway

Sharkey Meets the Tin Man

Sharkey had a chance to appear on Broadway. What were the odds? Playwright Gladys Hurlbut sees him at a small fair in Upstate New York, next thing you know, she has to have him. It mattered little that Mark Huling's rookie seal lacked theater experience and had made few public appearances. She saw something in Sharkey she was sure would be a hit.

While Hurlbut may have felt an animal is just what the show needed, previous appearances by members of the wild kingdom were not all that successful. The Broadway musical *Rainbow* had featured the lyrics of Oscar Hammerstein II, along with Fanny the Donkey, who turned violent under the lights and was guilty of other bodily indiscretions. Opening night was a shambles and the show quickly folded. In another Broadway disaster, a giant snake was to slither through a rear stage window during the second-act curtain of *White Cargo*. Police closed the show when the snake instead crept downstage accompanied by a screaming actress, scaring the daylights out of patrons in the front rows.

A trained seal had never been in a Broadway musical comedy. How Hurlbut thought she was going to convince Richard Rodgers and Lorenz Hart to go along with her idea is anybody's guess. But she remained optimistic that Sharkey was not only going to be in the show, he was going to steal the show.

On Sunday, February 4, 1940, Mark and Sharkey departed Kingston, New York. Awaiting them ninety miles due south was the world of Broadway. Rehearsals started next day. To say things got off to a shaky start is putting it mildly.

Lead actress Vera Zorina had already bailed due to a Hollywood contract conflict. Rodgers and Hart conceived much of the play as a vehicle to highlight her talents. They replaced her with Hungarian operetta singer and international film star, Marta Eggerth. Though a talent in her own right, the show needed major rework. Zorina was mainly a dancer; Eggerth was mainly a vocalist.

Further problems arose when Lorenz Hart found out that director and coauthor Joshua Logan had brought in Hurlbut without him knowing. And Hurlbut's crackpot idea of using a trained seal wasn't helping matters. As one colleague put it, Hart was "fuming."[1]

Hart was also boozing. His binge-drinking disappearing acts had become commonplace, this no exception. He up and left, a no-show for just about every rehearsal.

If only that was the extent of it. Logan was suffering from severe depression. It largely explained why he had enlisted Hurlbut to help write the book. "By the first day of rehearsal I was in such a state of despondency that I could hardly sit through a reading," he said. "I had no faith in what we had written."[2]

The show was quickly overhauled to accommodate Eggerth. With Lorenz Hart gone missing, Richard Rodgers did double-duty, reworking lyrics as well as music. And as if that wasn't enough, working Sharkey into the show posed other challenges. Interviewed some sixty years later, Eggerth's understudy, Marie Nash, said, "I can remember this seal coming up and putting his head on my lap, and I was supposed to be feeding him fish, and his breath was enough to knock you over."[3]

Gladys Hurlbut nonetheless insisted on using Sharkey. Everyone reluctantly agreed. In the words of Lorenz Hart biographer Frederick Nolan, "That everyone agreed to this nonsense is some indication of how bad things were."[4]

It wasn't all gloom and doom. The other leads were Shirley Ross and Jack Haley. Both had impressive resumes. Shirley Ross had recently done five films with Bing Crosby and Bob Hope, including *The Big Broadcast of 1938*, which featured her singing "Thanks for the Memory" in duet with Hope, his career signature tune. Jack Haley was a song-and-dance man and comedian. A big-time vaudevillian in his early career, he had later appeared in films, been on Broadway, and hosted a radio show. But that all paled in comparison to his most recent success. Haley was fresh off filming a movie in the role for which he is most remembered: the Tin Man in *The Wizard of Oz*.

Oz was still in first-run theaters when rumors circulated of Haley desiring a return to Broadway after a seven-year hiatus. Reports surfaced he had landed the lead role in an upcoming Broadway play; a role he soon learned involved a routine with a trained seal. Haley visited Seal College a week before rehearsals. Mark developed material tailored for the play and suited to Sharkey's unusual intellect and flair for comedy.

There was at least *some* hope. Though, with the original lead actress gone, director Joshua Logan depressed, lyricist Lorenz Hart on a drinking binge, and a trained seal with hygiene issues thrown in for good measure, the show must have felt more like a Shakespearean tragedy than a musical comedy.

"Sally" the Male-Impersonating Seal

Circumstances had dealt a mess to producer Dwight Deere Wiman, one that neither his Yale degree nor family pedigree (of John Deere fame) could fix. Wiman couldn't even come up with a title for the play. He chose *Nice Work*, but decided against it and ran a contest in the New York dailies, offering a pair of opening-night tickets to anyone who came up with a winning name. Wiman's press agent concealed himself as a foreign student under the alias Sregdor Drahcir (Richard Rodgers backward) and mailed in the winner: *Higher and Higher*.

Wiman, known for his even keel, stitched together the play. Asked his formula during the show's preparation, he said, "The most important thing I can think of is getting the most efficient staff together that I can find and then hoping for the best."[5]

True to his word, Wiman surrounded himself with the finest in stagecraft. He hired Jo Mielziner, now considered "the most successful set designer of the Golden era of Broadway."[6] He hired Lucinda Ballard, who later received the first Tony Award for costume design. He hired seasoned Broadway conductor Al Goodman and his orchestra. And he hired future

Tony Award–winning choreographer Robert Alton, who, in turn, hired some twenty dancers, among them, three upstarts in their late teens and early twenties who would later become major show-business personalities: Vera-Ellen, Miriam Nelson, and June Allyson.

Alton rehearsed dancers at the Imperial on Forty-Fourth Street. Logan, still mired in a funk, worked separately with the principals, first at the old Playhouse, then at the Majestic. Richard Rodgers tinkered with melodies at the piano and did his best to rework lyrics. Lorenz Hart, for the most part, remained lyricist in drunken absentia.

Wiman announced that tryouts would start in Boston, then go to Washington, DC, in early March. But come mid-February, Wiman was still casting lead roles, Alton was still auditioning dancers, and Hurlbut was still doing script rewrites. Wiman delayed Boston and cancelled DC. It took until late February for the itinerary to finalize: Tryouts would be at the New Haven and Boston Shubert Theaters before going to the Broadway Shubert, which was running *The Philadelphia Story*, a comedy starring Katharine Hepburn, set to close the last Saturday in March. *Higher and Higher* would open the following Thursday. The drill was a familiar one for Wiman. He had produced two recent Rodgers and Hart hit plays, *Babes in Arms* and *I Married an Angel*, using Shubert Theaters for both tryouts and Broadway.

Tech week started the last week of February at the Majestic. The play was as chaotic as ever. Dancers had met the lead actors only once and hadn't even seen the script. As dancers pranced in their practice rompers, an attending theater critic romanticized the rehearsal as being "in a state of pleasantly smooth confusion . . . with everyone delightfully unaware of what the show is all about."[7] The dancers likely saw it differently. Alton's tech-week drills left Miriam Nelson so tired that she napped on top of the stage piano during breaks. Others relied on Vera-Ellen's homemade fudge for sustenance. With just days before the cast faced a live audience, the story line finally revealed itself to the company.

Its Cinderella plot involved servants working in a mansion who get in a pickle when their wealthy employers lose their family fortune. The servants, led by butler Zachary (Jack Haley) and maid Sandy (Shirley Ross), persuade one of their own, a scullery maid named Minnie (Marta Eggerth), to pose as a debutante and win over a wealthy young man in the hope he can pay the staff and keep the mansion running. Minnie instead falls for a lowbrow watchman, creating a dilemma, complicated by the exploits of Sharkey. Eventually, true love prevails. As for living happily ever after, Broadway historian Dan Dietz writes, "Hopefully the staff finds financial security and Sharkey always has seafood to dine on."[8]

On March 7, the play opened in New Haven to a packed house. Sharkey's first theater show was a tall order. He needed to be onstage without a trainer, remember his cues, and interact with the cast per the script. Alas, he missed his first entrance. Naysayers quickly had their I-told-you-so-moment. But as was later explained, Sharkey "became confused upon seeing the scenery for the first time, an alibi that even experienced troupers use today when they muff an entrance on the out-of-town tryout."[9] Sharkey, fortunately, regained his composure. The *New Haven Journal-Courier* described his scene with Haley as "unforgettable."[10] The *Yale Daily News* wrote of Sharkey: "There is an ease and abandon in his acting that borders on the alarming!"[11]

Sharkey soon received more press. The backstory began two months prior when, for reasons unknown, the show's publicist promoted Sharkey as "Sally" even though the script called for him to play "himself." In January, the *Daily News* had twice gaffed at the hands of the publicist, once reporting the play included "a whiskered beast named Sally,"[12] another time reporting the play included "a fat girl seal named Sally."[13] But there was no Sally nor would there be. The misnomer might have squeaked by relatively unnoticed had that been the extent. But it continued, oddly enough, on the occasion of Marta Eggerth and Shirley Ross having modeled for the women's high society fashion magazine, *Harper's Bazaar*.

Marta modeled a gold, silk chiffon dress with a white-dotted top—an outfit from Jay Thorpe, a luxury store on Fifty-Seventh Street that specialized in custom-made clothing crafted by French designers. Shirley modeled a white dress fitted close in the midriff—an outfit from Marshall Field's department store out of Chicago. Both wore accessories made by the American jewelry firm of Trabert & Hoeffer, in partnership with the Parisian firm, Mauboussin.

Sharkey also participated in the photo shoot. The camera-friendly seal could strike a pose and mood for a given situation, as if grasping the task and intended outcome. His unexplained skill before a camera lasted his entire career. Apparently, anything that gave Sharkey a chance to show off was fair game.

Behind the camera was Martin Munkácsi. The Hungarian-born Jew and former Berliner had been a preeminent European photographer before fleeing Germany after Hitler's rise to power. He had since come to New York and signed a whopping contract with *Harper's Bazaar*. Often publicized as the world's highest-paid photographer, many today consider him the father of fashion photography.

Munkácsi made short work of integrating a seal into the realm of high-society glamour. He situated Sharkey next to Marta. Sharkey posed in a full front-profile, with his head gracefully held high. Marta leaned back ever so slightly, with an understated smile. In another shot, he situated Sharkey next to Shirley. Sharkey posed in a distinguished side-profile, facing right. Shirley modestly glanced left. In both shots, Munkácsi took creative advantage of the contrast between the dark-skinned seal and white backdrop such that Sharkey's smooth body contours interacted with the surrounding negative space in a uniquely engaging manner.

Harper's Bazaar featured the pictures in a two-page spread that ran in their March issue, timed to create buzz ahead of *Higher and Higher*'s Broadway open. Included was a blurb about the show, with the seal designated its *deus ex machina*, a Latin phrase connoting an unforeseen power that rescues a seemingly hopeless situation. It was great exposure except for one thing. The publicist had given the magazine his made-up seal name—with an alternate spelling to boot. *Harper's Bazaar* thus ran the piece headlined "Sallie the Seal."[14]

Now faced with fashion lovers around the globe reading about a wrongly identified seal (and theatergoers wondering who on earth Sallie was), the publicist took corrective action. Under the canon of "there is no such thing as bad publicity," he doubled down with a fanciful press release, clarifying "unsubstantiated whisperings" about Sallie being unhappy with her role. The story hit newsstands right after the last show in New Haven. "Now, the whole scandalous affair has come to light," wrote the *Brooklyn Daily Eagle*. The paper offered a blow-by-blow account.

> Mark Huling, her trainer, swore that she could play the part of a male impersonator. In fact, being an old experienced seal-skinner, he even went so far as to guarantee the deception. A grievous error on his part, as subsequent shenanigans have sadly shown. Right from the first day of rehearsal, it was apparent to every-

body that Sallie had a crush on Jack Haley. And as the days lengthened into weeks, the infatuation-at-first-sight ripened into a deep, undying love. Instead of following Miss Eggerth, as the script demanded, Sallie had an adoring ambulation for no one but Haley. Huling commanded and cajoled, but to no avail. Sallie just wouldn't sacrifice her true feelings for art, and at last, Huling had to admit defeat. There was just one thing to do, and sadly, Mr. Wiman did it. Sallie got her notice along with two weeks' supply of butterfish.[15]

The article made clear that the role belonged to "a sleek young male named Sharkey." With the Sallie ordeal settled, the cast and crew packed their bags and headed to Boston, set to open in two days. Unfortunately for Mark and Sharkey, the bizarre of *Harper's Bazaar* was about to give way to something even more bizarre.

Shanghaied Seal

Opening night in Boston was a sellout. The hometown favorite was a poor Irish kid from Boston who had made it big: Jack Haley. By one account, Sharkey provided Haley with "a grand ad libbing opportunity which he milks throughout the show." When Sharkey entered ahead of cue, Haley acted unaware and turned to another actor, "Do you feel a draft that has halitosis?" When Sharkey refused to exit, Haley told jokes until the stage-struck seal plodded off.[16]

Reviews the next morning were passable, barely. The *Boston Globe* wrote, "There are slow spots and unnecessary dialogue, but there is no doubt in the world everything will be ironed out in the next two weeks. It will be a faster and smoother show a week from now, and nearly perfect by the time it's ready to leave Boston."[17]

Lorenz Hart returned during Boston tryouts after his rash of unexcused absences. Richard Rodgers had his lyricist back, and not a moment too soon. The song "Life! Liberty!" was so bad they axed it. One Boston-area critic called it "one of the worst musical-comedy songs ever written."[18] During an interview, Rodgers admitted the song "was all wrong from the start," adding, "The only excuse I have to offer is that we had to write the show in a terrific hurry." Wiman interjected, artfully making light.

"Larry [Hart] told me that aside from the fact that the song was bad, the lyrics worse, that the people who were doing the show were baffled by its inappropriateness and couldn't put it across, and that it didn't belong in the show at all, it was a good song."[19] Hart silently smirked. Some later speculated that Rodgers had penned the lyrics, given Hart's prior truancy. They replaced the song with another called "I'm Afraid."

The play improved. But in the days that followed, it became more and more apparent that *Higher and Higher* was having difficulty living up to the *Globe*'s rosy forecast. Then came the unthinkable. Police reports, newspaper articles, a picture, eyewitness accounts, and subsequent mention in books, memoirs, and autobiographies all document a seemingly fantastical event, something the *Boston Globe* called "the strangest odyssey known to seal or man": Sharkey was kidnapped.[20]

Mark woke up unknowingly the next morning. He went to the Shubert basement where Sharkey was lodged at night in a combination tank and pen, under lock and key. There, he found the lock broken and Sharkey missing. Mark notified the police.

Sure enough, early that morning, at about sunrise, across the Charles River in Cambridge, police had received an anonymous tip informing them of the whereabouts of a stolen seal. Earlier still, in the wee hours of the night, Boston Police had answered a call from "a startled witness" who claimed to have seen a seal scampering down a city sidewalk.

The mischief had its origins in the days preceding. Word came that some of the Specialty Girl dancers were mingling off hours with undergrads from nearby Harvard University. "The Harvard lads stand around the stage door and wait, the cold Back Bay wind whistling through their whiffle haircuts," a journalist observed.[21]

Introductions and pleasantries having been cordially dispensed, and time clearly of the essence, what better way to demonstrate one's masculinity and impress the chorine of one's desire than by stealing the seal presently a part of the show in which she is appearing.

And so that first Saturday night in Boston, after the show, three brawny Harvard boys secretly stowed themselves in the theater. When at last the coast was clear, they hacked the lock to the basement seal pen and freed Sharkey. Acting with the cunning and urgency of a bank heist, and aided by a barrel of fish, the hoodlums led Sharkey, fish by fish, step by step, up a circular staircase and out a backstage door. Sharkey snacked his way right into the back of a getaway car.

The captors had gone but a few blocks when plans went horribly awry. Accruing odor inside the vehicle is likely to blame, for at the crossing of Stuart and Dartmouth, Sharkey sprang out a carelessly opened car window, then flopped onto the sidewalk and bolted.

A startled eyewitness phoned the police.

Cruisers raced to the scene.

Sharkey meanwhile scampered through the streets of Boston, eluding his abductors, his mayday barks reverberating through the otherwise tranquil nighttime air. Three blocks henceforth, the boys caught up. Aided by more fish, they coaxed Sharkey into their arms, wrapped him in a blanket, and put him back in the getaway car. The car vanished into the night.

Moments later, two squad cars arrived.

Police were soon on the lookout for three white males and a chocolate-brown sea lion traveling in a sedan with New York plates, last seen near the Boston Public Library. The aggressors continued on their malodorous joyride, undetected. After an undisclosed amount of time, they returned to campus.

One story held that the caper involved Harvard's undergrad humor club, the Harvard Lampoon, its alumni rich with notables like John Updike, George Plimpton, and Conan O'Brien, and others associated with shows like *The Office*, *Saturday Night Live*, and *30 Rock*. Most relevant to this story, however, is the Lampoon's age-old reputation, to this day, of being pranksters of the highest order.

Sharkey was whisked to Lampoon president Russell Bowie's dorm. When that didn't work, the captors hustled him to Lampoon headquarters, the Lampoon Building, a cylindrical structure with a castle-like facade and satirical appurtenances approximating a face wearing a Prussian helmet. (A Cambridge mayor once called it "one of the ugliest buildings in the world."[22] It is now on the National Register of Historic Places.)

When that too proved disagreeable to Sharkey, his abductors brought him to nearby Claverly Hall, where they hoisted him through a window that spilled into the dorm suite of one Jesse Cleveland, an underclassman trying to join the Lampoon, a trial-by-fire period of pledging known on Harvard campus as "comping."

Cambridge Police soon received what was described as "a mysterious telephone call" directing them to Cleveland's dorm, where they would find a stolen seal.[23] Sharkey meanwhile meandered to the dorm bathroom. The tumult awoke Cleveland, who, not long after, was greeted with a knock on his door. It was the police.

Cleveland relayed his story: "I heard a noise in the bathroom. It sounded something like barking. I got up and snapped on the light and there was what looked like a seal on the washstand. It reached a flipper down into the tub and turned on the water full blast. Then, a few seconds ago, it dove in." (Within the realm of possibility given that Sharkey's training had included a comedy skit with him independently drawing and taking a bath.)

The cops scratched their heads and gazed strangely at Cleveland. "Let's take a look," suggested one of the officers. They opened the bathroom door and peered inside. In plain view was Sharkey, who, by one account, was "having a swell time" in Cleveland's bathtub.[24]

The underclassman quickly became a person of interest. "But I didn't go anywhere last night," he pleaded.[25]

The police contacted the Animal Rescue League. Agents rushed to the scene and leashed Sharkey. But as they exited the dorm, he broke free. Agents fruitlessly gave pursuit. Students poured out of their dorms to view the spectacle, which was like something out of the Keystone Kops.

Over a hundred students gathered to cheer Sharkey as he snaked under one parked car after another, a dozen in all, evading frustrated rescuers, sweat dripping from their foreheads. After much excitement, an agent resecured Sharkey on a leash.

Mark hurried to Cambridge. To use a wordplay on a line Jack Haley was surely familiar with and Mark must have surely been thinking: "Sharkey, I've a feeling we're not in Kingston anymore."

Rumor had it the captors were put up to the task as a publicity stunt. If such the case, it worked. Newspapers nationwide ran a photo showing Sharkey in front of a Harvard dorm, next to a rescue agent, a policeman, and grinning students. The *New York Times* ran a story titled "Seal Found in Harvard Bathtub." A front-page headline in the *Boston Globe* read "Sharkey, Shanghaied Seal." And the *Harvard Crimson*, in another case of mistaken gender, ran a piece: "Coppers Undercover Kidnapped Actress in

Dorm Bathtub: Trick Seal, Star of Musical Show Disappears from Shubert in Publicity Stunt."[26] (John F. Kennedy was then a Harvard senior. Though hardly a suspect, less certain is whether he played a part in the article. The future president was then an editor for *The Crimson*.)

In another twist, a competing narrative surfaced involving Hollywood starlet Ann Sheridan, known as "the Oomph Girl," oomph in this case meaning sexually alluring. The Lampoon had ridiculed Sheridan the month before by awarding her "the most unlikely to succeed."[27] That sparked a nationally covered feud between the actress and the Ivy League humorists. Hearsay on campus was that a Sheridan agent had instigated the seal napping as retribution to embarrass the Lampoon. *The Crimson* ran a second article, claiming that "Only yesterday a Warner Brothers operative in Boston persuaded some undergraduates to steal a seal, and . . . tried to drag Ann Sheridan in the picture by saying, 'This seal has more oomph than the Lampoon' to every reporter he could find."[28]

It is hard to know whether Sharkey's kidnapping was a *Higher and Higher* publicity prank or Lampoon jokesters simply trying to impress some dancing gals or a Sheridan publicist trying to settle a score. In any case, three Harvard boys had pulled a doozy.

There was just one problem. Nobody had told Mark about the "joke" beforehand, and he wasn't laughing afterward.

Mark was not much for swearing, but on those rare occasions when suitably agitated, he used one particular word, a word he always repeated for effect, which in this case would have gone something like: "Goddamn those goddamn kids."[29]

We might expect this to have been such an occasion, for no sooner did Mark find out than he filed a complaint with Judge Joseph Zottoli, who issued a warrant, charging "John Doe" with larceny of a trained seal. Mark dropped the charges once he determined that Sharkey was unharmed. As far as can be told, Sharkey was back onstage at the Shubert without having missed a performance.

Tryouts continued without further incident though *Boston Herald* critic Elinor Hughes did raise concerns about lighting and costumes, these on top of previous concerns by others regarding the music and dialogue. Yet despite its glitches, Joshua Logan, of all people, saw potential, later writing, "Even in my despondency, I knew [Rodgers's] music was superb, that Robert Alton had devised some amusing dances, and Larry Hart had supplied brilliant lyrics. And so I worked on as well as I could to put *Higher* on its feet."[30]

But it still wasn't sitting quite right. And with Broadway a week away, having a trained seal onboard was the least of anyone's worries. Boston tryouts went through March, with fixes made right up until the very end. From there it was off to New York.

Opening Night: Act I

Thursday, April 4, 1940: opening night on Broadway. Previews and advertising had been plentiful; advance sales were encouraging. Ticket prices ranged from $1.10 to $6.60. Patrons situated for an evening of entertainment. Reviewers readied their notepads. In attendance were critics from the city's biggest newspapers—the *Times*, *Herald Tribune*, *Daily News*, *Sun*, *Daily Mirror*, *Post*, and *World-Telegram*—the toughest and most influential critics in theater.

The playbill listed all two dozen cast members, including Shirley Ross as Sandy Moore, Jack Haley as Zachary Ash, Marta Eggerth as Minnie Sorenson, and Sharkey as himself. The playbill stopped short of listing Sharkey in any of the scenes. It may not have been the star billing Gladys Hurlbut had imagined, but Sharkey had made it to Broadway, albeit, only slated to appear in two scenes in Act II.

At 8:40 p.m., Al Goodman and his orchestra went into full swing. The curtain rose. Into view came a hotel ballroom during the closing minutes of the annual Butler's Ball. A tall archway framed the entire stage. Two semicircular staircases met center-stage. Behind that, a floor-to-ceiling backdrop portrayed majestic columns. A banner, draped high in the air, ran the width of the stage. In total, the set called to mind an opulent ballroom.

Twenty-two dancers, billed as the Specialty Girls and Specialty Boys, paired off and whirled in stunning evening dress. Adding to the gaiety were stage platforms that moved. A sequence of dance turns followed: two couples in Scottish outfits; a couple doing an Irish jig; a pair of jitterbug dancers; and pairs of waltzers. After much festive stepping and skipping, the boys got their top hats and brought the girls their capes. Choreographer Robert Alton had designed a gem. Burns Mantle of the *Daily News* called the ballroom scene "as good as any musical comedy opening that I remember."[31]

Act I moved to the lavish kitchen of the Drake family mansion, where servants learned that the Drakes had just lost their fortune. When the servants realized that Mr. Drake had a daughter named Deborah who'd been living in Iceland for fifteen years, they plotted to pass off one of their own, a scullery maid played by Marta Eggerth, as Deborah. The servants, led by Jack Haley, schemed to send Eggerth to a swank singles nightclub in hopes of her landing a wealthy bachelor to provide money to keep the mansion afloat. A millionaire bachelor fell for the debutante imposter, resulting in the bachelor's father placing a newspaper notice announcing his son's forthcoming marriage to the lovely Deborah Drake, who, of course, was not at all Deborah Drake. "Deborah," however, instead fell for a night watchman, and he for her. The Hungarian-born soprano professed her love in two songs: "Nothing but You" and "From Another World." The music was splendid, as one could only expect from Richard Rodgers, but the lyrics, according to some, fell short. Conjecture was that some of the lyrics might have been the handiwork of Rodgers, given Hart's malingering during the show's preparation; though "Nothing but You" was apparently good enough for Judy Garland, who would later record the song.

Act I closed with "Disgustingly Rich," a barn burner full of movement, featuring vocals ping-ponging among cast members, interspersed with ensemble refrains. The participants declared in rhyme their plans once Eggerth marries the duped millionaire and they all become disgustingly rich: dining on salmon, playing backgammon; buying clothes at Saks, evading income tax; going to Miami to have salami.

But Haley dropped a bomb just before the curtain fell. He refused to have Eggerth marry if she wasn't truly in love.

Poof went the millionaire wedding.

Intermission. Patrons congregated in the lobby for cocktails and a smoke. The consensus seemed to be that the music was good and the dancing great, but the story was a dud, serviceable at best, lacking in the laugh department, a musical comedy without much comedy.

Director Joshua Logan had watched from his theater box, unsurprised that the first half had dragged, equally unsurprised by some of the reviews that would follow, later writing that they "were as gruesome as I knew they would be."[32] He had been unabatedly dejected for some time. So much so, that the set designer had suggested he seek help.

Logan attributed his gloom to be a byproduct of the story that he had helped craft and had directed, which he considered a failure. He would come to learn his unrelenting glumness had nothing to do with the play, but complicating his ill-placed blame was the fact that the first-act story line had indeed laid an egg.

Not all reviews would be as bad as Logan imagined, though two of the attending New York newspaper critics were brutal in their assessment of the first act. The *Herald Tribune* critic said, "It has a terrible time starting and then limps along between musical numbers," adding, "it isn't very funny." The *Post* critic said the story was "downright soporific [sleep inducing] in its slow-moving first-half."[33] The worst would come eleven days later when *Time* pronounced the plot "as much of an outright menace as maggots in cheese."[34]

There was at least the music and dancing, which practically everybody liked. And there was always the hope of a funnier second act.

Opening Night: Act II

Act II unfortunately didn't start much better. The watchman broke up with Eggerth because he didn't want the debutante socializing with the lower class, not knowing she was a maid. The servants, minus Haley, reinstated their scheme of having Eggerth pose as Deborah Drake to reel in a millionaire. Haley met with the watchman to inform him of Eggerth's real identity, setting up a spat between the watchman and Eggerth. Then one of Deborah's workers from Iceland—who happened to be in town and had seen the newspaper notice about her wedding—paid a visit to the Drakes in search of his debutante boss, not knowing that the Deborah at the mansion was an imposter. The Iceland fellow mentioned he was traveling with Deborah's baby, prompting one of the servants to reassess their charade as she wondered aloud whether the time had come to reveal their secret ploy. (Is it any wonder that much of the plot criticism stemmed from its being too complicated for a Broadway musical?)

That's when the worker from Iceland called out, "Come, Sharkey,"[35] and introduced the servants to Deborah's baby: her baby pet seal. Out lumbered Sharkey. Chaos ensued.

Shirley Ross climbed a chair and demanded that Sharkey be removed from the premises. Servants directed Sharkey to a secret door that led to the mansion east wing, allegedly haunted, where he could stay. Sharkey exited through the secret door.

Unceremonious though his first entrance was—after having been dismissed as a runt, after having been accused of impersonating a "fat girl seal," and after having been kidnapped—Sharkey had done something no seal had ever done. He had appeared in a Broadway musical comedy, a Rodgers and Hart musical comedy, no less.

Onward marched the convoluted plot. Eggerth and the watchman joyously reunited in a rooftop rendezvous, only to have Eggerth fall through a skylight into the east wing. She went missing just as a Drake family historian set out to scour that same wing in search of lost family records. This against the advice of Haley, who, playing the quintessential scaredy-cat, cautioned him that the east wing was haunted.

Act 2, scene 3 opened to a darkened stage. Moonlight shone through a window, scarcely revealing a dungeon-like cellar. A slight breeze stirred heavy cobwebs. Eerie critters climbed backdrop walls. Onstage was an old horse carriage and trunk chest, along with equipment brought by Deborah Drake's worker from Iceland: sealskin crates and a seal stand covered by a white sheet.

Three men crept into the room, each with a flashlight: the historian, searching for archeological treasure; the watchman, searching for his missing true love; and Haley, looking to bail at every opportunity, acting more like the Cowardly Lion than the Tin Man. And lurking about unbeknownst to any of them: Deborah Drake's pet seal, Sharkey, his very existence of which they were unaware.

Haley turned on the lights. The watchman grabbed a lantern and went on his way. The historian eyed the old horse carriage and told the tale of the coachman's ghost. Drake family legend held that, in 1824, revelers exiting a festive ball trampled to death a coachman who had operated the carriage that now stood before the historian and Haley. The revelers had shot the coachman's horse right where Haley was now standing. According to lore, every midnight brought forth the sounds of the coachman's whip. It being midnight, whip cracking sounds pierced the air, heard only by Haley.

Focus then turned to the old trunk chest near the carriage. At the urging of the historian, Haley dragged over the chest to see what was inside.

He found a grubby book that he gave to the historian. Looking for more, Haley leaned into the chest—head down, bum up.

Just then, Sharkey snuck onstage.

The historian remained preoccupied with the grubby book. Haley remained bent over, his elevated rump directly in sight.

Sharkey mulled the situation and coyly glanced at the audience, as if to convey his mischievous intent.

The crowd watched, agape, a flood of kindred thoughts no doubt silently coalescing at lightning speed: "Oh my, he's not, he wouldn't."

He did. Sharkey took dead aim and barreled nose-long into Haley's ass. A split second later, Sharkey turned around and scurried offstage with the prowess of an Olympic sprinter.

The crowd laughed—and laughed, and laughed, and laughed. One critic remarked that no other show on Broadway offered an "instant quite so shatteringly funny."[36]

Haley flung himself upright and looked accusingly at the historian. The two stared at each other, trying not to laugh themselves, that most delectable of situations for any comedian, the crowd howling wildly. As the howls lessened, Haley laid in to the historian and spoke of behavior "that no gentleman does to another gentleman."

The historian maintained his innocence. Haley twice circled the chest in search of the culprit. Finding none, and if not the historian, he convinced himself that the ghost of the coachman had appeared with his whip. "He gave me the butt end of it," Haley exclaimed.

After dismissing Haley as crazy, the historian spotted a package of dusty letters tied in a blue ribbon at the bottom of the chest. The two peered down. Thinking the documents might be of significance, the historian bent over to reach them.

Spot on cue, Sharkey snuck back onstage and gave the crowd another devilish glance. He then plowed nose-long into the historian's backside and immediately raced offstage. The theater again exploded into extended hilarity. In two short comic turns, Sharkey had pumped life into the play like a shot of adrenaline to the heart.

The historian laid into Haley. "Cut that out."

"Cut what out?" Haley replied.

"Didn't you just do to me what you just asked me if I did to you?"

The two looked at each other, perplexed, the crowd in a fit of hysterics. They closed the lid on the chest and sat down. The historian then read aloud a found letter. Haley listened, by now both scared and hungry. He peeled a banana and looked over the historian's shoulder. With the banana resting in Haley's hand, off to his side, out crept Sharkey, who, ever so subtly, approached Haley, ate half the banana, and dashed offstage.

The crowd again burst into laughter.

Haley turned to take a bite, only to find the banana half eaten, the crowd still in stitches. He did a double take, gave a protracted google-eyed look, then blamed the historian, who, of course, denied any misconduct.

The historian resumed reading the letter. Haley, now holding a half-eaten banana, again looked over the historian's shoulder.

Once more, out crept Sharkey, who snuck up on Haley, ate the rest of the banana, and scuttled offstage, drawing another round of hysterical laughter. Haley turned and stared at the fully eaten banana. He gave another google-eyed look—even more google-eyed than his first google-eyed look—and begged to leave as the crowd continued laughing.

The historian, bent on further investigating, carried downstage the Iceland fellow's stored seal-stand. He removed its white sheet cover and tossed it offstage. Moments later, a ghostly figure appeared onstage wearing the discarded white sheet. It was Sharkey.

Sharkey patiently stood upright on his stand while Haley and the historian gabbed, unaware of his presence. Each time Haley spoke, he turned not quite far enough to see Sharkey, until finally he turned and saw the ghostlike seal.

Sharkey leapt.

Haley screamed.

The script called for a quick chase-off, but the pair abandoned their parts and improvised a comic delight. Sharkey raced after Haley, nipping at his trousers, nosing his behind. Each time he goosed him, Haley squealed in falsetto, parodying Eggerth's operatic soprano. Round and round they went, Haley yelping, Sharkey in hot pursuit.

The theater again broke out in bellyaching laughter. "Convulsed" was the word used by multiple critics. Brooks Atkinson of the *New York Times* noted that among those convulsed in laughter were the orchestra pit musicians. (Some were convinced Haley had smeared his pants with salmon. Others guessed the use of a trick device. Neither was the case, as was later confirmed in the *Herald Tribune*. "Contrary to popular belief, no fish oil or any other lures are affixed on Jack Haley's trousers to induce Sharkey to nip him at the psychological moment." Others wondered how Sharkey could perform so independently. As one observer noted, "Nobody apparently has to threaten him with whips or seduce him with fish." When asked how he got Sharkey to play his part, Mark replied, "I just tell him what to do, show him a few times and he does it." How he got Sharkey to eat the banana was kept a trade secret.[37])

Having scared the bejesus out of Haley, Sharkey scooted offstage, whereupon Shirley Ross entered and complained the racket had awoken the entire household. Haley told of his escapades with a mysterious creature residing in the east wing.

"You dope. That was a trained seal," Ross explained.

After some convincing, Haley accepted her explanation. "All I can say is—he's been trained to do the damnedest things!"

Now clued in, Haley sang a novelty number with Ross called "I'm Afraid," in which they revealed their innermost fears. Among them, for Ross, rain, fogs, and touching frogs. For Haley, catching cold, growing old, and—trained seals.

There was still the task of finding Eggerth. The watchman spotted her in a dumbwaiter. Reuniting, he learned she had uncovered thousands of bottles of fine wines and Napoleon brandies hidden in a secret cellar.

Eggerth stumbled into view carrying a bottle of brandy. The ensemble rejoiced. Haley offered some friendly advice: "While you're down here, don't bend over."

The servants decided to open a nightclub in the east wing and sell the stockpile of booze to solve their money woes. Eggerth would supply singing entertainment and pretend to be Deborah Drake, providing the name recognition needed to attract business.

But in the seemingly never-ending series of plot twists, a powerful busybody named Ellen reappeared. She had long suspected that Eggerth was an imposter and was determined to prove she was a fake, thus foiling the servants' plan to exploit the Deborah Drake name. If the servants were to open their club, they would first need to convince Ellen that Eggerth was truly Deborah.

When Ellen found out about Deborah's pet seal, her foolproof test became whether he would recognize Eggerth. (Sharkey and Eggerth, according to the plot, had never crossed paths.) The servants stammered excuses to avoid Sharkey having to meet her. Shirley Ross added to the list. "Well, I'm afraid he's gone to bed."

Ellen was sure she had them on the ropes. "What's the matter? Are you afraid he won't recognize her?"

After some hemming and hawing, Eggerth nervously came forth. In her best broken-English Hungarian accent, she took a chance. "Yes, I call him. Here Sharkey—Sharkey—Sharkey."

Out came Sharkey, the fate of the servants' future on the line. Haley dangled a fish, visible to Sharkey and the audience but not to Ellen. Not above a succulent bribe, Sharkey waltzed over to Eggerth, let out some cheerful yaps, and put his head on her lap. Eggerth grabbed her bottle of Napoleon brandy and the two of them got sloshed as Sharkey convincingly played the part of a slobbering, spitting, drunkard seal.

Mission accomplished.

Sharkey had tricked Ellen, who left in a huff, muttering something about her boss now likely wanting a penguin. Haley went to Sharkey and quipped à la Groucho Marx, "For that, you get sturgeon." Haley fed Sharkey a fish, as if dropping a letter down a mail chute.

Shirley Ross announced that Sharkey was immediately hired to work at Club 22, a takeoff on the Manhattan former speakeasy turned celebrity hangout, the 21 Club. Thanks to Sharkey, the servants now had a prosperous nightclub to supply them their needed money.

The finale returned to the annual Butler's Ball. Cast members gathered on two staircases set in the same ballroom as the opening scene. A year had elapsed since the start of the play and couples were again in evening dress. Only this time, the scullery maid played by Marta Eggerth was at the ball, thus having realized her dream.

Atop the right staircase stood Eggerth, Europe's leading coloratura, soon to be one of the ten highest box-office draws in the world, on Broadway for the first time, ready to reprise her vocal feature, "Ev'ry Sunday Afternoon." But her spotlight moment was not to be. In the words of one journalist, "When Miss Eggerth began to sing, Sharkey diverted attention from her by diving into [his] tank . . . hell-bent on swiping [the] scene from her."[38]

Eggerth sang, assisted by Sharkey's background splashes. The curtain descended on her last note and went right back up, allowing the company to sing a final refrain to end the play. Cast members lined downstage. In the middle was Sharkey, who took a bow, the practice of which was standard coursework at Seal College.

Joshua Logan later wrote about the final curtain that night, candidly recounting his struggles with depression: "Sharkey the seal was on his little stand, stage center, and when the audience applauded, he slapped his fins together, which caused the audience to applaud and laugh more. . . . [It] gave me the only laugh I had had in months."[39]

(Logan would soon be diagnosed and receive treatment. He stayed in theater and film for decades more, coauthoring and directing the original Broadway production of *South Pacific*, for which he received a Pulitzer Prize and Tony Award. He later spoke openly about his depression, extolling the use of medications to manage his bipolar condition.)

Logan also later recalled the house lights coming up that opening night. Everyone was quietly exiting out the center aisle when a woman's voice rang out.

"Darling, zat ees zee muss wanderful f-ck in zee worl."

Heads turned from every direction. A French wife was talking to her American husband. Much to his embarrassment, she was using the French word for seal: *phoque*.

He tried to hush her but she kept talking. Loudly.

"I deed not say zee show was good, I shuzz say zee f-ck was good, zee f-ck, only zee f-ck, and oh, how I loved zat f-ck."[40]

"By this time, the whole aisle was laughing," Logan recalled.[41]

With new meaning uniquely bestowed upon "pardon my French," theatergoers continued their opening-night exit amid the sounds of chuckles and *phoques*.

Chapter 5

Higher and Higher

A Star Is Born

Sharkey's career was poised to go *Higher and Higher*, literally and figuratively. The next morning, millions read about the latest Rodgers and Hart Broadway musical comedy. Reviews were mixed, though critics reached overwhelming consensus on one point: Everybody loved Sharkey. And it wasn't as if he got lost in the fine print. Here's how it read, starting with the *New York Post*, which opened its review:

**SHARKEY AND JACK HALEY
IN "HIGHER AND HIGHER"**

Sharkey? Do you know who Sharkey is? Well, at any rate he is well worth knowing. Unquestionably he is one of the most gifted members of the family of Phocidae. And the Phocidae can be gifted, indeed. Even so, Sharkey is different . . . it is impossible not to have a feeling of affectionate gratitude for him. Come to think of it, it almost seems as though Sharkey must be the Great Seal of the Republic. He has troublesome habits. No one can deny that. Still, one rejoices at his being nosey. Although he may not know his Book of Etiquette, Sharkey's lack of manners can nonetheless put some laughs in a book where laughs are badly needed. The truth is that he and Jack Haley provide Mr. Wiman's new musical with its funniest episode and with one of the most uproarious scenes the winter has disclosed.[1]

The *Herald Tribune* likened "Mr. Sharkey" to the United States Marine Corps, "For certainly he comes rushing with valiance and dispatch, just in time to join Mr. Haley in saving the evening." The *World-Telegram* wrote, "The most hilarious interlude is provided by the exploits of a trained seal answering to the name Sharkey, who has picked up some astonishing tricks, perhaps from attending burlesque shows too often." *Daily Mirror* columnist Walter Winchell wrote about "Sharkey, a trained seal, who is so comical, he actually makes Haley seem like a straight man." The *Sun* noted nothing sensational, "always excepting Sharkey."[2]

New Yorker drama critic Wolcott Gibbs, an owlish and prickly sort, began his column as follows:

> A week or so ago in this space, I said that nobody wanted to watch a trained seal all night. This was a hasty and ill-considered statement, and I would like to retract it. There is a seal called Sharkey in Dwight Wiman's *Higher and Higher* that I could look at with the greatest pleasure practically forever. It is hard to define the exact quality that sets Sharkey apart from all other seals, except that his heart seems to be so complete in his work. . . . He is the natural artist, performing his magic for nothing but love.[3]

The *New Yorker* theater listings bear out Gibbs's change of heart. After initially failing to mention Sharkey, he revised the listing after the show opened: "Sharkey the Seal is supported by a fine cast, including Jack Haley, Shirley Ross and Marta Eggerth."[4]

Newsweek called Sharkey "a saucy seal." *Time* said he was the "biggest thing in the show." The Associated Press wrote that Sharkey "gives a performance that all human actors could study well for technique." United Press said he was "congesting the aisles of the Shubert." And Alice Hughes, in her widely read women's society column, called Sharkey "a real star," adding, "The crowd adores him."[5]

Gladys Hurlbut was a fool no longer. A prognosticator of most striking ability, she had called it right from the start.

Sharkey had stolen the show.

Sardi's Restaurant

Producer Dwight Deere Wiman arranged for a gala honorary luncheon as a token of his "esteem and appreciation for [Sharkey's] noble support."[6] The jacket-and-tie affair was to be at Sardi's.

On Wednesday, April 10, 1940, with the show about to complete its first week on Broadway, Sharkey and his escort Jack Haley sauntered over to the thirteen-year-old restaurant, a celebrity hangout across from the Shubert. Wiman directed Sharkey, cast members, and reporters past a little bar in the front alcove, on into the dining area. The modest-sized room had an air of decorum without being pretentious. Small tables draped in white cloth were meticulously set to accept the attending celebs and press.

Jack Haley and Sharkey heading to Sardi's. National Library of Australia, nla.obj-449711907.

A crew from the Hearst Corporation situated themselves to film a newsreel piece for their long running series, *News of the Week*.[7]

Sharkey leaned against his custom seal-stand. He then proudly lifted his head high and rested his flippers on a dining table, completely at ease. By one account, "Sharkey's table manner was refined and self-assured." Behind him, lining the walls, were caricatures featuring celebrities who had dined there, Sardi's trademark decor to this day.[8]

Jack Haley, Shirley Ross, and Marta Eggerth joined Sharkey at the head table. It all looked oddly matter of fact. Indeed, formal dining was nothing new for Huling seals. A 1927 silent newsreel showed a seal at a tea party, accompanied by Mark's wife, Lillian, and their twelve-year-old daughter, Marjorie. The seal wore a table napkin around his neck as he nosed his way through a fine china arrangement, sniffing dinner rolls and eating fish alternately delivered via fork by Lillian and Marjorie.

Haley, Ross, and Eggerth each gave a short speech befitting the occasion. After that, a Sardi's waiter appeared in a black suit and bow tie. Draped over his left arm was a white service towel. With great ceremony, the waiter delivered to the guest of honor a gourmet entrée of matjes herring

Sharkey's luncheon at Sardi's. National Library of Australia, nla.obj-449711907.

on a silver platter. Jack Haley gently took hold of the platter and eased it toward Sharkey, who eyed the proceedings like a black Lab watching a T-bone steak coming off the grill. Marta Eggerth observed as Shirley Ross happily fed the flippered VIP.⁹

News of the event raced across the nation. Sharkey had dined at Sardi's. Or had he? A columnist soon added to the story in his "Now-It-Can-Be-Told Department." According to an inside source, "There was a seal present but he wasn't Sharkey." The informant, claiming he never forgets a face, confronted one of Wiman's men, who "hemmed and hawed a minute and broke down." The man confessed. "Nope, that was Sharkey's understudy by the name of Teddy."¹⁰

Sharkey in fact did have an understudy named Teddy, a fellow Seal College graduate. Whether Mark had kept Sharkey at the theater, perhaps to rest him for the afternoon matinee, is unknown, leaving the true seal identity at the Sardi's luncheon an unsolved mystery. Sharkey, however, was unquestionably a regular at Sardi's after evening theater performances. Vincent Sardi Jr. later recalled Sharkey regularly clomping into his barroom. "Of course, Sardi's bar has always been ahead of the times," Sardi reminisced. "We've had our share of unusual customers." Sharkey once even bellied up to the bar and drank beer from a saucer.¹¹

Four days after the Sardi's luncheon, Sharkey appeared in the widely circulated Sunday *Herald Tribune*. Al Hirschfeld—who for eight decades famously drew caricatures of celebrities and Broadway stars—inked a caricature of Marta Eggerth comforting Sharkey as he yearned for a fish held by Jack Haley. The paper noted that "Sharkey, the seal is not a member of the Actor's Equity, but the cast of 'Higher and Higher' enthusiastically concedes that his acting talents entitle him to be."¹²

Days later, syndicated columnist Dorothy Kilgallen weighed in. For twenty-seven years, she penned "The Voice of Broadway." Able to make or break an actor's career, she also reported on current events; the *New York Post* once called her the most powerful female voice in America. On the show's two-week anniversary, Kilgallen gushed, "Broadway's current glamor boy, in my book, is not Desi Arnaz, Maurice Evans, or Franchot Tone, but that new, sleek, come-hither brunette dream prince of 'Higher and Higher'—Sharkey the Seal. The other boys can sing and dance of course, but can they act with flippers?"¹³

Jack Haley, Sharkey, and Marta Eggerth, drawn by Al Hirschfeld. © The Al Hirschfeld Foundation, www.AlHirschfeldFoundation.org.

Phony War

World War II was eight months old. Military actions had been quiet, so much so that many had been calling it the phony war. But five days after *Higher and Higher* opened on Broadway, Germany attacked Norway and Denmark. Luxembourg was next, then Belgium, the Netherlands, and France. They all fell to Germany that spring, stunning the world. Over the years, the Hulings and their seals had been no strangers to Germany's militaristic aspirations.

In 1914, terrorists killed the heir to the Austro-Hungarian throne. That sparked a diplomatic crisis that spiraled out of control. A military conflict ensued, marking the start of World War I. Frank Huling was in Europe at the time, his seals billed as international jugglers.[14] As the first shots rang out, Frank found himself caught in Germany.

"It was while I was showing in Breslau that the storm broke," Frank said. "I went to the manager and said 'I'm off!' and I started to go to Berlin all right; and there my troubles started. I had my American passports all right, but as I could speak little German, I had great difficulty in explaining who and what I was."[15]

Berlin authorities incarcerated Frank under suspicion that he was an English spy. Germans feared espionage. Circus types were apparently on their watch list, perhaps because the Germans themselves were disguising operatives as circus performers who traveled with contraband hidden in tent poles.[16] Officials detained Frank for three days. He eventually boarded a train headed out of the country.

During the trip, German officers inspected passengers every few stations. "To convince one officer that I really was a seal trainer," Frank said, "I had to get my animals out on the station and make them do some tricks." A few stops later, German authorities forcibly removed Frank from the train, his coarse treatment a precursor to the Gestapo under the Third Reich, whose men directed "suspicious individuals" to train station police barracks for interrogation.

Whatever Frank may have said or done, or perhaps how he looked, was deemed objectionable. Officers locked him up, overnight. Frank described it as "about the worst experience I have had."

Frank finally escaped from Germany and fled to England, where he and the seals boarded an ocean liner at the Port of Manchester.[17] Returning home, the animals took up residence in the newly established Huling seal quarters in Kingston, New York.

"I never want to see Germany again," Frank said shortly afterward. There are no records indicating he ever returned.

World War I continued for four years. The US ultimately became militarily involved; Allied forces ultimately prevailed.

Months later, the British Navy revealed "one of the most surprising secrets of the war." A leading British news agency wrote, "The British Government has just permitted the news to leak out that seals were trained to hunt German submarines, and they achieved some remarkable successes." Literary journals and newspapers throughout the United States and Britain published an article about California sea lions from someone the article claimed "probably knows more about them than any man alive."[18] That someone was Frank Huling.

It is unknown to what extent Frank contributed to the British military program. The seal trainer most credited is Frank's counterpart in England, Joseph Woodward. If Frank was involved, he was coy about it during his interview with the British press. "From my own experience," Frank said,

> I can at once understand how the British officers were able to train sea lions to follow submarines with unerring efficiency. In fact, there is scarcely any work these beasts cannot be trained to do. I am of the opinion that for short distances he can swim almost as fast as a porpoise. Considering the average speed of a submarine under water to be about twelve to fourteen miles an hour, it appears to me that the full-grown sea lion can easily catch and pass a submarine if within reasonable distance of the vessel at the start.[19]

German submarines (*Unterseeboots*, undersea boats, Anglicized "U-boats") crippled Allied shipping lanes during the war. They torpedoed and sank ships, both military and civilian, most infamously, the *Lusitania*, which killed about 1,200 (mostly civilians) and foretold the US declaring war on Germany. Countermanding U-boats was nigh impossible using traditional means. Admiral Jellicoe, head of the British Royal Navy, considered U-boats "the gravest peril which ever threatened the population of this country." Winston Churchill said, "It was in scale and in stake the greatest conflict ever decided at sea."[20]

British naval officers trained California sea lions to detect the sound of a U-boat propeller. A sea lion chased the submarine by swimming toward the noise. The animal carried a red float on a line and marked the U-boat position so that British sailors "could hasten to the spot and drop a depth bomb where it could wipe the German undersea pirate out of existence. . . . The intelligent sea lion was usually killed in the operation, but that is only one of the innumerable cruelties of war."[21]

Recent scholars have challenged the veracity of some of these claims, but there is no disputing that the British Royal Navy trained California sea lions to hunt German U-boats, and early results succeeded. There is also no disputing—at least in the eyes of Great Britain right after World War I—that the world's foremost authority on sea lions was one Frank Huling.

~

Jumping forward to January 1936—three years after Hitler's rise to power and three years before the start of World War II—Ray Huling and Charlie were in Berlin for a month of shows at Germany's top variety venue, the Scala Theater. Sharing the bill was singer and cabaret superstar Claire Waldoff. Feisty and openly gay, Waldoff's "non-Aryan" deeds and associations had earned her prior censorship under Germany's propaganda minister and right-hand man to Hitler, Joseph Goebbels.

Although cabaret had flourished under the Weimar Republic preceding the Third Reich, Goebbels, in less than three years, had shut down every cabaret hall in Germany; their sexually progressive and anti-Nazi undertones hardly in line with his objectives. *Die Katakombe*—an underground cabaret annex to the Scala and frequented by Waldoff—was the last to survive, having closed eight months earlier.

Goebbels remained wary of Waldoff. And many others.

On January 8, 1936, Goebbels paid a conspicuous visit to the Scala "celebrity" loge. That Waldoff would attract his presence was hardly cause for celebration. By then, there was already hushed talk of Nazi dissenters, and at times their incidental associates, having vanished at the hands of the Third Reich. Back home, US Western European Affairs Chief Jay Pierrepont Moffat had assured Americans traveling to Germany that they should have "no cause for worry if they mind their own business and keep out of trouble's way."[22] And here was Ray and Charlie, in Germany, sharing the bill with a Nazi dissident, staring into the crowd at one of trouble's most sinister incarnates.

The evening opened with twenty-four high-kicking showgirls known as the Scala Girls, the German equivalent of the Rockettes. Ray and Charlie appeared later in the first half of the show, performing against a backdrop of smiling cartoon animals. Ray wore a tuxedo; Charlie wore a decorative collar with a big bow on top. Their act closed per usual with Charlie in a grass skirt, doing his hula dance to orchestral accompaniment.[23]

During intermission, Goebbels stormed backstage. The feared Nazi leader let loose a diatribe directed at Waldoff, describing the show as *groben quatsch*, gross nonsense.[24]

Goebbels, however, didn't shut the show down, perhaps because the Olympics were coming to Germany and the Third Reich was putting on false airs of tolerance for the world to behold. The show played as planned through the end of January.

On February 4, two days before the start of the Olympics, Ray and Charlie boarded the SS *Bremen*, a luxury liner that was the pride of Germany. Bigger, more powerful, and faster than the *Titanic*, it departed

"Berlin: Scala—Ray Huling mit Seehund Charly." © Freiburg State Archives. Licensed under Creative Commons, CC BY 4.0, retrieved from *Europeana*.

Bremen, Germany, for its six-day overseas trek. Proudly hung high on its bow was an oversized swastika flag. Whether the ship arrived to a salutation of Nazi protesters, as was often the case when it docked in Manhattan, cannot be known with certainty.[25]

Ray and Charlie never returned to Germany. Claire Waldoff and her partner Olga von Roeder ultimately fled Berlin.

By spring 1940, the Scala Girls were high kicking in full military uniform, singing nationalistic songs on the Scala stage while Germany marched through Europe, conquering one country after the next. A phony war no longer, the US nevertheless maintained its policy of neutrality, determined to avoid another global military conflict, given the loss of blood and treasure that had accompanied World War I. The country went about its business.

Higher and Higher continued its run.

Autographs and Bronx Cheers

Higher and Higher had just about completed a month on Broadway when syndicated columnist George Tucker wrote, "Do you know that the most popular entertainer on Broadway is neither a Romeo or Juliet, but a trained seal, named Sharkey?" Even the cast conceded him top billing upon overhearing word on the street, "Let's go to see 'Higher and Higher'—you know, the one with that seal in it?"[26]

Sharkey received more backstage visitors than anyone. "Jeweled sophisticates on their way to the El Morocco after performance drop backstage to congratulate the stars . . . and they are not in their stellar dressing rooms two minutes before they are looking over the actors' shoulders and stretching their necks and beginning, 'Uh—I say, they don't keep that seal anywhere around here do they?' "[27]

Imagine their surprise when they saw not one, but two seals, Sharkey and understudy Teddy. According to Dorothy Kilgallen, there was even more to the story: "Now, I regret to report a crisis has arisen backstage. Teddy is getting temperamental. The applause virus has spread through the seal's soul, and he and Sharkey have terrible fights because Teddy is jealous over the star's success. . . . He just stands in the wings every night, flipping his flippers and whisking his whiskers, waiting for the moment when Sharkey, dazzled with adulation, will miss a cue, and therefore a fish."[28]

Most nights Teddy made but one appearance. He stood in and took bows to end the show. The swinging curtains unnerved Sharkey. So out came Teddy, relegated to accepting applause for all of Sharkey's efforts.[29] To make matters worse, the crew got in the habit of calling Sharkey, "Sharkey I," and Teddy, "Sharkey II."

It reached the point where Teddy had trouble responding to his real name. Everything came to a head during an actual performance. Jack Haley and Shirley Ross were onstage, expressing their innermost feelings toward one another. An attending playwright recalled what happened next.

> Sharkey II, apparently overcome with jealousy by the acclaim given Sharkey I, went racing out before the footlights, flipping around in a magnificent display of seal histrionics, bowing, honking, and rolling acrobatically from one side of the theater to the other . . . resisting all blandishments of trainers and stagehands to lure him off.[30]

If there is such a thing as a seal "roll eyes," Sharkey no doubt provided one from the wings. There was only room for one celebrity seal. Sharkey knew it. And poor Teddy, he knew it, too.

∼

Sharkey's photo shoot happened right at the theater. Shirley Ross arrived wearing a long pleasant dress. Her white formal gloves and elegant hat added a touch of savoir fare. She was all in.

Seven of the Specialty Girl dancers arrived in showy costumes, each outfit slightly different, though each exposing ample amounts of their long, talented legs. Stagehands brought out a dressing room chair, the one inscribed "This Seat Reserved for Sharkey."

The photographer positioned Shirley Ross and the chair in front of his camera. Dancers stood on either side. Sharkey waddled over and leaned upright against his chair; Shirley Ross graciously smiled.

Two of the dancers nearest Sharkey petted him. Another looked on pensively, having placed herself as far away as possible from the pungent mammal. Others giggled, wearing expressions that said, "I can't believe I'm doing this."

Sharkey's Broadway publicity shot. Billy Rose Theatre Division, The New York Public Library for the Performing Arts.

Sharkey, the center of attention; this is what he lived for. The immodest seal made easy work of the situation. (Sharkey never met a camera he didn't like.) He held his head high, with body language that was all swagger. And with the opening and closing click of a shutter, the world of Broadway fame now included a publicity shot of a trained seal.

On Saturday, May 4, *Higher and Higher* celebrated a month on Broadway. The following Wednesday, Sharkey was guest of honor at Rockefeller Center. Gorgeous weather brought out a large midday crowd. Spectators packed into the sunken plaza as well as the street-level balcony overlooking the Rockefeller Plaza skating rink.

Eight *Higher and Higher* Specialty Girls emerged on roller skates, wearing light jackets, skirts, and knee-high socks, courtesy of Lord and Taylor. They formed a line, each with their hands on the waist of the dancer in front of them. At the head of the line was Sharkey.

Sharkey and the Specialty Dancing Girls at Rockefeller Center. Billy Rose Theatre Division, The New York Public Library for the Performing Arts.

    Sharkey stood on his stand, which rested on a four-wheel dolly pushed by the lead dancer. The dancers skated around the rink, wheeling him around like a king. Sharkey basked in his glory; his look debonair. He surveyed the crowd confidently and coolly, as if broadcasting to the world that this was indeed his destiny.

    The dance troupe glided under the watchful eye of Prometheus. The famed eighteen-foot statue was then six years old. Sunbeams glimmered off the golden bronze effigy. Surrounding the statue was the Rockefeller Center Plaza fountain. Cascades of water streamed from all directions, collecting in the pool at the base of the fountain.

All went according to plan. That is, until Sharkey finessed a surprise dismount and made a beeline for the fountain. The dancers skated after their wayward colleague to no avail. By the time they reached water's edge, he had already taken his unauthorized plunge. Sharkey splashed and cavorted as laughs and cheers permeated the sun-drenched air.[31]

∽

Sharkey's next special event was at the New York World's Fair, now in its second and final year. On Monday, May 20, the fair opened its week with a noontime flag-raising ceremony and an address delivered by Mayor Fiorello La Guardia. Lunchtime programming featured Sharkey, who was joined by Jack Haley, Marta Eggerth, and Shirley Ross. They did a show at the Carrier Igloo, a five-story, white stucco, igloo-like structure, promoting a fast-rising technology: air conditioning. Sharkey stayed afterward with Jack Haley and his six-year-old son, Jack Jr. (future husband of Liza Minnelli). They gazed at the forty-eight-foot-high dual-thermometer next to the Carrier Igloo, which depicted the outside and inside temperatures side-by-side, highlighting the difference, a hook that would become ever more persuasive in the summer days ahead. The three of them next went inside the air-conditioned igloo. Crowds trailed them, as did a press photographer who took shots of the popular entertainer enjoying a day off with his young boy and sea lion costar.[32]

That same month brought autograph seekers. A Manhattan society column reported that "Since his opening night success, an ever-swelling demand for Sharkey's signature has rent the Broadway air. At first, Sharkey modestly declined on the grounds that he really didn't rate the attention. But the more he refused, the more insistent their clamor grew."[33] Jack Haley soon bought a gift for Sharkey: a special rubber stamp and inkpad that fit in his right and left front flippers. Sharkey practiced assiduously for weeks, pressing stamp to pad, until he had mastered his technique. Fans of Broadway now had another autograph to add to their collection, one that read:

SHARKEY
GRADUATE, SEAL COLLEGE
KINGSTON, N.Y.

Fame also brought gossip. One reporter wrote of a chat among starving actors, overheard at Sardi's, the topic being Sharkey. "If we had him in the show I just closed in, we'd have eaten him during the Cleveland run." Another wrote of Haley, seen about town with a lady friend whose dog "broke his leash and nipped Haley in the spot generally reserved for Sharkey, the seal."[34]

Sharkey-gossip of the most sensational variety—most sensational because the incident never actually happened—involved a lost valuable. The lost valuable hoax was so clichéd it had all but become a parody of itself. Shirley Ross allegedly dropped and lost a diamond ring during a scene with Sharkey. The "news" was unashamedly leaked the next day.

Sharkey, Jack Haley, and Jack Jr. at the New York World's Fair. Manuscripts and Archives Division, The New York Public Library.

Sharkey saw the ring fall and before anyone could interfere, he slithered over to where it lay and swallowed it in one gulp. Now, distinguished assayers of seal on the hoof place Sharkey's valuation at $3500, which added to the $2500 ring now inside of him raises his total dollar worth to a neat six grand—or indubitably the most valuable seal in captivity. Day and night guards have been placed in charge of Sharkey until the ring can be retrieved through the due process of nature.[35]

Credit the *Daily News* for reporting its own version, writing that Sharkey ate the ring "before anyone could say *Publicity*." The story ran under the headline, "Well, Maybe."[36]

Publicity stunts aside, Sharkey and Teddy settled into a routine. Mark set up makeshift quarters in the alley between the Shubert and Broadhurst Theaters. Their daily ritual included a bath, exercise, and plenty of play. Mealtimes were 10:00 a.m. and 4:00 p.m. Mark cleaned their teeth afterward using a triple-sized toothbrush dipped in saline. Their workload was Broadway-standard, eight shows a week.

"Members of the cast enjoyed playing with Sharkey in the interim they were off-stage," Mark said. "Right in the midst of all the fun, he would start moving off in the direction of his next entrance, without a word of command. Sharkey never missed a cue during the entire run of the show." Sharkey knew from the music score when he was due on stage.[37]

Broadway's frolic with sea lion celebrity brought with it unique moments, like when Sharkey did a WABC radio broadcast promoting *Higher and Higher* and he "first looked at the mike carefully (it was an ordinary one, no frills), took a practice bark into it next, and then raised up and took a bite out of it."[38]

Topping that was the time Sharkey learned that most uncultured of human customs, imitating fart noises. In an interview granted to the Associated Press, Mark said that "Sharkey was awaiting his turn in a dressing room when some of the boys, to pass the time away, began experimenting with various modulations of Bronx cheers. Without hesitation, Sharkey placed his flippers to his nose and began blowing a variety that would have made any Brooklyn fan green with envy."[39]

With his haunted mansion scene just minutes away, Sharkey became a virtual backstage flatulence machine. "I had a tough time stopping him,"

Mark admitted. The dressing room gestures were quelled just in time; Sharkey did the scene as scripted. It wasn't until he had finished and had almost cleared the stage when he stopped (audience in plain view), put his flippers to his nose, and as Mark put it, "gave an elongated cheer and trundled for his herring."[40]

∽

May became June. *Higher and Higher* was now the fourth-longest active running musical on Broadway, among the "golden dozen" theater attractions listed in the *Daily News*. Ads for Chesterfield cigarettes featured *Higher and Higher* in bold print, bragging that it embodied "Chesterfield's increasing popularity and the new Broadway hit of the same name."[41]

On June 9, the *Herald Tribune* ran an article titled "Backstage Life of Sharkey the Seal." Included were three drawings of Sharkey preparing for his haunted mansion scene, drawn by Don Freeman, an illustrator and author best known for his children's book, *Corduroy*.[42]

Time published its Broadway annual report the next day. They doled out nine Best Awards, whose recipients included Cole Porter, John Barrymore, and Sharkey, the only recipient from *Higher and Higher*.[43]

But things hit a major snag that same day. Producer Dwight Wiman confirmed rumors that Marta Eggerth was withdrawing from the show. He shut down the box office and announced he was suspending performances effective the end of the week. The show would restart in August. Ticket holders left in the lurch were guaranteed new ticket accommodations upon his reopening of the box office. Eggerth was booked for a tour of opera houses with her husband, acclaimed Polish tenor Jan Kiepura. Net receipts for a majority of the concerts were for Polish relief.[44] Wiman had known of the tour all along.

Eggerth would go on to have the longest career of anyone in *Higher and Higher*. After a brief Hollywood stint, she returned to operetta, touring the world for decades to much acclaim, especially with her husband in Franz Lehar's *The Merry Widow*. She performed into her eighties and nineties, here and in Europe, teaching master classes, giving recitals, and making appearances at Café Sabarsky, a renowned cabaret venue on the Upper East Side of Manhattan. Her last public performance was in 2011 at the

One of three illustrations of Sharkey drawn by Don Freeman. Billy Rose Theatre Division, The New York Public Library for the Performing Arts, Astor, Lenox and Tilden Foundations, used with permission from Roy Freeman.

age of ninety-nine; she died two years later. When this author contacted Marta Eggerth's son, Marjan Kiepura, himself a noted concert pianist, to inquire whether his mother had ever shared any memories of Sharkey, his response was quick and enthusiastic.

> Oh, yes! My mother often spoke of Sharkey! I grew up hearing about Sharkey and that she loved him very much. She remembered that Sharkey was a good "actor" and very well trained. He was a regular member of the cast. She told me that she always wanted to hug and kiss him but he smelled of fish. Regardless, my mother felt that he was human. They had a great relationship and she always told me "he was a good colleague."[45]

Eggerth's last night with *Higher and Higher* was Thursday, June 13. Her understudy covered Friday evening, the Saturday matinee, and Saturday evening. With that, the play ended its inaugural run. The scheduled reopen was to be seven weeks later.

Sharkey made one last cameo before going on break. He presided at a bathing suit contest sponsored by Saks Fifth Avenue. His celebrity arrival frustrated journalist Alice Hughes, who wrote that it caused "an especially dandy traffic jam on 39th Street. . . . Sharkey eyed the swim suits carefully, allowed they were right pretty, ate a few little dead fish on the house and then galloped away, playing 'Home Sweet Home' on a little tin horn. Doesn't take much to amuse a New Yorker."[46]

Richard Rodgers's Irrefutable Rule

Sharkey returned to Seal College and did a Fourth of July carnival in nearby Rosendale. In August, he returned to the Woodstock Library Fair, which observed the anniversary of his discovery there by Gladys Hurlbut, who joined him. The two greeted a receiving line of fans. Sharkey was billed as "the seal that set all New York talking."[47] Three days later, Associated Press theater critic Mark Barron opened his nationally syndicated Sunday newspaper column as follows:

> Sharkey, the seal, flapped out of his luxurious pool at Kingston N.Y. today and prepared to resume his lucrative and glamor-

ous engagement. . . . Sharkey can boast of several triumphs. He is the first seal to play a return engagement as a dramatic actor on Broadway, and he will probably think that this is his farewell tour. He is the only member of the Pinnipedia group of mammals to win a half dozen medals for his acting; and he is the one representative of wild life on the Rialto who has conducted himself a perfect gentleman through such ordeals as being fed champagne and tickled by blondes at nightclubs and being guest of honor at a skating party in Rockefeller Center.[48]

Higher and Higher reopened at the Shubert, minus Eggerth. Turnout was unenthusiastic, as were the few reviews that appeared. The *New York Times* reported that the show "does not really warm up until Haley and his pals toss the book out the window somewhere toward the last third of the evening [and] Sharkey, who is one of Broadway's current celebrities, starts waddling and flipping in the midst of the rumpus."[49] The play closed three weeks later, "collapsing in a quiet heap," as one Richard Rodgers biographer put it.[50] All told, it ran for 108 Broadway performances, not bad for those days, though not nearly up to the standards of Rodgers and Hart.

Thirty-five years later, Richard Rodgers lamented in his autobiography: "If *Higher and Higher* is remembered at all today it is probably not because of its cast or songs but because of a trained seal. This leads to another of Rodgers' Irrefutable Rules: If a trained seal steals your show, you don't have a show."[51]

It Never Entered My Mind

Richard Rodgers may have been a little too hard on himself. If nothing else, *Higher and Higher* left behind one of Broadway's most enduring songs, the melancholy "It Never Entered My Mind"; a tune of a sort that if one focuses on Rodgers's beautifully simple melody, it is easy to forget there are lyrics, and if one focuses on Hart's poignant lyrics, it is easy to forget there is melody. In total, a piece that is greater than the sum of its formidable parts.

Originally sung by Shirley Ross just before Sharkey's haunted mansion scene, "It Never Entered My Mind" remains a well-covered show tune, recorded over the years by the likes of Frank Sinatra, Linda Ronstadt,

Wynton Marsalis, and, more recently, Chris Botti and *American Idol* finalist turned Broadway star, Katharine McPhee.

The 1954 and 1956 instrumental versions by Miles Davis are the most well-known. Lauded among jazz enthusiasts, Miles's earlier recording has twice made it into a major film score: once in the dramatic final scene in the 1974 movie *Lenny*, a tell-all biopic about comedian Lenny Bruce starring Dustin Hoffman; and again in the marriage proposal scene in the 1999 movie *Runaway Bride*, starring Julia Roberts and Richard Gere. That same Miles version also made it into the 2017 season finale of *Better Call Saul*.

As for vocal versions, there is none more breathtaking than Sarah Vaughan's off her album *Sarah Vaughan Sings Broadway*. Included is the oft-omitted introductory verse along with the standard chorus; her treatment of the melody more than capable of sending chills down the spine of even the most casual of listeners.

Higher and Higher made it to the big screen. The 1943 film starred Jack Haley and also Frank Sinatra in his first leading movie role. Only one Rodgers and Hart tune, "Disgustingly Rich," made it from the stage show into the movie. There was no trained seal.

Rodgers and Hart rebounded with *Pal Joey*. It opened on Broadway four months after the close of *Higher and Higher* and was their third-longest running musical. Robert Alton again choreographed, discovering Gene Kelly, who played the part of Joey. The show was one of Rodgers and Hart's last collaborations. Hart's lifestyle caught up with him; he died three years later at age forty-eight.

As for what happened to Sharkey?

Well, his career was just getting started.

Chapter 6

Dry Act, Wet Act

Scribner's Commentator

It is with some hesitation that the adventures of a trained seal continue to be chronicled during a period involving the deadliest military conflict in human history. Over 50 million people died during World War II, unspeakable military and civilian casualties, including the murder of 6 million Jews in concentration camps. Against this backdrop, what possible relevance could the story of a trained seal have? How does entertainment and fun square with the horrors of World War II? Perhaps these are not fair questions. Fair or not, they seem relevant to ponder at the very least.

The United States was a country sharply divided. Isolationists thought the country was better off minding its own business by avoiding the military conflict altogether. Interventionists thought that Germany and the other Axis powers posed an existential threat to democracy everywhere, arguing the time had come to join in the overseas fight.

Scribner's Commentator, self-described as "The National Magazine for an Independent American Destiny," was the nation's leading isolationist periodical and the leading voice for the nation's largest antiwar organization, the America First movement. They argued that Germany and the other Axis powers had no interest in harming the United States. Moreover, they felt the US was ill prepared militarily, which was reasonably accurate. (America's military meagerly ranked as the eighteenth largest in the world.)

Automobile giant Henry Ford and aviation hero Charles Lindbergh were the movement's leading supporters, believing Europe should decide its own fate. Their detractors often viewed them as anti-Semitic. Some accused them, not entirely unfairly, of being Nazi sympathizers. But the America First movement made for strange bedfellows. Right-wingers like Ford and Lindbergh found common ground with left-wing pacifist groups like the Keep America Out of War Committee. As a matter of national policy, isolationism was the country's official position, as it had been for some time, articulated by congressional passage of several Neutrality Acts.

Scribner's Commentator beat the isolationist drum loudly. Its December 1940 issue had Ford on the cover, who contributed an article, "An American Foreign Policy." Also included was a transcript of Lindbergh's latest radio address, "A Plea for American Independence." That same issue had an article, "War or Peace, America's Decision," and one with the teaser, "Who has had a finger in more interventionist pies than anyone else? This revealing article will tell you what one man and his associates are doing to push this country into war." The magazine derided interventionists, a group that had found increasing support in response to escalated Axis military aggression and persecution of innocent civilians. Interventionists, however, were still in the minority, a point not lost in that same issue. A cartoon on the inside cover depicted a radio labeled the Noisy Minority that cynically blared, "Don't bother about swords, fight 'em with feather dusters. Go after Japan! Crush Hitler! Blah, blah, blah." Commenting in the foreground was Uncle Sam. "Maybe the Noisy Minority would like to do the fighting."

Scribner's Commentator was unquestionably a hotbed for the America First movement. The magazine also sprinkled in human-interest stories completely unrelated from the politically charged material that otherwise filled its pages. In what is arguably the most bizarre placement of a seal-training article ever found in a magazine, that same December 1940 issue had a four-page piece on Seal College.

"Don't try to train a seal unless you have plenty of time and limitless patience," the article started. "Let's go to the Seal College and see why."

Mentioned was "gentle soft-spoken Mark Huling," along with his partner, Walter Jennier, and staff members William Roe and Lew Bohan. Readers learned of Dean Huling and Professor Roe training Pal and Rocket. Sharkey got his due, described as "the smartest graduate of probably the oddest college ever founded."[1]

The piece ended, "You'll probably catch one of the acts some time. If you do, give it the big hand it deserves."

Odiva the Samoan Nymph

Sharkey may have been out of the Broadway limelight, but the press aristocracy kept writing. Lucius Beebe—a flamboyant intellectual, esteemed journalist, and self-proclaimed snob—issued several Broadway awards that year. Most Gratifying Performance went to "obviously Sharkey, [with whom] Roscius, Salvini, or the elder Barrymore should be glad to be associated." It was good company: Roscius, a famous actor during the Roman Empire; Salvini, a noted nineteenth-century Italian actor; and Maurice Barrymore, patriarch of the famed American acting family. Dorothy Kilgallen also issued her own awards. Most Bizarre went to Orson Welles, Prettiest Legs went to Betty Grable, and Most Original New Comedian went to Sharkey, who "has returned to Kingston, N.Y., Seal College—for post graduate courses!"[2]

Indeed, Sharkey was working on advanced material. "I've never seen an animal with his brains," Mark said. "He catches on like lightning. His ambition knows no bounds, and his self-satisfaction is plainly evident whenever a new feat is mastered."[3]

Within a month after the close of *Higher and Higher*, Sharkey worked a New Jersey theater as part of a five-act variety bill, where he was awarded "topline honors." He headlined a seven-act bill at another Jersey theater, where the press called him "a wow."[4] At another theater, he was billed as "Jack Haley's Wonder Seal," though Mark was none too pleased with the wording; Haley wasn't even on the program. It was the first and last time Sharkey came so advertised.

During each performance, while lying on his back, Sharkey balanced a glass of water on a pole balanced on his nose. He then craned his neck and rolled over on his back 360 degrees without spilling a drop. The stunt looked to be a physical impossibility. One critic praised it "the most difficult trick of balancing that can be contrived by man."[5]

Sharkey also roared like Leo the MGM Lion, so loud and realistically, one was hard-pressed to tell the difference. Mark set up another bit: "And now, we're going to have Sharkey do his imitation of a nagging wife." Mark played a soused husband, coming home after a long night. Sharkey greeted him in "a pretty pair of pink underthings" and unleashed a barrage of remarkably human-like though utterly incoherent vocalizations. One observer likened it to "a chattering, vixenish wife giving her stay-out-late husband a hunk of her mind." The press called Sharkey's imitations "amazing."[6]

Along with the new stage act, Mark developed a water-tank act. He claimed it a first in sea lion training, which wasn't entirely true. In the early 1900s, an old codger named Captain C. F. Adams had developed a sea lion water-tank act that featured his attractive, young assistant, Miss Alma Beaumont, better known as Odiva the Samoan Nymph.[7]

Odiva did a striptease act. The shapely artiste undressed to reveal a form-fitting mermaid suit, then dove into what was billed as the largest water tank ever constructed for a stage. Fans admired her large lungs, which is to say, she could hold her breath underwater for a long time, upward of two minutes. While submerged, spectators (men in particular) watched as she sewed, ate, and demonstrated underwater acrobatics, all while a dozen or so sea lions swam around her. The novelty made it all the way to the Palace Theater.

History does not record whether Captain Adams and his assistant ever became intimately acquainted, though the act did run into trouble on at least one occasion. After coming off the road, the captain made the mistake of asking his wife to launder Odiva's eight mermaid outfits. He then went on an ill-advised night on the town. Returning the following afternoon, the captain found the eight mermaid suits in a charred mass.

"What is this?" he asked.

"Tut-tut!" replied his wife. "Can't you see? They're burned."

Odiva hauled the captain's wife into court on charges of malicious mischief. During the proceedings, the blackened swim outfits made their way around the courtroom. As they did, the wife "merely sniffed."

A witness testified that he had seen the wife at the scene that fateful night, at which time he rescued the smoldering attire. He further testified that, afterward, "she would not thank me for putting out that fire."[8] Fortunately for the captain's wife, the court magistrate dismissed the charges, absent any proof she was the one who had started the blaze.

Mark contemplated no such assistant-mermaid aspirations. Rather, he envisioned Sharkey in a water tank, by himself, performing complex stunts. In that regard, he holds claim as the first to develop a seal water-tank act. The task was challenging in that it required the seal to perform while distant from his trainer.

Mark taught Sharkey to retrieve a Frisbee-sized ring from the Seal College pool. Mark first placed the ring around his own neck while Sharkey looked on. After a few repetitions, Mark put the ring around Sharkey's neck and requested he do the same once in the water. Mark tossed the ring in the pool. Sharkey dove in; moments later, he surfaced with the ring around his neck. Without prompting, he jumped from the pool, jerked his neck, and flipped the ring back to his trainer like an old pro. Success on his first try, noteworthy even for Sharkey, and a story Mark often retold.

Sharkey soon learned to balance objects high in the air while in the water. He swam with an object on his nose, highlighted by his exiting the pool while keeping the object balanced. He also learned a stunt that would become his specialty: hurdling.

Mark constructed a hurdle. (Mark built all his props in the Seal College workshop. They were never more than they needed to be, but always everything they had to be.) He fashioned two vertical boards spaced a few feet apart, attached to a common wooden base. Pegs ran up both boards, one set of pegs slightly higher than the other, allowing him to sleeve the end of a pole through a pair of pegs. The pole rested on the lower peg. The higher peg secured the pole from above. He placed the apparatus near the pool such that the pole cantilevered over the water like a high-jump bar. Raising or lowering the pole was as simple as moving it to a different pair of pegs.

Next came the tricky part, getting Sharkey to hurdle. He had the physical ability; the issue was timing. More fundamental was getting him to comprehend the task. Mark considered it "one of Sharkey's most difficult feats."[9] A smoothened tree limb served as a hurdling pole. Mark put the tree limb a foot above the water. With Sharkey in the pool, Mark waved a baton over the makeshift pole to simulate the desired action. Untold amounts of patient instruction followed.

At last, it happened. Sharkey barreled through the water toward the horizontal barrier. Mark waved his baton at the crucial moment, throwing in some body English for good measure. Sharkey leapt out of the water and cleared the hurdle. Delighted with his accomplishment, he sped out of the pool and received an enthusiastic "job well done" hand-flipper shake from his trainer. The era of hurdling seals had begun.

Mark raised the pole. Sharkey rose to the challenge. His graceful approach and the sheer physicality of his leaps were a thrill to behold.

His highest jump was initially four feet. He would later reliably clear a five-foot-high hurdle. Mark replaced the tree limb with a white wooden pole about twice the diameter and length of a broomstick. He wrapped electrical tape around the pole in a candy cane pattern as a visual aid for Sharkey. Numerical markers on the vertical boards denoted the height of the jump. At times, Mark added a question mark on top, as if the sky was the limit. The apparatus remained a prop for the rest of Sharkey's career.

Other pool tricks followed. Sharkey dove from a seven-foot-high platform and jumped through a flaming hoop.

Mark noted that the tank act "provides Sharkey with the means of displaying his most spectacular talents. Sharkey is the only seal in the world 'under control' at all times. In this medium he has the opportunity to show off the high degree of his intelligence and the scope and extent of skillful training."[10]

Sharkey now had two acts, one for stage, one for water. Mark called the stage routine Sharkey's dry act and the water routine his wet act.

Sharkey hurdling in the Seal College pool under the direction of Mark Huling. Photo by Stan Lee.

More practice at Seal College. National Library of Australia. nla.obj-429964785.

Sportsmen's (a.k.a. Sports) Shows

At about this time, Mark entered into an arrangement with Shilling Theatrical Enterprises, an entertainment agency in Midtown Manhattan, on Broadway. It was run by Bill Shilling, a former vaudevillian who specialized in booking acts for sportsmen's shows, also known as sports shows.

Sportsmen's shows were outdoor recreation trade shows that took place in indoor arenas and lasted about ten days. Scores of booths displayed the latest in fishing, hunting, and camping gear. Motorboat displays often accompanied the show, as did fish and wildlife exhibits, workshops, and demonstrations. The event highlight was a daily variety show in an indoor pool and attached stage. Acts included everything from expert archers to pistol sharpshooters, Ping-Pong champions, indoor ski jumpers, and trained animals. Other acts featured canoe tilters (two people standing in separate canoes, with each canoe oared by a teammate as the two jousted with padded poles) and log rollers (two people exhibiting fancy footwork on a log that feverishly spun until one of them fell in the water). An emcee and orchestra accompanied the entire show.

Although big-time vaudeville was long gone, its legacy, the variety show, remained an ingrained part of American popular culture. Variety-act presentations at sportsmen's shows were but one of many ways that vaudeville redefined itself in the post two-a-day era: vaudeville for hunters and fishermen, as it were.

Sportsmen's shows played in cities large and small. Bill Shilling handled practically all of the entertainment contracting, a bonanza for Seal College, especially because the sportsmen's show season was during the otherwise light winter and early spring months. Shilling booked Mark to present Sharkey and Teddy in a string of six shows. Sharkey had his first tour, advertised as "The World's Greatest Seal."

St. Louis was first. In its coverage of opening day, the *Post-Dispatch* headline was "Sharkey the Seal, Out to Steal Popularity from Sportsmen's Show Dogs." The article said that the dog trainer "may have to teach one of his black Labrador retrievers to applaud with his paws or a slippery fellow named Sharkey will steal the spotlight from him. . . . Sharkey's stage presence and timing is quite precise. After each trick by Teddy, there's Sharkey applauding for all he's worth and looking around at the audience as though to say, 'See, isn't this all wonderful?' . . . Sharkey himself provides a highlight when he does a high jump out of the water."[11] Another reporter said that Sharkey's act "seems to be receiving more attention than any other at the show." Sharkey's success earned him a guest appearance on the radio show, *In St. Louis This Week*.[12]

Chicago was next, drawing 50,000 paid admissions. Critics declared Sharkey "the show's biggest applause winner . . . a master at pantomime . . . his human like gesticulations are rib ticklers."[13] Sharkey again put himself in charge of applause after every feat by Teddy. Although if Teddy muffed one, Sharkey used his flippers to hide his face in embarrassment. Poor Teddy must have wondered what he had done to deserve working with Sharkey, first as his underappreciated Broadway understudy, now as his bumbling comic foil.

Sharkey was a neatnik. A tank had to be in pristine condition before his act could begin. Prior to performing, he removed debris from the pool. It wasn't part of the act or anything that Mark directed. During one show,

Sharkey was to follow a comedy diver, but he first brought Mark some scrap pieces of paper that had been floating in the tank. He then submerged. Mark called for him. Sharkey surfaced but resubmerged, this time for an extended period. Mark grew nervous and called again, later recalling that "This time the little fellow appeared and came bounding up on to the stage and deposited a pair of gaudy striped socks at my feet. The comedy diver had forgotten them when he finished his act."[14]

New Orleans was next. The music mecca seemed an ideal spot for Sharkey, for in addition to being a juggler, a comedian, and a hurdler, he was an accomplished instrumentalist, a skill that would provide the next memorable event in his career.

Where the River Shannon Flows

Mark had taught Sharkey to play music on a homemade instrument. The metal-framed device was three feet wide, four feet high, and four inches deep. Nine differently tuned buzzer bells were arranged in two horizontal rows: five on top, four just below. A dry-cell battery pack powered the bells. Sharkey played notes by pressing his nose against buttons arranged on the opposite side of the metal frame; each button activated a corresponding bell. Mark's brother Frank had introduced the concept over twenty years prior, stating the following:

> In a class by itself . . . in the world of performing animals is the bell solo performance performed by my star sea lion musician. A series of buttons rigged up to bells present somewhat the appearance of the manual of a piano. In this number, he actually picks out the notes of a musical piece, nodding his head when he presses the right one and growling softly to himself if he by any chance plays the wrong note. He really seems pleased at his capability.[15]

Mark built on this concept in the 1920s by teaching music of increased complexity. One reporter called it "the most intelligent thing a seal has ever done."[16] Some fifteen years later, Mark recycled the routine for Sharkey by teaching him the Irish song, "Where the River Shannon Flows." It was timely. Bing Crosby had just recorded the tune.

The song consists of thirty-one notes of various pitches and rhythms. Sharkey learned to play the individual notes by following Mark's baton as he pointed to the instrument buttons. Sharkey then graduated to playing the entire sequence from memory. Mark then taught him rhythm and pacing, again using a baton to provide guidance, much like an orchestra conductor. "Sharkey knows his notes, but requires assistance with tempo," Mark said.[17]

After forty minutes of daily tutoring for three months, Sharkey mastered the tune. He played the song with conviction at a bright tempo, without the slightest bit of herky-jerky in his treatment of the melody. It required keen memory, physical dexterity, and deft interaction with a trainer, an accomplishment unsurpassed to this day. It was also about to make national headlines, but not for the reasons one might think.

New Orleans sponsors planned a promotional radio broadcast to air locally the night before the open of their sportsmen's show. Sharkey's music

Mark prepares Sharkey to play "Where the River Shannon Flows." Press photo from the author's collection via Gary Bohan Sr.

feature seemed like a perfect fit, and so they decided he would perform on the radio, playing "Where the River Shannon Flows." There was just one hitch: one big hitch.

For years, a rift had been brewing between radio stations and the American Society of Composers, Authors, and Publishers (ASCAP), an agency that collected royalties for composers when radio stations broadcast their music. ASCAP enjoyed a virtual broadcast-rights monopoly—they had contracted with the period's most renowned popular composers. ASCAP had also steadily increased broadcasting fees. Everything came to a head in 1940 when ASCAP declared that fees would double at the end of the year. Radio stations decided enough was enough. They banded together and chose not to renew their ASCAP licenses.

On December 31, 1940, at the stroke of midnight, popular music vanished off the air: the music of George Gershwin, Cole Porter, Jerome Kern, and countless other notables, gone, just like that. Absent a licensing agreement, ASCAP refused to let radio stations broadcast their music, even prohibiting patriotic tunes like Kate Smith's beloved signature song, Irving Berlin's "God Bless America."

ASCAP figured outcry over the mass exodus of popular music would force stations to cave. They also kept a firm hold on their elite composers; ASCAP had limited its membership and had been the only agency that paid radio royalties. Broadcasters turned to their own newly formed licensing agency, Broadcast Music Incorporated (BMI), which signed unproven composers and welcomed genres shunned by ASCAP, such as blues and roots music, dismissed by ASCAP as lowbrow and valueless.

With the dispute at the height of its storm, Sharkey was to do his radio broadcast. That is, until someone realized that ASCAP controlled the rights to "Where the River Shannon Flows." Acting with due diligence, and looking to avoid a steep fine, the station contacted ASCAP to see if they might make an exception and allow Sharkey to play his music feature. After all, it wasn't as if he was Bing Crosby or Kate Smith. He was a trained seal pressing buttons with his nose on a homemade instrument.

ASCAP swiftly issued their response: no deal. The Associated Press released a wire picked up by practically every newspaper in the country, including this in the *New York Times*:

TRAINED SEAL IS OFF THE AIR
HIS SOLE TUNE IS ASCAP

NEW ORLEANS, March 6 (AP)—Sharkey, the trained seal, is going to have to broaden his repertoire to get back on the air unless the ASCAP–BMI controversy ends shortly. He knows how to play "Where the River Shannon Flows," and that's all. It's an ASCAP tune. He was due to broadcast here tonight on a program of the Southern Sportsman show, but the lawyers said no.[18]

Headlines appeared from coast to coast: "Sharkey is Out of Job"; "Woe Is Musical Seal"; "Sharkey Stumped." One small town newspaper, showing not a whiff of melodramatic restraint, ran the headline, "ASCAP Puts End to Radio Career of Trained Seal."[19]

Mary Bostwick of the *Indianapolis Star* added to the coverage. The future Indiana Journalism Hall of Fame inductee was among the country's foremost women reporters. One of her brands was covering topical events in rhyme. She devoted an entire column to Sharkey and composed a lengthy poem, a snippet of which follows, dedicated to his plight as a result of ASCAP "bannin' . . . the River Shannon."

> The owner of this seal was in an awful fix then, brother!
> The seal just knew the "Shannon" and couldn't learn another—
> Oh, you may balance articles with ease upon your nose—
> What good is that to listeners around their radios?[20]

The licensing feud lasted for months. Surprisingly, the public didn't miss listening to ASCAP composers nearly as much as ASCAP had hoped. Radio producers used theme songs in the public domain; thus, the Lone Ranger rode to the "William Tell Overture" and the Green Hornet flew to "Flight of the Bumblebee." Glenn Miller used the same tactic with his swing version hit of "American Patrol," an 1885 march in the public domain and out of the grasp of ASCAP, one of many public domain melodies that rapidly filled the radio airwaves.

Duke Ellington, an ASCAP-registered composer, kept broadcast royalties flowing by having his cohort Billy Strayhorn and son Mercer write for his orchestra and publish with BMI. The two went on a tear. Ellington quickly abandoned his ASCAP repertoire in favor of his new BMI repertoire. Among the new tunes was Strayhorn's "Take the 'A' Train," first broadcast two weeks after the boycott started, Ellington's theme song for the rest of his life.

Unknown composers like Arthur Herzog Jr. and others long ignored by ASCAP seized the moment. Herzog and Billie Holiday had written "God Bless the Child," which BMI gladly published. Holiday recorded it that spring, a radio hit that entered the Grammy Hall of Fame thirty-five years later in recognition of its lasting historical significance.

The boycott concluded that fall with a new licensing agreement that left ASCAP with less-profitable terms than before. Even worse, they lost their industry foothold, a miscalculation that set them back for decades. BMI meanwhile continued publishing styles eschewed by their elitist competitor, styles like "hillbilly" music, which developed into western and later country music; and "race" music, which developed into rhythm and blues, laying the groundwork for early rock and roll. It is not an exaggeration to say that the ASCAP boycott and emergence of BMI shaped popular music for the next generation and beyond.

Water Circus

Minneapolis was the next stop on the sportsmen's tour. Sharkey got right back on the radio. Whatever musical number he may have played is unknown. Rest assured it wasn't registered with ASCAP. Reviews stayed positive; a journalist wrote that Sharkey "has been stopping the floor shows with his high-hurdling in the indoor pool." Mark brought about the only media blemish. In an apparently laborious interview with popular local columnist Virginia Safford, asked if it takes much patience to train a seal, he replied, "It takes more patience to answer your questions." The exchange found its way into next day's *Minneapolis Star*.[21]

Sharkey and Teddy concluded their tour with stops in Madison and Kansas City. After a return home and a short break, it was off to the Jersey Shore for three months in Atlantic City at the summer entertainment capital of the country: Steel Pier.

Steel Pier had been part of the plan ever since Mark had returned to seal training. His inside track likely came from George Hamid, a man with a successful booking agency who had previously represented "Huling's Sea Lions," promoting them as "a troupe of animals that are unsurpassed in sagacity and alacrity."[22] For years Hamid had booked entertainment for Steel Pier. Landing a summer there afforded Sharkey more great exposure, consistent with the city and pier's history of shining the spotlight on the brightest stars in show business.

Boardwalk Empire author Nelson Johnson writes, "Among those who received their first big break in Atlantic City on the road to stardom were W. C. Fields, Abbott & Costello . . . Bing Crosby, Bob Hope, Ed Sullivan [and] Jackie Gleason." Steel Pier historian Steve Liebowitz puts it like this: "If you were headlining Steel Pier, you had made it. . . . To 'play the Pier' was the goal of all great entertainers."[23]

Steel Pier was over seven football fields long and in spots was wider than a football field. It went from the Boardwalk, over the beach, and extended 1,000 feet over the ocean. Fronting the pier was an exhibition hall, a movie theater, and six funhouses. Further down was a theater for children's shows, a hall for stage shows, and a theater for feature movies. Over the ocean was the Marine Ballroom, one of the largest ballrooms in the country. Directly behind that, at the end of the pier, was the outdoor Ocean Stadium. Interspersed were reading rooms, smoking lounges, and areas for outdoor relaxing. All told, the pier could handle 20,000 patrons. Movies and shows ran repeatedly, day and night. Best of all, for one low admission price, you could go from one pier attraction to another. A large sign on the pier read, "Where Else Can You See So Much for So Little Money."

Nighttime evoked a seaside Times Square. The wraparound marquee fronting the pier was the world's largest. Towering illuminated billboards displayed both current and upcoming attractions. More light came from the Marine Ballroom in the form of a 50-by-120-foot neon sign on its roof that spelled STEEL PIER.

The pier's music lineup that year was a who's who of entertainers: Frank Sinatra, Harry James, the Ink Spots, Tommy Dorsey, Dinah Shore, Gene Krupa, and others. Fresh talent arrived each week, musicians as well as famous comedians like Eddie Cantor and upstarts like twenty-three-year-old comedian Art Carney. Indeed, the pier that summer more than lived up to its motto: Showplace of the Nation.

Sharkey and Teddy worked the Water Circus attraction at Ocean Stadium. The show had high divers, a high-wire act, an aerialist, and vaudeville's premier slapstick artists, Willie, West, and McGinty, who performed a bit as three blundering Steel Pier carpenters. Ending the program was the Diving Horse: rider and horse diving from a forty-foot-high platform into a water tank. Shows ran afternoon and evening, seven days a week, four and five shows a day, more on holidays. Each was about forty-five-minutes long, if not a tad longer, depending on how the horse felt about plunging from the diving platform. Crowds regularly filled the 5,000-seat outdoor venue, many in their Sunday best. Grandstand seating offered a superb look at the action, augmented by the sights, sounds, and smells of the surrounding Atlantic Ocean.

Emcee Jack Montez opened the show, "Ladies and gentlemen, prepare yourself for the thrill of a lifetime!"[24] When it came time, he brought out Mark and the seals. Mark took to the stage dressed in a blue blazer (trimmed in gold), tan slacks, and white dress shoes. Using a white baton, he led Sharkey and Teddy through their wet act.

Mark conversed nonstop with his sea lion friends. After each trick, he heaped praise like a football coach pumping up players after a big play. His relaxed farmboy twang (mixed with a dash of showbiz pizzazz) complimented the act by just the right amount.

After one trick, Mark sang out, "That was *allll* right." After another, he bellowed, "By Jove, you got *that*, all right." Mark beamed after another, "Very nicely done. Yes sir, you're a wonderful man, that's all there is to it. How 'bout a piece of fish for that?" Congratulatory seal head-pats and backslaps were the norm. Fist pumps and reflexive leg kicks accompanied Sharkey's hurdles. After one inspired leap, Sharkey proudly bolted back to his trainer. Mark held out his hand as Sharkey threw out a flipper. "Let's have a little shake on that."[25]

Mark's idiosyncratic lingo was as endearing as the affection his seal colleagues offered in return. They enjoyed sneaking playful rubs up against the boss as well as receiving his constant compliments. Bond between trainer and seals was the special ingredient that made it all work. And it all made for a splendid presentation.

Sharkey became the talk of the pier. He swam at breakneck speed. Mark regularly clocked him at forty miles per hour, at times faster. (Current literature assigns California sea lions an average speed of fifteen miles per hour and a top speed of twenty-five miles per hour.) Crowds were spellbound. But what mesmerized crowds the most was Sharkey's hurdling.

Steel Pier's publicity department added to Sharkey's cachet by publicizing a daredevil stunt: he would attempt to hurdle a canoe in the open waters of the Atlantic. Spectators gathered, as did a press photographer. Diving champion Lois Zahn stood waist-deep in the ocean and steadied a canoe with her hands. Sharkey charged through the water like Evel Knievel at Caesar's Palace. Out of the water he soared. He spread his four flippers like wings and cleared the obstacle with ease. How he managed a smile for the camera while in flight cannot be known. Steel Pier released a captioned photo, "He Flies through the Air." The caption ended, "Sharkey is to trained seals what Babe Ruth was to baseball sluggers."[26]

Picture and caption ran in papers across the northeast, enticing would-be vacationers to visit the pier. Those who came were quick to see his name. On the pier's mammoth entrance marquee were two rows of lights in three-foot-high block lettering: SEE SHARKEY, WONDER SEAL. The side of the pier was lit up in similar fashion: SHARKEY THE HURDLING SEAL.

Business roared. Good weather helped, as did efforts by the mayor to rid the city of gambling, and, as he put it, other "undesirables." He boasted, "There is no question that money spent on horse joints and the numbers racket is now going into legitimate channels."[27] Steel Pier owner Frank Gravatt, known around town as the saltwater Barnum, said that pier attendance that year was the highest in its forty-three-year history.

Universal Newsreel showed up that July. Given everything to choose from, they did a segment titled "Seals Perform Amazing Stunts." Graham McNamee, radio's foremost voice during its formative years, narrated. "Meet Teddy and Sharkey, clever seals, just back from college. What a round of stunts they perform at the Steel Pier. Juggling, hurdling and many others—all sure-fire laughs."[28] The one-minute clip was a lighthearted close to an otherwise somber newsreel that opened with British troops fighting Italian and German forces on the frontlines of Libya and Egypt.

Sharkey also found time to mingle with the stars. Sammy Kaye had a hit that summer with "Daddy," composed by one of his sidemen, and published, of course, with BMI. The tune stayed number one on the *Billboard* charts for eight weeks during which Sammy played the pier. Between sets, behind the Marine Ballroom, the bandleader could be found teaching Sharkey to play trumpet.

Abbott and Costello played the pier for nine days in August, promoting the release of their movie, *Hold That Ghost*, which world-premiered at the pier. The comedy duo had four hit movies that year and was Hollywood's third-highest box office draw, behind only Clark Gable and Mickey Rooney. During their stint, beachgoers and those on the Boardwalk couldn't miss the two adjacent billboards on the pier pavilion roof, one advertising Abbott and Costello in person, the other advertising "Sharkey the Wonder Seal!"

On one occasion, Lou Costello (sporting a half-chewed cigar out the left side of his mouth) brought a lucky fan backstage to meet the celebrity seal. He kindly escorted a little girl about ten years old, who was wearing a summer dress, white ruffled dress socks, and T-strap shoes. Sharkey cheerfully extended his flipper for her to hold, bringing a warm smile to both Lou and the star-struck youngster.

Sharkey and Sammy Kaye behind the Marine Ballroom. Press photo from the author's collection via Gary Bohan Sr.

Dry Act, Wet Act

Labor Day weekend was a madhouse. The Andrews Sisters played the Steel Pier Music Hall, singing their recent hit, "Boogie Woogie Bugle Boy," a tune from the Abbott and Costello movie musical comedy *Buck Privates* that costarred the three sisters. Crowds were so big, they did ten shows a day. Over at the Marine Ballroom, packed houses danced to the sounds of Glenn Miller and His Orchestra.

The weekend lineup also included an impromptu bit by the Three Stooges. Moe and Curley lay on their bellies. Between them was Sharkey. Using their hands to mimic flippers, Moe and Curley lifted their torsos and struck a seal pose. Mouths open and eyes closed, Moe, Curley, and Sharkey belted out a tune while Larry amusedly observed.

It remains a matter of interpretation whether the melodious howls were Moe and Curley imitating Sharkey, or vice versa.

It was a summer to remember. Radios broadcast the songs of unsung BMI composers; baseball fans marveled at DiMaggio's fifty-six-game hitting streak and Williams's .406 batting average; moviegoers flocked to see *Citizen Kane*; and Sharkey "played the Pier" with the biggest names in popular music and show business.

Sharkey and the Three Stooges. Photo by Mark Huling. From the author's collection via Michael Reilly.

Unity for Victory

Sharkey finished at Steel Pier the weekend after Labor Day. His final fling of summer coincided with the Miss America Pageant, held at nearby Boardwalk Hall.

Three weeks later, Sharkey opened a monthlong engagement at the Roxy, a 6,000-seat theater just outside Times Square, built in the 1920s by Samuel "Roxy" Rothafel, the largest movie palace of its day, later surpassed only by Radio City Music Hall, also built by Roxy. On the bill with Sharkey were the Nicholas Brothers, legendary African American tap dancers. Also appearing was Miss America and the house dance troupe, the Roxyettes, predecessors of the spinoff Rockettes. Accompanying the stage show was the world-premiere screening of *A Yank in the RAF* starring Betty Grable, who attended opening night, along with many other stars. Marquee lights glittered and flashed. News outlets interviewed celebrities. The gala occasion also featured a street festival outside the theater, a military flyover, and a midnight ball attended by high-ranking politicians and military officials. Fox Movietone News called it "a news headline in New York because of the record-breaking crowds that jammed to attend." *Variety* reported that a "super hoopla" attended opening night, adding that "Sharkey is as amazing as ever with his balancing, catching plates on the end of his nose and ability to play tunes on the electric bells."[29]

Sharkey's tour moved to Pittsburgh at the historic William Penn Hotel for a fund-raiser with Latin bandleader Xavier Cugat and other celebrities. The ballroom was reportedly "bulging on all sides."[30] Sharkey stayed in Pittsburgh and worked a nightclub that held him over for two weeks, interrupted only by his doing a lucrative one-nighter in Philadelphia. Club dates followed in Cleveland, Detroit, and New York.

One night, Sharkey came out on a stage that had mirrored pillars, floor to ceiling. He saw his reflection, yelped in surprise, then dashed into the crowd onto a woman's lap. The crowd laughed so hard that Sharkey did it again next show. Mark said that "aside from the lady's dignity, no one was hurt." Another time, Sharkey was derailed when he noticed a lady's fur coat on a front row seat. "Sharkey apparently mistook it for a bear, and wouldn't do his act until the fur coat was removed."[31]

But thoughts of trained seals soon moved to the nation's collective backburner. On December 7, 1941, Japan attacked Pearl Harbor. The next day, the United States declared war on Japan. Three days later, Germany and Italy declared war on the United States. Hours later, the United States declared war on Germany and Italy. The nation rallied behind President Franklin D. Roosevelt. Citizens came together in ways previously unimaginable.

Do you remember *Scribner's Commentator*, the nation's leading isolationist magazine and voice of the America First movement that had oddly run a story the year before on Seal College? Right after Pearl Harbor, an issue was due to come to subscribers. It never arrived. Some now think the publisher had prepared an issue before the attack, but wisely refrained afterward from mailing out its antiwar vitriol. A new issue arrived a month later minus the usual isolationist rhetoric. Pictured on the cover was General MacArthur, commander of US Army Forces in the Far East. The magazine offered refunds to subscribers and never published again. On the top of the first page read "Unity for Victory."[32]

Chapter 7

Sharkey Goes Hollywood

All Sealed Up

If one had to guess Sharkey's next big feat in the days after the attack on Pearl Harbor, his appearing in a major motion picture comedy would not be on the top of the list. Yet that's exactly what happened—with the hottest comedy team in Hollywood.

It wasn't the first time a Huling-trained seal had been in a major motion picture comedy. Ten years earlier, movies with sound were the latest craze. Like many vaudevillians adapting to changing times, Ray Huling and Charlie ventured into talkies.

Charlie's first film was a two-reel short, twenty minutes long, a popular format of its day. Short films were shown before the main feature. This one starred Al St. John, one of the original Keystone Kops. The slapstick comedian and actor appeared in 346 movies, silent and talking, earning him a star on the Hollywood Walk of Fame. He was also fond of animals and got along famously with Charlie. By one account, he spent a "hunk of his paycheck buying fish to keep in good with his supporting player."[1] Paramount Pictures, the country's oldest major film studio, released the movie under the title *All Sealed Up*. A movie synopsis reads as follows:

> Al St. John is getting married, but there are problems. The minister only speaks Polish and the wedding guests are bums.

However, it all turns out to be a joke played on the couple by the best man. . . . At the wedding itself, an unexpected guest wants to know what to do about "her"—the one waiting for Al. The "her" referred to, is in fact his playful pet seal, so there's not going to be much chance for a peaceful honeymoon![2]

Charlie starred in another two-reeler two years later, filmed in Brooklyn at Warner Brothers's Vitagraph Studios as part of their Vitaphone "Big Five" Comedy series. This one costarred big-time comedian Ben Blue. Charlie played an aquarium seal befriended by aquarium worker Ben Blue, who soon lost his job. Ben's misfortune continued when Charlie followed him onto a train. Confusion ensued in a case of mistaken seal identity. Authorities accused Ben of stealing a government seal. Fortunately for Ben, Charlie took to "protecting him from all danger" and ultimately caught the real

Ben Blue and Charlie in *All Sealed Up*. Lobby card from the author's collection.

thief.³ Warner Brothers released the short under the spectacularly unoriginal title, *All Sealed Up*, not to be confused with Paramount's film of the same title.

Charlie returned to Vitagraph a year later to film *Vitaphone Music Hall*, a two-reeler with four vaudeville acts. (Ironically, the very technology largely responsible for vaudeville's demise—talking motion pictures—preserved for posterity many vaudeville acts.) *Motion Picture Daily* wrote, "The seal is by far the most amusing performer and his tricks are numerous and amazing."⁴ Warner Brothers released the movie under its Broadway Brevities banner, a film series featuring well-known artists such as Sammy Davis Jr., who had made his film debut two years earlier as a seven-year-old dance sensation in the Broadway Brevities short, *Rufus Jones for President*, a satire about a black child elected president of the United States.

Shirley Temple next came calling for Charlie. The curly-haired child actress was in a four-year streak as Hollywood's top box office draw. Only Bing Crosby and Burt Reynolds have had longer streaks. Charlie regrettably had an impending overseas tour. But Ms. Temple was so intent on having him in her next movie that the casting director "kept the wires hot between Hollywood and Kingston, pleading with Ray and Charlie."⁵ The director even offered them a transcontinental flight, but the schedule conflict proved too difficult to overcome.

Impressive though Charlie's motion picture credentials were, one feat had eluded him over his long and distinguished career—acting in a full-length motion picture. Enter onto the scene, Sharkey.

Within weeks after Pearl Harbor, President Franklin D. Roosevelt appointed a liaison between the government and motion picture industry. In effect, he struck a deal. Hollywood could continue with no government interference in return for its full support of the war effort. Hollywood obliged. It made countless movies propping up US and Allied forces, it churned out war-related newsreels, and it made films encouraging patriotism. Hollywood's support of the war effort was unequivocal. With Hollywood and FDR in lockstep, the movie industry didn't miss a beat after Pearl Harbor—nor did Sharkey.

Abbott and Costello were casting for their next movie and wanted a role for Sharkey. "Universal Studio executives listened to their arguments and consented." Irene Thirer, motion picture editor for the *New York Post*, wrote that Sharkey "was doing his act at the Atlantic City Steel Pier last summer when Abbott and Costello were visiting celebs. At that time, Lou and Bud appeared in a newsreel shot with Sharkey and they immediately sensed the seal's photogenic possibilities. Came a chance to write the aquatic mammal into a script—which was forthwith done."[6]

And so in January 1942, a month after Pearl Harbor, Seal College inked a deal. A press release spread the news nationwide.[7]

Sharkey was going to Hollywood.

Pardon My Sarong

Sharkey was to arrive at Universal Studios in March. There, he would join the cast and crew in filming the upcoming Abbott and Costello musical comedy, *Pardon My Sarong*.

Mark and Sharkey left Kingston and stopped in St. Louis so Mark could meet with his partner, Walter Jennier, who was presenting a string of shows. Walter premiered a stunt with Buddy, who, while on his back, leveled his flippers and let Walter do a handstand. (The stunt worked great except for an earlier practice mishap at Seal College when Buddy unexpectedly tossed Walter into the pool.) Mark's partnership with Walter amicably ended soon after. Walter and Buddy returned to circus life, performing for years to much acclaim.

After St. Louis, it was off to Hollywood. Mark and Sharkey made the trip in a van that Mark had designed. It had a water tank in the back, big enough for Sharkey to relax while traveling. It also had side viewports so Sharkey could enjoy the scenery along the way. Seal College grads each received a vehicle, an innovation that Mark said was "but one of the many scientific improvements" he had recently considered.[8]

No sooner did Sharkey arrive in Hollywood than he ran into his former Broadway colleague, Marta Eggerth, who was filming MGM's *For Me and My Gal*, a song-and-dance World War I throwback, starring Eggerth, Judy Garland, Ben Blue, and Gene Kelly. *Hollywood* magazine wrote, "The day Sharkey first appeared on a rival lot to do his turns before the camera, Miss E. rushed over to wish him luck. Sharkey took one look, flapped his fins [and] unleashed a string of joyous yips."[9] Sharkey also reunited with Leif Erickson, Eggerth's beau in *Higher and Higher*. Erickson now had a leading role in *Pardon My Sarong*.

Pardon My Sarong was classic screwball Abbott and Costello. The comedy duo had cut their teeth doing stage shows, honing their bits to perfection, many of which made it onto the big screen. They were at ease doing knockabout physical comedy—Bud Abbott, the mean, bossy, straight man and victim of circumstance at the hands of stooge Lou Costello—and were equally at ease with word play and double entendre, most notably in their version of "Who's on First?" which was later honored by *Time* as the best comedy routine of the twentieth century.

Pardon My Sarong involved a rich playboy who chartered a bus to take him and his cackling female admirers to Los Angeles so he could compete in a yacht race to Hawaii. The bus drivers, played by Abbott and Costello, drove the gang there, not realizing they had unwittingly stolen the bus. After dropping off the passengers, the bus drivers were chased by a detective. They avoided capture by driving the bus off a pier—with both of them still in the bus! The playboy, now on his yacht, pulled up anchor and unintentionally rescued the pair.

Abbott and Costello stood on the yacht, soaking wet, accompanied by the rich playboy captain, who promptly hired them as crew for the race. As they all peered out into the harbor, out popped Sharkey, cheerfully barking away. Costello shrieked. Abbott explained that it was a seal and that they make good fur coats.

"They make fur coats?" Costello replied. "How do they teach them that kind of work?"[10]

The captain told them the animal was a harbor seal named Sharkey. Costello asked if they could bring him on the yacht; the captain nodded. Costello sang out, "Shar-key! Shar-key!"

Sharkey swam over and joined the crew. Before long, the yacht set sail in the calm waters of the Pacific. Sharkey placed himself at the stern and gazed out to sea—to his right, straight ahead, to his left—keeping a dutiful lookout. At the helm were Abbott and Costello.

Hearing a lunch bell, Abbott grabbed a can of sardines, which received an inadvertent puncture. Abbott shoved the can in his back pocket, unaware that sardine juice was now dripping onto his trousers. Sharkey lifted his nose, reeled off several showy sniffs, then snuck up behind Abbott and tried to eat the can, comically goosing him in the process. Abbott flinched slapstick, glared at Costello, and smacked him, telling him to keep his hands to himself. Sharkey kept goosing Abbott, who kept smacking Costello.

Abbott lectured Costello to keep his hands on the wheel and to steer the ship northeast by southeast. When Costello questioned the illogical instruction, Abbott pointed to a compass and read off its markings, which included northeast and southeast.

But just as Abbott said *southeast*, Sharkey snuck up and rammed into a buttocks, this time Costello, who amusingly flapped and sang out high-pitched squeals.

"What's the matter? You nervous?" asked Abbott.

Costello gave an extended daggered stare.

"Only around southeast."

Costello stayed at the helm. As might be expected, the yacht veered off course, but by the time the captain noticed, it was too late. They fell into the path of a storm that blew them farther off-course until they were hopelessly lost. Food supplies dwindled. Costello went up on deck, dejected, joined by Sharkey.

"Sharkey, boy, am I hungry," Costello lamented. Abbott came on deck and gave Costello a gun, suggesting he kill himself to avoid starving to

Bud Abbott, Lou Costello, and Sharkey. Movie-still, *Pardon My Sarong*, Universal Pictures.

death. Sharkey disapprovingly barked and jumped up and down. "I don't think Sharkey likes the idea," Costello noted.

Abbott left, leaving Costello and Sharkey alone. Abbott then made his way to the galley and confidently told crew members there would soon be one less to worry about. Up above, Costello turned to Sharkey and asked if he was ashamed to see him take his own life.

Sharkey whimpered and gabbled. When Costello offered him a handkerchief, Sharkey blew his nose into it with several exaggerated honks. Costello yanked it away. "That's enough. It's the only handkerchief I've got." Sharkey let out a loud "*Bar-eck.*"

Costello put the gun to his head, "Goodbye, Sharkey." Sharkey rolled on his side and covered his face with his two front flippers. From between his flippers peeked one of his expressive big brown eyes. Costello said one last dramatic, "Aw, Sharkey."

The movie cut to the galley below where the crew heard a gunshot. Everybody raced to the deck. Costello looked at them, gun still in hand, sheepishly explaining he had missed. Nearby was Sharkey, still peeking from between his flippers. (Sharkey's cleverness aside, the gallows humor treatment of suicide has not aged well. One relatively recent critique condemned the macabre scene as being "too oppressive to be funny." A current blogger criticized it as being "beyond low."[11])

After the botched suicide attempt, the crew stumbled on an uncharted island inhabited by friendly natives, diabolical villains, and a sacred jewel. The crew went ashore where Costello was mistaken for an ancient god named Mullah.

The second half of the movie was a zany procession of island buffoonery. Toward the end, the main villain hopped in a motorboat, holding the heroine crew-member of the yacht captive. The boat sped into the ocean. Costello swam in pursuit but quickly fell behind. Out of nowhere came a helper—Sharkey—who dashed from the beach into the water. Costello gave one of his signature wails. "Shar-key!"

Sharkey darted toward Costello, who directed his helper. "Closer Sharkey, closer. Good boy, I've got you. Go ahead!" Sharkey towed Costello to the motorboat at breakneck speed. Costello caught the villain and thwarted him in a thrilling and amusing chase scene.

The final scene paired hero Lou Costello on the yacht deck with the island princess. "Attempting to kiss her, he instead planted one on Sharkey, and then fell headfirst into the galley," writes an Abbott and Costello historian.[12] The film ended with Sharkey applauding.

Universal, regrettably, cut the final scene during editing. Mark later commented,

> Sharkey did some outstanding work. Unfortunately, the best of Sharkey's scenes got no further than the cutting-room floor, it being necessary to cut the running time of the picture. Sharkey learned his part well and quickly, and seldom required a retake of a scene, nor did he cause the studio any loss of time or money with temperamental outbursts, as so often happens in the case of actors of human genre.[13]

Sharkey, however, did require at least one retake of the suicide attempt scene. Cameras rolling, he let out an unscripted bark. Costello played along. "Are you really?" Sharkey again barked. Costello gently ad-libbed, "You are? I think I am too."

Costello then got down to business and sternly pointed his finger. "Look it, Sharkey—" Sharkey, none too happy about getting a dress down, even if pretend, lunged and nipped the lecturing forefinger. Costello yowled (for real) and improvised his way forward with raised voice, "Now Sharkey, don't eat *me*, I saved your—"

Sharkey thrust at Costello's face. Costello ducked and cried out, "I saved your life, ya lug." Sharkey lunged again. Costello finally broke character. "GET . . . THE . . . HELL . . ."

Sharkey thrust once more. Costello recoiled, both grimacing and smirking, and yelled, "Get the hell outta here." A chorus of laughs bellowed from behind the cameras.[14]

∽

Charles Previn—a composer, Broadway arranger, and the music director for Universal—put together four numbers for *Pardon My Sarong*. Featured were the Ink Spots, future inductees into the Rock & Roll Hall of Fame. They had headlined at Steel Pier the prior summer as they had done before, a first for any black entertainer. *Pardon My Sarong* is worth watching if only to see them sing "Shout Brother Shout" while dancers Tip, Tap, and Toe hoof atop a table, at times doing moonwalk-type moves forty years ahead of their time.

Also featured was "Vingo Jingo," a mysterious drumbeat that morphed into a big-band burner. The scene was choreographed on a stage with 20,000 exotic plants. Male "jungle" dancers intermingled with beautiful island natives called the Saronga Dancing Girls, who gyrated in sexy sarongs and skimpy tops. A cutaway shot showed Sharkey whirling about, boogying his best hoochie coochie.

Not everyone was so impressed. Long before the Motion Picture Association of America issued suitability guidelines like PG-13 and R, the American Association of University Women issued their own guidelines. They called the Saronga Dancing Girls "slightly vulgar." They didn't have a problem with Sharkey though, stating that he "puts in an original performance which seems practically human." For children eight to twelve, they rated the movie "not so good." For adolescents twelve to sixteen: "passable, but rather trashy."[15] Censors in Pennsylvania, Massachusetts, and Ohio deleted the racier dance sequences. The Motion Picture Producers and Distributors Association of America simply rated the movie "Approved," as was customary at the time, meaning it was generally deemed moral. *Pardon My Sarong*'s current rating, in Australia anyway, is G.

In addition to receiving praise from the American Association of University Women, Sharkey received praise from Bud Abbott and Lou Costello. Both admitted "they were licked" when it came to trying to steal a scene from him.[16] Director Erle Kenton said that Sharkey was the only cast member able to direct attention to himself, away from the other comedians. And Kenton knew a thing or two about comedy, having mentored under Mack Sennett, a filmmaker considered the king of comedy during the silent film and early talking film eras. Kenton, who himself directed over 100 movies, scored Sharkey higher than any other animal actor he had directed, including Rin Tin Tin. "Sharkey, the seal, is the best comedian of all," Kenton said. "I'll swear Sharkey thinks. He always works to the camera and often ad-libs a piece of business that throws us on the floor. He can even steal a scene from Lou Costello."[17]

Universal released the movie that August. It was just the kind of comic relief and musical razzmatazz the country needed at a time when more and more Americans were in dread of a Western Union deliveryman showing up at their door with a telegram from the secretary of War, expressing his sincere regret. Contemporary sources indicate that *Pardon My Sarong* was Abbott and Costello's biggest hit movie to date, the second biggest Hollywood moneymaker of the year, one of four hit movies the comedy duo released that year.

Abbott and Costello were a top-ten Hollywood box office draw eight different years. In 1942, the year Sharkey was in *Pardon My Sarong* in their biggest hit movie to date, they were Hollywood's number-one box office draw, the only year they achieved that distinction.

Dimouts and War Bonds

Sharkey didn't play Steel Pier that summer. Atlantic City was now a basic training center for the Army Air Corps and Coast Guard. Hotels became barracks; Steel Pier's exhibition hall became a recruitment center. Over 300,000 soldiers spent time in the city during the war. The area had also come under fire; a German U-boat sunk a US Navy destroyer off the southern tip of New Jersey. Records also indicate that "one U-boat surfaced and, without opposition, sent shells into Atlantic City."[18]

Along the East Coast, the government instituted mandatory "dimouts." Outdoor lights were shut off and windows were covered with blackened material. The darkness prevented potential enemy aircraft from identifying targets and also avoided silhouetting ships, providing cover for critical US coastal shipping lanes. Atlantic City—a year ago a seaside Times Square, the Steel Pier marquee lit up "SEE SHARKEY, WONDER SEAL"—now had tower guards on the lookout for a possible sneak attack, the nighttime cityscape an eerie pitch black.

Sharkey worked little that summer. He went to Upstate New York to raise money for the war effort and did his wet act at a New Jersey pool club. He also did a nationally broadcast show on CBS. A greater breadth of musical expression over the radio airwaves there has never been, for in addition to Sharkey playing his newfangled bell instrument, the show had a Chinese student performing on an ancient musical instrument traditionally played by Taoist monks during meditation.

Meanwhile, the overseas fight raged. The US government issued war bonds to help finance the war. Although rates were below market, people embraced the concept and bought bonds as a patriotic way of having a moral and financial stake in the war. Hollywood greatly assisted. For the month of September 1942 alone, the motion picture industry pledged to help sell a billion dollars' worth of bonds.

Hartford, Connecticut kicked off Labor Day weekend with a "Salute to Our Heroes" bond rally in front of the Old State House. People gathered at a specially set-up Victory House. The "victory" moniker was omnipresent during the war. Sponsors promised the Friday noontime arrival of a movie star. Celebrities and dignitaries were often happy to help. Those who came to Hartford to drum up war bond sales included everyone from First Lady Eleanor Roosevelt to bandleader Glenn Miller.

At Friday noon, a taxi pulled up in front of the Old State House. A back-passenger door swung open. Out came Sharkey.

The first thing one noticed, after one noticed that a seal had just exited a taxi, was the neatly tied, thick wad of cash between his lips. The bundle totaled $375.

Sharkey sauntered over to the Hall of Heroes and plopped himself in front of a booth marked BONDS, where he gave the money to a representative from the Volunteer Office of the Hartford Defense Council. Sharkey received his bond, much to the glee of onlookers, except for the one woman who was unapologetically using her left hand to cover her nose. Most thrilled was a nearby volunteer Cub Scout, his smile a blissful blend of awe and joy.

Sharkey next went into the crowd and selected a uniformed soldier. The two mingled among the masses. Sharkey carried a hat in his mouth and solicited donations. When the hat filled, he returned to the booth and bought another bond, which, according to the *Hartford Courant*, was "presented to the soldier with the seal's compliments."[19]

Worth Going into Debt

That fall, Sharkey appeared at a war-relief fund-raiser in Kingston, marked by patriotic decorations, blackened windows, and a "noticeable absence of young men."[20] He also did a corporate dinner party at nearby Williams Lake Hotel and a short theater stint in New Jersey. Though he was chief entertainer each time, it was small consolation. That summer and fall would go down as the slowest work period ever for Seal College.

In December, Sharkey was a late addition to a four-day Christmas show in Miami at the Olympia, the grandest theater palace in South

Florida. The holiday stage production was said to have "an impressive array of attractions," including the Watson Sisters, big-timers of yesteryear in a rare showbiz configuration, a comedy sister act.[21]

During opening night, Sharkey came onstage with a suitcase, opened it, grabbed a pillow using his mouth, then crawled into his custom bed and started snoring. The crowd burst out laughing, only to laugh even harder when he "awoke" to a ringing alarm clock, wriggled out of bed, and scratched himself something shameless. Mark feigned his displeasure, seeing Sharkey's lewd behavior. Sharkey put his flippers over his eyes in mock embarrassment, then bowed and gave himself self-congratulatory slaps on his posterior as he took his applause.

A woman in the crowd whispered, "I know a small man is working in the sealskin." A man behind her agreed. "It does seem that way."[22]

"It's Worth Going into Debt for a Gander at Sharkey, the Seal" was the headline in the next day's *Miami News*. The advice stemmed from an opening night remark by a critic: "If you don't have the price of a ticket, borrow it. But catch Sharkey the Seal at the Olympia this week." By the end of the run, his mention in the newspaper rose from "added attraction" to "top performer on the bill."[23]

Mark and Sharkey returned to Upstate New York. Wintertime was fun time. The seals enjoyed romps in the snow. A harnessed seal sometimes pulled a lucky tot through the woods on a metal-runner sled while Mark ran alongside. Snowball fights were a favorite pastime. They were lopsided affairs, more like Mark lobbing snowballs against the seals' backsides. The family cat joined in the action, happily coexisting among the seals. The animals thrived on all the attention. Generous food rations accompanied winter play. Seals jostled for position in the packed snow, crowding around fish-filled metal bowls, eating and barking, barking and eating. After mealtime, Mark went to the back porch, opened the door, and nodded inside. The seals, without exception, scampered to their trainer in anticipation of the next activity.[24]

Seal College enrollment peaked at sixteen seals. But the college had downsized due to decreased demand and loss of staff. The US Army drafted Mark's assistant Billy Roe, and would later draft Mark's other assistant, his son-in-law, Lew Bohan, both of whom would serve overseas. With former partner Walter Jennier having returned to circus life, Mark was the sole trainer for a period, with help from his daughter, Marjorie, who tended to the facility when he was on the road.

By winter of 1942–1943, the operation was down to three seals: Sharkey, Teddy, and Jumbo. That number soon became two.

Teddy was next to go, though where he went is unknown. His last documented event was with Sharkey at a wartime-tinged show. Exhibitors included the American Red Cross, the Women's Army Auxiliary Corps, and the Women Accepted for Volunteer Emergency Service. The seals did their wet act in a water tank at Chicago Stadium, a 15,000-seat indoor arena. So ends our story of Teddy. A standout that first year, along with Sharkey and Jumbo, Teddy had settled into his support role like an able second-string quarterback on a championship football team. Talent though he was, his lasting claim in the annals of trained seal history will forever be having endured its most humbling assignment, that of being Sharkey's understudy and sidekick for three years.

Meanwhile, in an office just outside of Times Square, Seal College agent Bill Shilling was busy securing work. He booked Sharkey solid, with an itinerary any top entertainer would have craved. In February 1943, Mark gassed up the custom seal van, departed Kingston, New York, and embarked with Sharkey on the road trip of a lifetime.

Seal College parking lot, Kingston, New York. Photo by Mark Huling. From the author's collection via Gary Bohan Sr.

Chapter 8

Movie Palaces and Nightclubs

Tojo and Hitler

After Pearl Harbor, the entertainment world could be summed up in two words: movie theaters. During 1943, over 60 percent of Americans went to a movie theater at least once a week, a number unmatched since. Compare that to 3 percent in 2017.[1] A booming wartime economy coupled with limited entertainment options provided a Hollywood jackpot. Theaters were social hubs where people participated in war bond rallies, held scrap drives, and flocked to see their favorite stars on the silver screen. Hollywood film production soared, which also aided live variety acts. Movie palaces presented stage revues with A-list bands and entertainers who preceded the feature film and were big draws themselves. Although devotees of vaudeville, then and now, will argue that stage presentations at movie palaces lacked the purity and stature of straight vaudeville during its heyday, many movie palace entertainers identified as vaudevillians; theater operators often billed them as such. Many become stars. Vaudeville, however "impure," had lived to see another day.

Sharkey's 1943 schedule included stops at the country's biggest movie palaces—venues with spectacular architecture, ceiling murals, lavish ornamentation, and every other extravagance imaginable in a theater. He worked the 3,400-seat Capitol Theater in Washington, DC and the 3,300-seat Loew's State Theater in Times Square, doing a week with Ed Sullivan, who emceed a six-act stage revue accompanied by an onstage orchestra. He also played the 3,800-seat Chicago Theater, a venue so opulent it went by the name "The Wonder Theater of the World." Glowing notices followed Sharkey wherever he went. Scarcely a week went by without a review in one or both of the two big trades, *Variety* and *Billboard*.

During each performance, Sharkey imitated General Hideki Tojo; the prime minister and military leader of Japan, a man who wore distinctive and rather large unflattering round eyeglasses. Sharkey came onstage wearing similar huge eyeglasses and pranced senselessly, making loud grotesque belching sounds, ineptly doling out fighting orders. The audience howled watching Sharkey mock the despised military leader, a man later convicted of war crimes by an international military tribunal, crimes for which he was executed.

Tojo sufficiently ridiculed, Sharkey shuffled to his chair. Mark removed the oversized glasses and addressed the audience: "And now, ladies and gentlemen, we're going to have Sharkey do his imitation of a B-29 flying over enemy lines."[2]

Sharkey balanced his torso atop his chair-back and suspended his body horizontally. He then spread his front flippers like airplane wings and arched his head and back flippers like a dive bomber, all while vocalizing a loud rumbling noise that bore an uncanny resemblance to a propeller-driven airplane engine. The crowd burst into applause in midroutine. As Sharkey finished, Mark showered him with praise and affection, repeatedly patting his head, "That's the idea. Very nice. Very, very nice."

Mark next presented an old routine, repurposed with a new punch line. The gag was based on Sharkey's ability to make remarkably humanlike though wholly unintelligible verbal utterances. Mark addressed the audience, "And now we're going to have Sharkey do his imitation of Hitler giving a radio address."

Sharkey thrust up his right flipper, gave a Hitler salute, then went to a microphone and delivered a mock Hitler radio address by spewing an extended nonsensical gabble of "wild and weird jabbering noises."[3] Laughs and cheers filled the theater. Night after night, city after city, Sharkey's imitation of Hitler was a showstopper.

Sharkey's wartime political imitations rivaled the rest of the entertainment world. Lampooning enemy oppressors was considered a vital morale booster. Charlie Chaplin mocked Hitler in his movie *The Great Dictator*.

The Three Stooges ridiculed the Third Reich in *You Nazty Spy!* (Moe, of Jewish descent, played Hitler and later said it was his favorite Stooges film.) Bugs Bunny and Popeye both derided the Japanese (Bugs in Warner Brothers' *Bugs Bunny Nips the Nips* and Popeye in Paramount's *You're a Sap, Mr. Jap*). Walt Disney employed Donald Duck in the Oscar-winning *Der Fuehrer's Face*, and Bugs Bunny famously spoofed Hitler in the Looney Tunes classic, *Herr Meets Hare*.

In his 2018 article "Bugs Bunny at 80," Joe Sommerlad notes, "In fearlessly mocking the dictators then bestriding the world stage, puncturing their ballooning pomposity, the likes of Bugs, Donald and Popeye reassured the public that they had nothing to fear from such delusional tyrants."[4] Distribution of much of this material has been suppressed in recent years on the grounds of it being offensive by today's standards, including its lighthearted portrayal of Nazis and its unabashedly racist portrayal of the Japanese. But during the grueling years of World War II, the battlefield of satire took all comers, including leading comics, adored cartoon characters, and—the world's greatest seal.

On the warfront that spring, Allied forces triumphed in Tunisia. The operation culminated with the Nazi surrender of their *Afrika Korps* commanded by Erwin Rommel, known as the Desert Fox for his skillful maneuvering in the African desert. Rommel was a military genius of great tactical prowess, a Nazi field marshal who had earned the respect of many adversaries, including US General George S. Patton. Though the war was far from over, Patton and the Allies had scored a key victory over Rommel and the Nazis.

Mark worked the news into the act that very evening. An attending critic wrote, "It will be a long time before this reviewer is able to forget a trick performed by Sharkey . . . Sharkey's most hilarious stunt is an imitation of Hitler explaining the African defeat. The seal makes ranting sounds into the microphone which are so perfect a parody of Hitler's oratory that it strikes one as one of the funniest things that has ever been done on the vaudeville stage."[5]

Camp Boardwalk and Iceland

Sharkey did a long stint that summer at Atlantic City's Steel Pier. Entertainment had returned to the resort city, although Steel Pier's usual towering nighttime lights remained blackened to safeguard against potential German submarine attacks. Much was different since Sharkey's pier debut two years earlier. "The most amazing wartime change among American towns is in Atlantic City," wrote the *Saturday Evening Post*. "[It] has shucked its perpetual sports-coat and donned the grey-green jacket of the Army." "All you saw up and down the Boardwalk were military uniforms," a soldier later recalled.[6] Atlantic City also became home to the country's largest military hospital; the rationale being that the recovery and morale of wounded soldiers would be boosted by the salt air and proximity to the ocean. Vacationers still came to the ocean playground, albeit in fewer numbers due to government "pleasure driving bans" that limited family travel to one round-trip vacation destination.

Sharkey once again headlined. Fox Movietone News featured him in a newsreel, shot on location, and *Billboard* featured a picture of him on the pier, alongside bandleader Sammy Kaye, captioned, "A top-drawer ocean spot, a No. 1 performing animal and a leading orker [orchestra leader] furnish the ammunition to lure big coin."[7] Sharkey and the famous bandleader got along swimmingly, except for the time during a poolside performance when "Sammy Kaye had the temerity to peer over Sharkey's shoulder and received a juicy squirt in the face for his curiosity."[8] Sharkey, Sammy, and others like Jimmy Durante entertained vacationers and the thousands of military recruits who arrived every month for basic training in Atlantic City, known during the war as Camp Boardwalk.

The city embraced the military presence and provided overwhelming hospitality. Restaurants and theaters cut prices for those in uniform; locals provided meals. Beaches closed, allowing soldiers to perform military drills in the sand in preparation for overseas battle. Crowds collected on the Boardwalk to watch simulated amphibian assaults that included sounds of machine-gun fire and exploding bombs. Mothers and fathers saw their boys off to war, spending precious family time together before saying their emotional goodbyes.

Sharkey did his part to lighten the situation by mocking Tojo and Hitler. He also did his wet act. Mark fastened a doll to a post, "Come on, kiss your sweet baby." Sharkey leapt from the water tank and hugged the doll. He then came onstage and threw himself onto a long, wetted mat, like a baseball player sliding headfirst into home plate. More water stunts followed. After Sharkey's final pool exit, Mark made circular motions with his baton, rousing Sharkey into his final maneuver, a triple-revolution belly spin.[9]

Sharkey returned to movie palaces that fall. He started in Providence, Rhode Island, sharing the bill with the king of the one-liners, Henny Youngman. He also played the Baltimore Hippodrome and the Manhattan Academy of Music, later renamed the Palladium, a rock and roll venue during the 1970s. And he did another stint with Ed Sullivan at Loew's State Theater in Times Square, where *Billboard* assigned him high rank "among the flippered intelligentsia."[10]

Sharkey performed later that fall at Iceland, the largest restaurant in Manhattan's theater district. Located right on Broadway, its Scandinavian cuisine came with wall-to-wall posh maroon carpeting, matching maroon chairs, and an upscale decor. The restaurant presented a stage revue and two orchestras. Sharkey headlined the revue, billed "The Wonder of the Age." *Billboard* wrote, "Sharkey is as effective here as in a vaude house. The fishburner has plenty of tricks to amuse the customers."[11]

The *Village Voice* included Iceland in a 2011 story about ten forgotten New York City restaurants. The article ended with a poke at its northern theme: "As with other restaurants in the vicinity, there were nightly floor shows of a standard sort—sequined dancing girls, torch singers, comedians—but no polar bears, icebergs, or trained seals, alas."[12]

Sharkey would have begged to differ.

Jazz Meets Seal

Jazz and trained seals: a seemingly unlikely combination, but in our story, there are two points of historical interest. One involves Sharkey's tour of movie palaces that year; the other involves Ray Huling's standout seal, Charlie. Both involve Fletcher Henderson—a pianist, bandleader, and one of the most significant arrangers in the history of jazz, a major architect of big-band swing music.

The story begins in 1934. Prohibition had just ended, and drinking establishments sprang up everywhere, practically overnight. One ambitious endeavor was the creation of Billy Rose—a lyricist, producer, and a major player on the New York entertainment scene, a man described as "very shrewd, highly complex, and oddly likeable . . . never for want of boldness and imagination."[13]

Rose took an interest in a vacant theater in the heart of Midtown Manhattan. Arthur Hammerstein had built the playhouse (its first show benefitting from his nephew and budding lyricist, Oscar Hammerstein II) but lost it to bankruptcy after the 1929 stock market crash. That paved the way for Rose, who set his sights on turning it into a one-of-a-kind venue, with dinner, dancing, entertainment, and most importantly, booze.

Variety called it "a new phase in the evolution of post-repeal show business." Billy Rose put it thusly: "It will be the nuts."[14]

Rose hired big-timers Ben Blue and Charlie the seal as his main acts. They had recently worked together in Brooklyn, filming *All Sealed Up*. Rose next went looking for music and found a twenty-four-year-old clarinet virtuoso by the name of Benny Goodman, who hastily assembled a group in the hope of landing the high-profile gig, his first stab at leading a big band. After a dismal audition, Rose brought him back for a second try. Goodman returned better prepared. Rose hired him. And so was born the Benny Goodman Orchestra.

Rose also hired thirty-six seedy vaudeville acts. "I want the real corn," he said. "I don't care how stupid or silly the acts are. I want actors that look like they slept in dollar-a-night hotels all their life and played theaters in spots that even Rand McNally wouldn't print."[15]

On Thursday, June 21, 1934, six months after the repeal of Prohibition, Billy Rose's Music Hall opened its doors. Previews listed Ben Blue and "Ray Huling and his trained seal." Neglected from mention was Benny Goodman. Simply promised was a "sumptuous music show."[16] Opening night was the hottest ticket in town. "Celebs are glimpsed everywhere" wrote a reporter, among them, Irving Berlin, George Jessel, and Rose's wife, Fanny Brice.[17]

A massive crowd assembled outside the former theater. Towering above the entrance was a four-story illuminated sign with blinking lights that spelled BILLY ROSE. Upon entering, one's view was drawn to a fifty-foot-high vaulted cathedral dome, its breathtaking neo-Gothic architecture adorned with mosaic tiles, a huge chandelier, ornate plastering, and ten illuminated stained-glass panels depicting scenes from Hammerstein-produced operas.

Customers sweltered. Word was the air-cooling system "went berserk."[18] Regardless, after thirteen years of Prohibition, it was party time. Tables replaced theater seats in the balcony and floor sections, accommodating the 1,000 people now there for a show, dinner, and dancing. Rose dispatched 100 bulbous-nosed, thuggish-looking, mustachioed waiters, who wore white butcher smocks and Wild West bow ties. The waiters gathered en masse onstage and serenaded some old-timey tunes before dispersing to tables to inform of the evening's dinner special: an eight-course meal for a dollar. On the back of each menu was a cartoon illustration of Charlie, balancing on his nose an oversized bottle of Meukow Cognac.

Two bars provided ample access to booze. Fine liquors lined the mirrored shelves of the main-floor Silver Dollar Bar, its floor studded with silver dollars. Another bar downstairs came styled Wild West, complete with a sawdust floor, a picture of Milton Berle captioned "Wanted for Murder," and the sounds of ragtime piano king, Mike Bernard. The downstairs program assured a "rootin', tootin', shootin', old-time saloon—sawdust, smoke, sin-copation."[19]

Nakedness pervaded. Freshly painted gaudy nudes decorated the main floor walls. The wine menu had a front-cover sketch of a naked woman with her hands strategically covering her pubic area while a decked-out gangster pointed a gun at her, saying, "Hands up." Also available were wooden paddle clackers imprinted with a naked lady from whose left hand stemmed a thin metal strip to which was attached a small red ball that clacked against the paddle when merrymakers shook the apparatus. Not to be ignored was the popular Wishing Well attraction, located on the main floor, at which for a twenty-five-cent investment could be seen the rippled reflection of two topless live mermaids at the bottom of the well, made possible by the trickery of mirrors.

The venue centerpiece, however, was its mammoth stage, festooned with a backdrop embroidered with caricatures of wailing jazz musicians, a clown face, singing elves, and odd ghostlike figures. Accompanying the backdrop was a waterfall effect.

Festivities opened with newsreels, cartoons, and a short film by Billy Rose titled *Here's to Broadway*, that depicted the gaiety of the theater district before Prohibition. The film also highlighted "the lawlessness of Volsteadism and its blight on Broadway until the FDR era and its patriotic endeavor for national recovery."[20]

Charlie opened the live show by merrily galloping onto the stage, honking a horn and pulling a souped-up children's wagon labeled "Sea Going Taxi." Ray sat amusedly oversized on the front of the wagon. Wooden crates overhung the back, housing an assortment of props.[21]

The wagon rolled center stage.

"The only one seal-powered taxi," Ray told the crowd. His relaxed tone matched his gentle persona.

The slender and balding trainer dismounted the wagon, placed a large, decorative bow around Charlie's neck, and spilled some lemons on the floor. "Charlie, just a moment, I'll get you a ladder. Just juggle one of these lemons for now."

Ray left the stage while the orchestra broke into background music. Charlie picked up a lemon with his mouth and jerked his neck, sending the lemon in the air. On its descent, he caught it with his nose and moved about the vast stage, lemon on nose.

Ray returned with a ladder, a softball-sized ball, and a stick. "Now Charlie, I want you to carry this stick to the top of the ladder, let it fall, and catch the ball. All right?"

"All right," Charlie replied.

Charlie's pronunciation was crystal clear. The echo vocalization bit had long been a part of the Huling brothers' stock in trade.

"You better be careful," Ray continued. "You know all the ladies like sealskin coats."

Ray turned to the audience and told them the next trick was very difficult. He continued in a playful cadence. "But if anyone thinks it's easy, they might try it with their little pet dog at home."

Ray balanced a stick on Charlie's mouth, then placed a longer stick on top of the first stick on top of which was the softball-sized ball. The items swayed in an eight-foot-high vertical tower. Charlie kept everything balanced on his mouth.

"Now hold it steady and watch your step," Ray said.

Charlie kept an upward gaze. The articles remained in a state of precarious equilibrium.

"Take your time," Ray added.

Charlie climbed the ladder to the top fourth step while balancing a ball on a long stick balanced on the short stick held in his mouth. Upon Ray's command, Charlie let both sticks fall, caught the ball with his nose, and flicked the ball to his trainer. The crowd gave a big round of applause. Charlie supplemented the ovation with his own clapping.

Ray chuckled. "Well then, you can carry this balloon down the ladder, roll over, take your seat, and throw it to me. All right?"

"All right," Charlie replied.

Ray tapped a balloon up to Charlie then turned to the crowd and quipped, "Balancing as it appears in slow moving pictures."

Charlie descended the ladder, intermittently nudging the balloon with his nose, only as necessary to keep it afloat. As the balloon whimsically floated downward, Charlie made his way down the ladder to the stage, then rolled over and tapped the balloon to Ray.

Juggling followed. The pair also did gags. "Now Charlie," Ray asked, "what do you do when you wear your woolen underwear?" Charlie scratched his posterior several times. Loudly. The orchestra responded with a *Wah-wah-wah-waaah*.

Charlie also did a burlesque parody (for those wondering whether a trained-seal act was in keeping with such an atmosphere). Charlie dressed in drag, wearing a gold, metal-cupped bra affixed to his torso with leather strap bells. Accessorizing his eye-catching brassiere was a matching gold metal-fringed skirt, a tasseled sultan hat, and a stone-studded choker necklace.

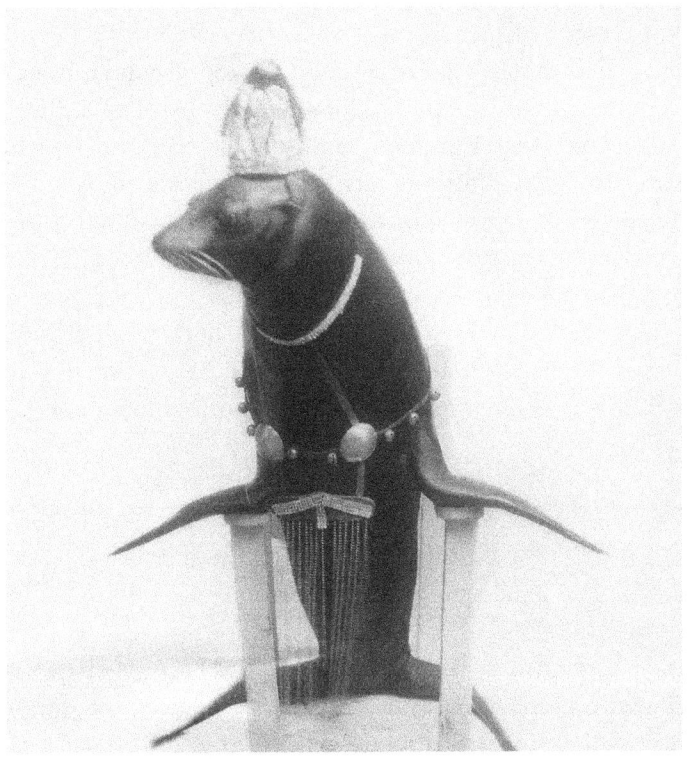

Charlie doing his burlesque takeoff. Press photo from the author's collection.

Charlie closed with an up-tempo dance number backed by the orchestra. Punctuating his exit cheers were no doubt the rat-a-tat-tats of unseemly wooden paddle clackers. *Variety* described Charlie's act that night as "more than usually effective."[22]

Billy Rose next introduced his Lonely Hearts Club, 100 hostesses "all with nifty figures and mostly easy on the eyes." Each wore a tight, black satin dress with an available-for-purchase heart covering her left breast. Among the hostesses' tasks was to provide fee-based companionship so "boys on the loose can always have company," flirtation services that also flirted with the boundaries of legality.[23]

Into the crowd they went.

Next up were Olive and George, vaudeville's famed song-and-dance duo of "highly attractive midgets." More acts followed: Ben Blue, Oscar the flea, chorus girls, a black tap-dance duo said to have "whammed 'em with their legmania," and a stage-screen production that ended with an onstage tableau of women, motionless and nude.[24]

Then came the thirty-six seedy vaudeville acts.

Rose unleashed them like a fireworks finale. Spellbound patrons watched as acts performed three at a time; each group allotted sixty seconds to give it their best. Out spewed a spoon band, fire-eaters, a "Fat Girl Ballet," a clown with electric eyes, minstrel men, a strong woman, a sword swallower, and a procession of other culls, castoffs, and misfits whom Rose termed the "Small Time Cavalcade."

For twelve solid bizarre minutes, acts came out in groups of three, pouring their hearts out. Then the grand finale: all thirty-six acts onstage at once. They took turns delivering a somber recitation, a lament coauthored by Billy Rose for the occasion, titled "Tank Town Trouper":

> For 20 years we've played the sticks
> For coffee and for cake,
> For 20 years we've played the sticks
> And never got the breaks[25]

The oration continued at length; the crowd visibly touched; one celebrity actress fought back tears. After delivering their oration, the thirty-six acts simultaneously reprised their routines in a massive, surreal burst of energy, something of an entertainment supernova, all while the orchestra blared "The Stars and Stripes Forever."

When the orchestra sounded its final note, the house lights dramatically blacked out. Amid the quasi-darkness, a parade of shadowy silhouettes solemnly marched offstage, the small-timers returning to the show business abyss from whence they had come. Evaporated into the stifling evening air was the final refrain of another verse Rose had coauthored for the occasion, sung by an Irish tenor.

> Give 'em that great big hand of yours
> This is their one big shot,
> May I present the Small Time Cavalcade
> The acts that Keith forgot.[26]

By one reporter's measure, their exit ovation lasted three minutes and twenty seconds. Goodman and his orchestra segued into dance music. The 100 beauties of the Lonely Hearts Club solicited business with an icebreaker special; a drink and a dance for a dollar. Customers assembled onstage on a woodland-themed set, alongside the orchestra, whose rhythmic melodies set into motion the sways of ballroom dancing. A set of music concluded the opening show. After three packed shows, the club completed its inaugural night, sometime around four in the morning.

Critics assessed the evening "absurd and engaging," "a monument of lunacy," "honky-tonk on a cosmic scale," "a roaring furnace of frivolity," "the maddest of madhouses."[27]

News of the nightclub spread nationwide, but lost in the ballyhoo was Benny Goodman, who had had trouble navigating his orchestra through the music cues prepared for the barrage of quirky entertainers. "We were terrible," Goodman recalled. "I don't know why, but we couldn't seem to work our way through the score." In the words of a sideman, "Benny could not conduct."[28]

Rose hired a separate orchestra for the stage show but kept the Goodman orchestra for dancing. Relieved from their duties as carnival accessory, Goodman's orchestra jelled in ways novel and profound. Critics took note. *DownBeat* magazine ran a cover story, "Benny Goodman and Orch. Big Success on Broadway."[29] It mattered not. Goodman received his notice the next month, later calling it "probably the toughest blow I ever received."[30]

The *New Yorker* wrote about Charlie in a Talk of the Town piece titled "The Great Seal," noting he was the only act at Rose's nightclub that had lasted the first two months.[31] Jinx in place, Rose soon remarked, "The best showman is the guy with the biggest knife, who cuts, cuts, cuts," boasting he had trimmed the seal act from fifteen to eight minutes.[32] Charlie got the ax shortly after. Not to worry; by October, he was playing the posh Chicago Theater and Chicago World's Fair.

Rose's theater nightclub meanwhile wobbled amid rumors of financial swindling, mobsters, and legal wrangling. Adding to its woes were the hard times of the Great Depression. Within six months of having opened, Billy Rose's Music Hall was history.

(What ultimately became of the theater is a whole other story. CBS started using it for radio two years later and later used it for television, including the variety show hosted by Ed Sullivan, for whom the theater is now named. David Letterman worked there for twenty-two years with his *Late Show*. The theater is now home to *The Late Show with Stephen Colbert*.)

A week after Rose's nightclub went dark, Benny Goodman premiered on *Let's Dance*, a new radio show broadcast out of New York on the NBC network. National Biscuit Company (later Nabisco) sponsored the program, promoting their latest product, the Ritz cracker. By then, word was out that Goodman's orchestra was being fueled by the hot arrangements of noted black bandleader Fletcher Henderson.

John Hammond, a young record producer who later discovered everyone from Aretha Franklin to Bruce Springsteen, had brought Goodman and Henderson together, describing Henderson's charts as "so far in advance of anything else around that a band playing them has a head start on its rivals that is insuperable."[33]

Let's Dance was a smash. So too was Benny Goodman, universally credited with giving birth to the swing era months later, a period from 1935 to 1946, when swing music dominated the hit parade. Goodman became a superstar, crowned the King of Swing.

Benny Goodman added two black musicians to his swing combo; pianist Teddy Wilson and vibraphonist Lionel Hampton. A racially mixed band was unheard of at the time. Goodman proceeded anyway, hampered by Jim Crow laws in the South that forbade racial integration in clubs and hotels. The musical result, however, was magical.

Recordings of the group are among the most cherished in the pantheon of jazz. Goodman's integrated band also provided a groundbreaking template for others. Hampton later said Goodman's "social approach to the racial problem in the United States was a total first," further noting that the band "made it possible for Jackie Robinson to get into major league baseball. This was such an important development that we just can't fluff it off or forget about it."[34] Indeed, Goodman's reign as the King of Swing was both musically and culturally pioneering, vis-à-vis his racially mixed combo and his larger orchestra, which, for years, played the arrangements of black maestro Fletcher Henderson.

With swing music still in fashion, in 1943, Henderson appeared with his own orchestra at the Apollo Theater in Harlem. The bill had a comedy tap act, Cuban dancers, a female impersonator, a scat singer, and Sharkey. *Variety* called the lineup "one of the neatest entertainment packages [the] house has had in weeks, clicking in almost every department. From Fletcher Henderson's polished boogie to Sharkey the Seal's amazing antics, there's scarcely a letup. . . . Henderson peddles a suave brand of melody flavored with enough jive to keep the 'cats' happy. . . . Sharkey the Seal continues to be an amazing stage personality."[35]

Fletcher Henderson's band included twenty-three-year-old drummer Art Blakey in his very first week touring with a major orchestra.[36] Blakey, a 2005 Grammy Lifetime Achievement Award recipient, would rise to fame as a bandleader who toured for decades with his Jazz Messengers, routinely turning unknowns like Wynton Marsalis into stars. Blakey and the rest of Henderson's band no doubt received plenty of hearty applause from fellow musician Sharkey.

Sharkey closed out 1943 by working Christmas week at the 2,500-seat Paradise Theater, a venue frequented by Detroit's black community. There, he shared the bill with another member of jazz legendary, the First Lady of Song, Ella Fitzgerald.

A most classy way to end another whirlwind year.

Advertisement in the *Detroit Tribune*. Library of Congress, Chronicling America: Historic American Newspapers.

The Great Stage

Two years had elapsed since Pearl Harbor. Victory overseas was anything but certain. The United States had become a veritable military production machine unlike anything the world had ever seen. The government partnered with private industry, manufacturing staggering amounts of armaments in record time. Ford built fighter bombers. Chrysler built tanks. Shipyards built battleships and submarines. Factories retooled for the army. Even the Lionel toy train company assisted by making warship compasses. And with so many men overseas, women entered the domestic workforce in record numbers, becoming welders and mechanics and doing other jobs traditionally done by men.

Government-enforced rationing of gasoline conserved fuel and rubber. Rationing of sugar and coffee offset import restrictions; rationing of meats, butter, and canned goods made these items available for US and Allied troops. Everything centered on the war.

Seal College clients in many cases were inactive. The Manhattan National Sportsmen's Show canceled its entire program. Fairgrounds became military depots, forcing the cancelation of annual fairs, some for the first time in over 100 years. Mainstay arena events refocused on supporting the war effort rather than having entertainment. As a practical matter, many arenas were unavailable, serving instead as storage and staging areas for the military.

Sharkey began 1944 in Boston. "Sharkey eclipsed every other act on the star-studded program," wrote the International News Service.[37]

Radio City Music Hall was next. At just twelve years old, it had already surpassed the Statue of Liberty as New York's number-one tourist stop. Its well-trod format—a stage show followed by a feature movie—ran until 1979, the last of its kind. The 6,000-seat indoor theater was the world's largest, as was its movie-projection screen, and its stage, known as the Great Stage. Framing the stage was the world's largest curtain, a three-ton contoured golden drapery. Hydraulic stage elevators, revolving turntable floors, and a high-tech lighting system enabled spectacular effects. The venue's permanent roster of performers was without peer: a seventy-five-piece symphony orchestra, a forty-member ballet corps, a thirty-six-member glee club, and its forty-six-member dance troupe, the Rockettes.

Mark and Sharkey arrived for rehearsal on a late January morning. Stomping about were choreographers, dancers, musicians, entertainers, and stagehands. Producer Leon Leonidoff corralled the troops to begin work on a new stage show, one of hundreds he produced over his forty-two-year career at Radio City Music Hall, this one titled *Smart Set*.

Rehearsals were crammed into the morning, before afternoon and evening box office performances of the ongoing show. Everyone ran ragged. Leonidoff teed off with Radio City Music Hall music director Ernö Rapée. Both were high-strung, passionate, workaholics. The two screamed at each other: "Pig"; "Peasant." A makeup embrace followed. The "travail of geniuses," said some. Others dismissed it as an act.[38] (Rapée died of a heart attack a year later at age fifty-four.) In either case, Mark and Sharkey were on the Radio City Music Hall rehearsal roller-coaster, strapped in for their next adventure with some of the most creative and volatile people in the business.

Among those at rehearsal was Jimmy Sileo. He owned the Cosmo-Sileo photo agency, the official photographer for the New York Yankees, responsible for the team shot of the famed 1927 Bronx Bombers and other iconic photos of players like Ruth, Gehrig, and DiMaggio. Jimmy was also the official photographer for Radio City Music Hall, earning him exclusive privilege to shoot rehearsals. That morning, Jimmy came upon Mark and Sharkey on the Great Stage.

Mark wore a screaming-loud, checkered suit jacket and spoke in a mild-mannered tone to his star pupil. "All right, time to take your stand, young fellow."

Sharkey shuffled to his stand and propped himself upright.

Mark again spoke to Sharkey. "Now, I want you to put this in your mouth, young man." Mark inserted a black rubber device into Sharkey's mouth. The prop was similar to a perfume atomizer bulb except more robust. Attached was a thin, hollow, tubular extension.

Mark lit a cigarette and placed it into the extension. Smoking was the epitome of Hollywood glamour and Mark had worked up a bit, explaining that although Sharkey smoked, he didn't smoke in bed.

With the apparatus hidden in Sharkey's mouth, the lit cigarette dangled from his lips with Humphrey Bogart–like suaveness, for Sharkey had long mastered his sophisticated look. Camera in sight, the prima donna seal was ready for action.

Sharkey and Mark at Radio City Music Hall. Press photo by Jimmy Sileo, from the author's collection via Michael Reilly.

Mark stepped back and stepped back again. A moment later, he issued a hand cue. Sharkey responded with a chew on the bulb.

Out came a puff of smoke.

Jimmy peered through his lens, Sharkey on his left, Mark on his right. In the background was the Seal College homemade bell instrument. When the cloud of cigarette smoke dissipated by just the right amount, Jimmy captured the image. Stage lights starkly lit both Sharkey and the wafting smoke pattern. A darkened side stage provided a contrasting backdrop.

And though he may not have realized it that instant, Jimmy Sileo had just added to his collection of iconic photos.[39]

~

Smart Set featured Robert Merrill, a twenty-six-year-old singer with the NBC Orchestra under Arturo Toscanini. Merrill would soon join the Metropolitan Opera, where he stayed for thirty years, eventually becoming their principal baritone. In late career, he often joked about Sharkey having upstaged him. He remembered well.

Ads read, "Smart Set—a spectacular panorama of metropolitan highlights produced by Leonidoff, settings by Bruno Maine, presenting the incredible comedy of Sharkey."[40]

Beginning the program was a bone-rattling overture on the Music Hall Mighty Wurlitzer, the largest pipe organ ever built for a movie house. Next was a Disney cartoon. Ernö Rapée then conducted the Music Hall Symphony Orchestra, performing the lively folk-tinged *Romanian Rhapsody No. 1*. After that came *Smart Set*. Robert Merrill soloed with the Music Hall Glee Club; the Music Hall Corps de Ballet danced amid a colorful backdrop inspired by French painter Edgar Degas; and Sharkey juggled, imitated, and did a music finale. *Variety* wrote that Sharkey was "set off to unusual advantage on the vast Music Hall stage." *Billboard* awarded kudos for his imitations of "Tojo the Jap" and "Hitler the Ranter."[41]

The stage show ended with the Rockettes. After that was the US movie premiere of *Jane Eyre*, starring Joan Fountain and Orson Welles. The stage-film combo fared well at the Music Hall box office, running four shows a day for four weeks.

Sharkey's appearance at Radio City Music Hall soon inspired a piece of art, though it was not a first for a Huling-trained seal. Charlie had posed

Sea Lion by Wheeler Williams (1897–1972), bronze, 1938, Collection of Brookgreen Gardens, gift of Mrs. E. Gerry Chadwick Jr.

for Wheeler Williams, a Yale and Harvard grad and longtime president of the National Sculpture Society. Williams sculpted a life-sized, bronze sea lion statue on a greenstone pedestal. Charlie's likeness balanced a copper ball that streamed cascades of water, keeping him sleek and wet. *Art Digest* praised the statue's naturalism: "Drops of water glisten on Charlie's crisp chromium steel whiskers." Critics found it "modern in its line and mass and elimination of unnecessary details."[42] The piece debuted at a New York City art exhibition, then traveled to England. It now resides at Brookgreen Gardens in South Carolina, home to one of the country's largest collections of outdoor animal sculptings.

Years later, just after Sharkey's 1944 debut at Radio City Music Hall, an artist named Billy Van painted an oil portrait of Sharkey posing in a stately side-profile, perched on his stand, deep in thought on a vast ocean beach. Behind him stood the Radio City Music Hall facade, reaching into dreamlike clouds against a backdrop of blue sky. The marquee read, "Featuring Sharkey, Wonder Seal." Mark hung the painting in the Seal College reception room, where it remained for the rest of Sharkey's career. On the wooden picture frame was inscribed "The Mirage."

Sharkey's appearance at Radio City Music Hall may have seemed like a mirage, but nothing could have been more real. After just four years in show business, he had starred on Broadway, headlined at Steel Pier, appeared in a Hollywood hit movie, and played the country's biggest theaters. About the only thing Sharkey hadn't done was entertain the president of the United States.

That came next.

Chapter 9

Sharkey Meets the President

Sharkey Goes to Washington

Secrecy shrouded the event. Security officials prohibited entertainers from seeking any advance publicity. The hush-hush list of performers included Sharkey, slated to perform at the event just three days after he wrapped up at Radio City Music Hall.

On Saturday, March 4, 1944, the big day arrived. Sharkey rolled into Washington, DC, where he shuffled about the newly opened Statler Hotel, thirteen stories of lodging offering the latest in luxury. Staff bustled to prepare for a dinner party in the main ballroom, a spacious 7,500-square-foot, two-story chamber that sparkled with extravagance.

President Franklin D. Roosevelt was to be the guest of honor. That in itself was significant. Social events of any kind were a rarity for the president, engrossed in the largest military conflict in human history, the stakes as big as they get. The president began his day that morning in the East Room of the White House at a religious service celebrating the eleventh anniversary of his first presidential inauguration (the last held in March before it moved to January). Clergy presided over the service, attended by government officials and their spouses. The president then went with First Lady Eleanor to see her off at Washington National Airport. She had appointments in the Caribbean to "assure soldiers in lonely outposts that their vigils were appreciated."[1] That the first lady would miss a rare night of socializing with her husband that evening was explainable for one simple reason: the guest list excluded women, the pretext being that "the ladies might hear dirty jokes and 'blue' language."[2]

The president returned to the White House for a quiet afternoon in his study; a cozy room with a fireplace and his favorite red leather chair, a replica of a chair used by Thomas Jefferson. Later that afternoon, he met with James Byrnes, head of the Office of War Mobilization. Later still, he met with his tailor, Samuel Scogna, a man who went to extraordinary lengths, literally, to mask the president's crippling affliction with polio. Scogna routinely made the president's pants legs extra-long so when the pants rode up his legs, his leg braces wouldn't show.

After Scogna had made his final alterations, the president left for his night out, joined by three others: his personal physician, his son-in-law, and a close friend. A clock on the wall read ten minutes to seven. Plenty of time to go the four blocks from the White House to the hotel for the eight o'clock start. History is silent regarding the president's mood in anticipation of the stag dinner, its twenty-first annual, which had become an insider beltway tradition. He had every reason to be subdued. Previous affairs had hardly been remarkable. Only fifty attended the inaugural banquet. Subsequent events often had empty seats, entertainment at times no more than sing-alongs around a piano. But the sponsoring association assured that this year would be different. It would be memorable. It would include a stage show, featuring celebrities of music, radio, film, and stage. With that in mind, the president went to the Statler Hotel main function room, aptly called the Presidential Ballroom. There, he situated himself at the head table for the annual White House Correspondents' Dinner.

The dinner drew record-breaking numbers. Seven hundred and fifty elites packed their way inside the ballroom. The big-ticket gala served as a fund-raiser, with proceeds going to the National Foundation for Infantile Paralysis, better known as polio.

Mealtime brought the requisite clinking of glasses and clanking of cutlery. Conversations competed with the sounds of the US Navy Band, there to provide dinner music. Servers navigated their way through a mass of people, tables, and chairs, bringing out courses of unrationed food items. The main course was roast duck.

After-dinner festivities excluded the usual tedium of speeches. Instead came the promised entertainers. Fritz Kreisler, the most celebrated concert violinist of his day, received a standing ovation. Gracie Fields, Britain's foremost film and stage celebrity, scored big with song novelties. Robert Merrill sang, as did Mexican sensation Pedro Bargas, touted "a cross between Bing Crosby and Caruso." Radio personages lent their gift of gab. Fifty-five-year-old Elsie Janis (a stage star turned Hollywood screenwriter) high-kicked her way to much applause, closing with a series of cartwheels that "pleased the President to no end."[3]

Then came Sharkey. Mark joined him, dressed in tails. In view were correspondents, politicians, and their male guests seated around tables, elbow to elbow, chairs adjusted to face the stage. At an elevated head table, situated off to the side, sat the president, vice president, five cabinet members including the secretary of state, a quorum of the Supreme Court, ranking military officers, and the speaker of the House. The Associated Press reported that the assembly was "the most complete turnout of the Nation's war leaders since Pearl Harbor."[4]

Mark and Sharkey whipped balls back and forth, looking like an old-time movie clip of two baseball players playing catch in fast motion. As the audience applauded, Mark tossed Sharkey a treat.

A reporter wisecracked from the crowd, taking aim at Hamilton Fish—a congressman and critic of the president. "The next time they throw him a fish, how about throwing him Hamilton!"[5] The gathering burst into a howl of bipartisan guffaws.

Sharkey next went up to the mike and did his wartime mimicries. He wore comically large glasses and mocked nearsighted Japanese General Tojo. He imitated an air-raid siren and a US fighter aircraft buzzing an enemy airfield. And, of course, he ridiculed Hitler. The Hitler parody extended to the many legislators in the room when Mark explained that Sharkey would be imitating Hitler giving an address to the Reichstag—Germany's rubberstamp parliament that assembled to listen to his speeches, unfailingly providing unanimous consent to his dictatorial decrees. Sharkey followed with his customary lampooning of Hitler bumbling his way through a nonsensical speech.

Sharkey finished with a number on his homemade instrument. Accompanying him, direct from New York, was the forty-piece NBC Orchestra. Sharkey then went to the head table and gave President Roosevelt a hand-flipper shake.

The evening's closing act employed a format that would come to define the event: a comedian doling out political zingers. Jester for the correspondents' first annual big-party affair was the conservative-minded Bob Hope, ready to roast the famously liberal president. Hope, later known for his TV specials and as host of the Academy Awards a record eighteen times, was set to go on a USO tour right after the dinner, one of fifty he made between 1941 and 1991. He later admitted being nervous in front of the president, but the barbs quickly flowed.

Hope cracked that DC stood for "damn confusing" and joked that "the highest ambition left for American youth is the vice-presidency."[6] (Roosevelt won a fourth term that fall, prompting a constitutional amendment establishing presidential term limits.) Hope told political gag after political gag. After each joke, the crowd turned their heads from the stage to the president, like spectators watching a tennis match, to see if the president was laughing. He was. Hope then poked fun at Roosevelt's media nemesis, conservative Robert McCormick, owner of the *Chicago Tribune*, who the president feuded with on a seemingly daily basis. Hope dragged the first family's Scottish terrier, Fala, into the fray. "And did you know . . . that Fala, the president's little Scottie, is the only dog ever housebroken on that newspaper?" Any concern that the comedian may have crossed the line disappeared when the crowd looked over at the president, who, by one account, "laughed so long and so hard that those at his table swear tears were running down his cheeks."[7]

The press was unanimous and magnanimous in their praise of the show. The *LA Times* called it "a killer-diller. . . . Something you see once in a thousand years. Maybe two thousand!" The paper added, "If you haven't seen Sharkey, the trained seal, you haven't seen anything." The *Indianapolis Star* wrote, "Was it any wonder that the President had a big night? Super entertainment ranged from a remarkable act by a seal—Sharkey, the seal of all seals—to Fritz Kreisler, now with snow white hair, the violinist of all violinists. . . . Charley Brendler, leader of the famous orchestra of the United States Navy, was entranced by the seal—the great Sharkey—who, with bells, played a beautiful waltz. . . . There are many performing seals, but Charley was so amazed by Sharkey that he would almost be willing to add him to the Navy Band."[8]

The president concluded the evening with a short, unscripted speech and a toast to the US Armed Forces. The crowd joined him in singing "Battle Hymn of the Republic."

That same night, the president called on a newly established elite military unit, the US Eighth Air Force, known as the Mighty Eighth, considered to this day the greatest air squadron in history. In a move resembling President Obama's covert military assassination of Osama bin Laden juxtaposed with the gaiety of the Correspondents' Dinner, that night, on March 4, 1944, the Mighty Eighth launched their first of many bombing raids on Berlin, Germany.

Return of an Old Grad

Two days later, Sharkey headlined a vaude-film bill. He so dominated the newspaper ad, it barely left room for the other four live acts. The notice stated, "Today, in person, Mark Huling presents Sharkey who just completed a command performance at the White House."[9]

Sharkey also caught the attention of NBC executive John Royal, later the first head of NBC-TV. Royal booked Sharkey for a New York City banquet at the most renowned function room in the world: the Waldorf Astoria Grand Ballroom. Sharkey once again had surpassed the achievements of Charlie, who, no slouch, had formerly garnered private bookings under management of Frances Rockefeller King, among the most powerful women in show business, an agent for the Keith circuit and later for NBC. Charlie, by the way, arrived at private functions in a limousine, "debonairly wearing a top hat and carrying a cane beneath its left flipper."[10] Those wishing a celebrity seal at their next party, be it Sharkey or Charlie, were well advised to bring their wallet. A private showing ran about $10,000 in today's dollars.

After the Waldorf Astoria, Sharkey did nine days in Chicago, headlining a floor show. The last leg of his itinerary was a movie palace in Michigan, where he once again topped the stage bill. All that remained of his long journey was the 700-mile ride home.

Mark and Sharkey had been inseparable throughout the tour. Sharkey's daily regimen included a bath, exercise, and plenty of play. He especially craved physical attention. His sensory diet included generous servings of Mark's back and tummy rubs. Sharkey also enjoyed nuzzling up to Mark's face, sharp canines exposed, delivering damp, toothy kisses to his trainer. "He wouldn't bite for anything," Mark said.[11]

The pair raised considerable sums of money. Sharkey would go to the lobby before shows and make the rounds, holding a donation bowl in his mouth, helping local causes like orphanages and national organizations like the March of Dimes. "Sharkey seems to get more of a thrill out of passing the hat for contributions than he does out of any trick," Mark noted.[12] War bond rallies were another popular fund-raising activity. Men, women, and children lined up to buy a bond from their favorite seal. Sharkey stood upright against a desk draped in an American flag and delivered bonds from between his lips, followed by a flipper handshake as a show of thanks for their patriotism.

Road trip activities were many and varied. Sharkey went on the radio show, *Truth or Consequences*. He promoted Encyclopedia Britannica by "reading" while Mark held open an encyclopedia. And he did several photo shoots, including playing a friendly game of cards with a starlet who lay on a table in a low-cut skimpy dress and high heels. Using his mouth, Sharkey plucked a card from a fanned-out deck of cards held in her hands. "Sharkey bids five aces," Mark said.[13]

Sharkey shows his poker face. Used with permission from the Embassy Theatre Foundation.

On the road, Sharkey enjoyed riding shotgun in the front of the truck, engaging in the familiar head-out-the-window pastime traditionally reserved for man's best friend. It came in handy one traffic jam when a vehicle was trying to give Mark the squeeze. Mark called over to his seal companion, "Sharkey, let's have it," which, for the unfortunate encroaching motorist, was the stage cue for Sharkey's imitation of Leo the MGM Lion. As if a 175-pound seal with its head out the window of a truck labeled Seal College wasn't freakish enough, the ensuing roar left little doubt which vehicle received the right of way.[14]

Sharkey returned home that May. Over a fifteen-month span, he had done about everything an entertainer could do, from playing places like the Apollo Theater and Steel Pier, to working with Bob Hope and Ella Fitzgerald, to amusing the president of the United States. *Parade* covered the homecoming with an article "Return of an Old Grad" that ran in Sunday papers everywhere: "Sharkey the seal comes back from his $1500 a week tour for a brush-up at Seal College, Kingston, N.Y."[15]

Sharkey received a big welcome-home smile from Jumbo, who awaited him on the Seal College porch. Sharkey swayed up the two front steps, which were nothing more than two rickety wooden planks on stacks of two-by-fours. The lack of lavishness did nothing to detract from the cheerful reunion. Mark looked on approvingly, wearing a suit and tie, with a handkerchief meticulously folded in a four-point configuration tucked in his top jacket pocket, evoking old-school showbiz norms—always dressing sharp, onstage and off.

Mark set up two outdoor pedestals so Jumbo and Sharkey could bat around a beach ball to each other. They also played together in the woodland backyard. Outdoor hose sprayings were another favorite pastime, especially when Mark placed the nozzle up close and directed jets of water onto the seals' faces. If Jumbo and Sharkey were particularly lucky, they might enjoy the occasional serenade of Mark playing his violin. He could play better than his lack of formal training or regular practice might have otherwise predicted.[16]

Elsewhere at home, Mark's wife, Lillian, was ill. Her mental health was in decline. She was in an infirmary, as she had been for some time, and would remain for the rest of her life. Mark visited regularly when in town, something that surely took its toll over the years, an emotional drain that may have explained, at least in part, his continued passion for spending time with seals. Those who knew Mark speak with a singular voice. The seals were his solace, his love, his pride. In an otherwise imperfect world, life was good whenever Mark entered the magical world of Seal College. There was nowhere on earth he'd rather be.

The American Fat Salvage Committee

On June 6, 1944—three months and two days after Sharkey's appearance at the White House Correspondents' Dinner, forever known as D-Day—Allied forces invaded the beaches of Normandy. Reports of inestimable casualties reached the US. The nation mourned. Major League Baseball canceled all of its scheduled games, something that wouldn't happen again (excluding labor halts) until September 11, 2001. Citizens united. People helped by collecting critical commodities to support the military effort, everything from scrap metal to scrap rubber, tin cans, rags, waste paper, and one other important item—fat.

Fat was essential for making glycerin, which, in turn, was needed to make explosives and certain medicines. Traditionally the US had imported fats from the Pacific. But with those areas now controlled by Japan, fat was in short supply, which became a matter of national security. As a result, the US government formed the American Fat Salvage Committee. The committee organized a fat drive, requesting that households bring used kitchen fat to local butchers in return for bonus ration points, which allowed for the purchase of items like meats and butter. Notices soon appeared urging the reclamation of fat.

As part of this effort, two captioned photos of Sharkey ran prominently in newspapers nationwide. One showed him using his nose to balance a tin can marked FATS. "Seal Sharkey knows that salvaged fat must balance with need of munitions and medicines at fighting fronts, and demonstrates point in own unique way." Another showed him in full bark, his mouth wide open. By his side was a tin can, marked USED FAT. "Sharkey, the talking seal, is making an announcement, and he hopes housewives will get four points waiting for them at the butchers for every pound of used fat they save and turn in. It's four red points now instead of two for a pound of kitchen grease. Save every drop and earn needed extra points."[17]

About 250,000 butchers participated as collection centers. Each pound of used cooking fat yielded enough glycerin to make a pound of explosives. The American Fat Salvage program recovered over 500 million pounds of household kitchen fat.

D-Day to V-J Day

D-Day was less than three weeks old when a motorcade of police cars, ambulances, and Red Cross vehicles snaked through the streets of Rhode Island. The caravan made its way to Narragansett Park, normally a Thoroughbred horse track. But on this day, its track and infield belonged to the Rhode Island Shriners' annual fund-raising circus. The motorcade transported hundreds of physically handicapped and infirmed children from hospitals and convalescent homes so they could attend a special matinee as guests of the Shriners. Each received novelties and goodies. On hand was Sharkey. After the show, Mark, a Shriner himself, stayed all afternoon as volunteers carried the special guests to the Seal College tank. Lensmen stood nearby, preserving images of the elated youngsters meeting Sharkey, who, by one account, repeatedly "extended his flipper in a greeting of friendship."[18]

After Rhode Island, Sharkey spent the summer at Steel Pier, again amusing vacationers and soldiers. Always the consummate perfectionist, shows went smoothly—except for the time when "a Navy blimp appeared on the horizon, and Sharkey, considerably intrigued, just stopped working until he had followed the progress of the blimp out of sight."[19] Sharkey's season ended the weekend after Labor Day. It was timely.

Moving north was a ferocious Category 4 storm, now known as the 1944 Great Atlantic hurricane. The hurricane hit Atlantic City four days later, destroying the end of Steel Pier where Sharkey performed (rebuilt shortly afterward). The nearby Heinz Pier, its patrons often seen wearing complementary pickle pins, did not fare as well. The storm washed away the forty-six-year-old attraction, which was never to return.

Hours later, the hurricane hit New York City, coinciding with the scheduled opening of Sharkey working again with Ed Sullivan on Broadway. Sullivan had added fresh acts to his theater variety show, including Sharkey and the Three Chocolateers, "Harlem Ambassadors of Fun." Gale winds and sheets of rain pummeled the city. Sullivan's new bill opened nonetheless. Ticket holders in surprising numbers braved the elements. *Billboard* made no mention of the hurricane in its review of the opening show, matter-of-factly noting, "Biz fair," further noting, "Mark Huling knows how to handle his fish eater."[20]

The storm ravaged the east coast from North Carolina to Maine. Sullivan reported on the aftermath in his popular *Daily News* column, "Little Old New York," writing that "the hurricane shrunk the supply of saltwater fish in the N.Y. market, cutting the daily shipments from 750,000 pounds to 200,000 pounds. Only performer on Broadway to be affected by this was Sharkey, the show-stopping seal."[21]

That December, Mark authored a piece that ran in *Reader's Digest*. He told the story, as he often did, of Sharkey's unspectacular arrival. "I almost sent him back he was such a runt. . . . Finally, I taught him a trick—and he learned it in record time."[22]

Sharkey finished the year in Chicago at a posh hotel. The extended nightclub resort gig ended just in time. A nationwide government midnight curfew on clubs came right after. The intent was to save on gas and coal. The unpopular wartime restriction all but eliminated nightclub entertainment during its tenure.

Sharkey went from nightclubs to sports shows, which were up against a different set of restrictions. The US Office of Defense Transportation (ODT) instituted a ban on trade shows in order to reduce congestion of public travel facilities, deemed crucial for military travel. Oddly, the ODT still allowed entertainment exhibitions. Not surprisingly, sports shows soon fancied themselves as entertainment exhibitions rather than trade shows.

Sharkey started 1945 at the National Sportsmen's Show, which had been canceled the previous two years due to war. Grand Central Palace, its usual Manhattan venue, was still in use as a military staging area, causing the event to relocate to Madison Square Garden. Upon later discovering that sponsors had illicitly run a trade show in addition to having entertainment, the ODT issued an after-the-fact reprimand, threatening cancelation of future events.

Next month was the International Sports Show at the Chicago Coliseum. The ODT, now on the lookout, raided the event and shut down the trade booths. People still came out in droves for the entertainment.

Sold-out performances resulted in an extra show. In the coliseum was a large pool. Sharkey raced through the water, then came out of the pool, performing before the section of the crowd that offered the highest bid, his currency measured in applause and cheers. Using homemade props, Mark also programmed the "shower routine." Sharkey went to a half-door prop, opened it, scampered to a bath area, operated a handle that activated a shower, took a shower, turned off the water, toweled off, then exited back through the half-door and closed it, milking every move. Having just dried, he splashed back into the pool, leaving the crowd in hysterics. *Billboard* wrote, "Bait casters, bird imitators, archery experts, baton twisters, canoe tilters, log rollers, dog mushers and retrievers went along with customary plan of this type of show, but Sharkey the Seal again stole the plaudits."[23]

During that same tour, Sharkey snuck in a four-day theater run in Indianapolis. The *Indianapolis Star* called him the "not-too-modest star of the show." *Variety* wrote that "top spot on bill is accorded Sharkey the Seal, who earns his honors."[24]

Minneapolis was two weeks later. Attending was future NFL Hall of Famer Bud Grant, then a high school senior, also a stellar athlete. Colleges were courting him, including the University of Minnesota. An avid hunter and fisherman, Grant particularly appreciated Sharkey's performance, recalling the experience decades later, at age eighty-six: "There was Sharkey the Seal and a pool in this building! And Sharkey was jumping in and out of the water. I was fascinated. . . . My thinking then was if I come to Minnesota, it won't be because of the recruiting efforts that were laid out for me. It would be because of the Sportsmen's Show. That was what sold me."[25] After military service, Grant became a star athlete at the University of Minnesota. He later played in the NBA and NFL before going on to become the winningest head coach in Minnesota Vikings history, a team he led to four Super Bowls.

Milwaukee was next. After performing before a capacity house, Sharkey met with Stoney McGlynn, sports editor for the *Sentinel*. Stoney sat at his typewriter, where his fingers generated a workmanlike tap dance of thin metal rods clacking against ink ribbon, engaging in their nightly race against the panting presses. Sharkey nudged his mouth right up to Stoney's ear. "He got the inside story right from Sharkey himself," Mark said. "Strictly confidential!"[26]

Sharkey and Stoney. Press photo from the author's collection via Gary Bohan Sr.

Stoney's article hit newsstands next morning:

SHARKEY CHIEF TONIC ON
SPORTS SHOW LAUGH MENU

As expected, Sharkey, THE SHARKEY, if you please, proves the chief crowd stealer. Sharkey, coming here rated as the world's greatest trained seal, more than lives up to his billing. He's a one-man show, a showoff, a comedian, a mimic, an orator, a hurdler, and a swimmer that puts speed-boats in the also-ran category. Above all, he is a showoff, a prima-donna sort o' a cuss, somewhat on the order of a Dizzy Dean when ol' Diz was the kingpin of the moundsmen and let all sundry know about it. From the time Sharkey takes the stage until he leaves, he's the master showman, the star of the show. And he knows it. He not only leads his own cheering and applauding section, but borders on the risqué by giving himself a pat on the tonneau if he believes he did something exceptionally well. And the crowd loves it![27]

A *Sentinel* photo taken during Sharkey's act showed not him, but rather, a candid of the crowd; men, women, and children laughing about as hard as humanly possible, one lady wiping tears from her eyes. The caption read, "Who—but Sharkey could make 'em laugh like this!"[28]

Sharkey also did a local radio spot. With a week of shows to go, sponsors were no doubt pleased to get the media coverage. Extenuating circumstances had canceled the opening weekend matinees. Franklin D. Roosevelt had died the prior Thursday. Cancelations of every stripe occurred nationwide. The weekend of solemn remembrance brought executive transition. After over twelve years of FDR as president, the country had a new leader, Harry Truman.

Hitler committed suicide three weeks later. The next day, his right-hand-man, Joseph Goebbels, committed suicide after poisoning his six children to death. A week later, Germany surrendered.

Japan surrendered three months later, following US atomic bomb drops on Nagasaki and Hiroshima.

World War II was over. A new era dawned for those fortunate enough to have survived. Optimism rejuvenated. A sailor kissed a woman in Times Square. Families reunited.

The baby boom began.

Chapter 10

A Postwar America

Victory Tour

World War II had ended in Europe. Back home, the United States celebrated victory and gave a heroes' welcome to those returning from overseas. Jumbo worked that entire summer at Steel Pier; each grandstand show ended with the entire company standing in line, offering a patriotic finale. Sharkey also worked in New Jersey in a one-week, thirty-act stadium fund-raiser for returning soldiers. The event attracted huge crowds. A journalist observed that audiences "particularly applauded Sharkey."[1]

That fall, Mark and Sharkey did one last war-bond tour. Eighty-five million people, over half the United States population, bought US bonds during and just after World War II. The program raised $185 billion ($2.5 trillion in today's dollars), a staggering amount, especially given their intentionally low interest-rate yields. Bonds functioned as a patriotic fund-raiser, vital to financing a war that had come at unprecedented cost. Bonds also removed money from circulation, helping to curb inflation, a key consideration given the volatile economics of bountiful wartime employment coupled with rationed goods. Victory Loan drives accompanied the eighth and final war-bond issuance. They went from late October 1945 to early December 1945. The effort raised 192 percent of its goal, the highest percentage of all the war-bond drives.

It was at a Midwest Red Cross bond rally where Sharkey eyed the buttocks of the wife of a famed mayor, who shall remain nameless for reasons soon apparent. Sharkey should have known better; perhaps he did, but he had made up his mind. His nose raced toward the unsuspecting posterior like an arrow from a Zen archer's bow that knows no other destination than that of a bull's-eye. Sharkey goosed her but good. Shrieks and flails emanated from the mayor's wife, providing the inescapable spectacle. News of the incident traveled courtesy of Walter Winchell, a gossip columnist of prodigious syndication, the most widely read journalist of his day, who dutifully informed his readership: "It killed all the people in the audience—they choked from laughing. The poor woman, the poor, poor woman."[2]

Sharkey's Victory Bond tour moved to the Fort Worth National Bank. Tellers beamed from ear to ear as they welcomed him to the front counter. Sharkey pulled himself upright, while Mark stood by his side, dressed in a button-down wool vest and matching trousers. Bystanders provided a mix of quizzical looks and grins. One man hoisted himself onto a back counter, towering over the tellers; others crowded around. Tellers directed Sharkey to a folding card table. Seated there were two young uniformed women from the Red Cross Motor Corps. They wore military belts with shoulder straps, as did a boy close by, outfitted in a miniature army uniform. People of all ages approached the table. Behind the table was a war-bond poster. Intentionally stamped over the word *war* was the word *victory*. The two Red Cross Motor Corps workers enlisted Sharkey as their helper by placing Victory Bond blanks between his lips, which he delivered to prospective buyers on the bank floor. The sequence repeated itself on end, much to the amusement of many, and much to the gratitude of Uncle Sam.[3]

Sharkey returned the next day. This time, he himself conducted the bond rally. Gatherers lined up to toss a rubber ring. The agreement was that if Sharkey caught the ring with his nose, the tosser would buy a bond. A flood of tosses ensued. One skillful young boy proudly clutched a bond bought with money from his savings account. An eleven-year-old girl whose brother was in the army tossed a ring and bought a bond for her parents. Another buyer admitted being particularly compelled to take a toss; her name being Catherine Sharkey.[4]

Sharkey's two days at the Fort Worth National Bank alone netted bond sales totaling over $350,000 in today's dollars. He did one last rally two days later at the nearby Continental National Bank, joined by the bank vice president and the chairman of a war-service committee.[5]

Sharkey at a Victory Bond rally. Courtesy, *Fort Worth Star-Telegram* Collection, Special Collections, University of Texas at Arlington Libraries.

From Texas, Mark and Sharkey hustled 1,500 miles to New York. Less than two weeks away was their next project, and it was a big one. Sharkey was to star in the thirteenth annual Christmas Spectacular at Radio City Music Hall.

Meanwhile, Mark's assistants, Billy Roe and Lew Bohan, returned home after having served overseas. Lew returned with a German Lugar pistol, a German saber, and a Nazi flag—spoils of war seized from enemy combatants while with his infantry division, as was allowed under international law and as was wildly popular among GIs. The US military decorated Lew with a Purple Heart for having received shrapnel head wounds while in France.

A Postwar America | 169

Seal College was back at full strength. The timing couldn't have been better. Things had been busy at Seal College—and were about to get even busier.

Christmas Seal

By 1945, the Radio City Christmas Spectacular was already a major tourist attraction. And with wartime gloom replaced by postwar enthusiasm, ticket requests poured in from around the country. Leon Leonidoff prepared a stage show called *Heigh Ho!* The boy-meets-girl plot had a cast of six: a boy, a girl, a toy maker, his apprentice, a mayor, and Sharkey. Ads described Sharkey with one word: incredible.

On December 6, the show opened to a capacity crowd. Included was a lavishly decorated live nativity scene and a colorfully costumed ballet. The Rockettes ended the stage show with a high-kicking number, prancing as reindeer pulling the sled of the newly married boy and girl. *Billboard* wrote that the show allowed "plenty of latitude for Sharkey to flip and flap his way thru his routines" and said his act "fit the scene like a nylon swim suit on a Varga model"[6] (the only instance, we may safely assume, of a trained seal act being compared to Peruvian artist Alberto Vargas's pinup paintings of "Varga Girls," regularly featured in *Esquire* and later in *Playboy*, often pasted on the nose of American aircraft during World War II).

Also on the bill was the world premiere screening of *The Bells of St. Mary's*, starring Bing Crosby and Ingrid Bergman, the most profitable film ever for RKO Pictures. The stage-film bill played for eight weeks, breaking Radio City Music Hall box office records.

Godfather movie buffs will recall the assassination attempt on godfather Vito Corleone, set in December 1945. His son and son's girlfriend were at Radio City Music Hall. A marquee read, "The Bells of St. Mary's and Famed Christmas Stage Spectacle." After exiting the theater, the two even talked about Ingrid Bergman. It's too bad they didn't talk about Sharkey. Odds are they would have said he was "incredible."

Sharkey later starred in another Radio City Christmas Spectacular. The Leon Leonidoff production included a ballet that ended with dancers depicting a gigantic Christmas card. A ballerina nimbly stepped forward and introduced the next act. "You have seen our Christmas card. We now present our Christmas seal."[7]

Variety wrote that Sharkey "performed brilliantly. . . . It's a perfect attraction for the kids who will be flocking to the house during the holiday vacation. Adults, too, find the intelligence of this mammal to be of an uncanny human quality."[8]

Meet Jumbo!

Meanwhile, Jumbo resumed performing with Mark's assistant and son-in-law, Lew Bohan. Prior to Pearl Harbor, Lew regularly had handled Jumbo, but they had worked little together since, other than some fairs, a Veterans Welfare Fund fund-raiser, and a Ringling Brothers patriotic show called *Spangles* that played at Madison Square Garden and boosted morale in grand circus style; admitted free were purchasers of war bonds, disadvantaged children, and members of the Armed Services.[9]

Given the light post–Pearl Harbor seal workload, Lew had returned to music in a USO tour of military camps with a dance band he directed under his given surname, Bohunicki. Lew next entered the military and went overseas. Like many World War II vets, he later spoke little about the war, though the little spoken spoke volumes: coming upon unmarked roadside package bombs, sneaking up on Nazi pillbox bunkers (narrowly escaping capture), and recalling instructions on how to effectively fire into an enemy line—memories that would come back to haunt.[10]

Returning home, Lew reunited with Jumbo. It was a cheery one judging from a journalist who wrote that "when Lew entered military service [and] said good-bye to Jumbo, the latter seemed to know there was danger in the air. He brooded constantly while Lew was in service. When Lew came back, the joy that he exhibited would have brought tears to the most hard-boiled individual."[11]

Lew henceforth worked with seals, never again as a musician. And as if to leave his wartime identity on the battlefield, he dropped his given name of Bohunicki, solely using his seal handler stage name, Bohan, which he also adopted for his family.[12]

Lew Bohan and Jumbo began their postwar activities in Ohio, doing free Christmas shows for infirmed children. They next worked at Mark's

Lew receives a cheerful welcome home after serving overseas. Press photo from the author's collection via Gary Bohan Sr.

former club, renamed from Huling's Barn to The Barn, where they performed in a New Year's Eve revue, *Barnyard Frolics*.

Lew and Jumbo did sports shows that first winter after the war. They started in Philadelphia, then jumped to Louisville, Indianapolis, and Omaha. Ads read: "Jumbo the Seal headlining a parade of outdoor champions."[13] Sports shows were more popular than ever. Gas rationing had ended, manufacturing of leisure goods had resumed, and interest in outdoor recreation was renewed with vigor. Pent-up demand for outdoor gear turned shows into veritable shopping jamborees (indoor malls still ten years away and internet shopping not even the stuff of science fiction). Crowds were so dense that police at times ordered arena doors closed. Shows promised "new equipment galore."[14] "Are you ready for your war-won vacation?" read a sports show promo. "Dad will get to see that new outboard motor he has spent the last five years dreaming about."[15]

Lew and Jumbo also worked at movie palaces in vaude-film presentations. US movie theater turnout that year rose to 90 million weekly admissions, spurred to new heights by returning vets. Although the US population has since more than doubled, 1946 set movie theater attendance records unbroken to this day.

Lew's favorite story was when Jumbo shared a bill with a theater company performing a Western melodrama. Crowds watched with moistened eyes as an injured cowboy lay on the floor during the final dramatic scene. One night, Jumbo accidently joined him on stage. Lew recalled what happened next. "The poor cowboy was dying bravely when Jumbo came up and stuck his nose in his face. Then, when this didn't stop the show, Jumbo walked over to a box, climbed on it, and started applauding."

Lew added: "The cowboy was almost sore enough to fight about it. But what could I do? That Jumbo is all ham and a yard wide. Nobody can stop him from acting."[16]

Lew and Jumbo spent that summer at Steel Pier, the first peacetime summer in five years. The ocean playground drew record crowds. Fourth of July weekend alone drew 300,000 people to Atlantic City, "swarming over beach and Boardwalk."[17] Featured that week at the Steel Pier Marine Ballroom was Benny Goodman.

The pier next brought in bandleader Tony Pastor, featuring his new vocalist, eighteen-year-old Rosemary Clooney, who delighted thousands, yet another for whom Steel Pier provided the big break. (Clooney later had number-one hit songs and was an actress, appearing as late as 1994 in the television drama *ER* alongside her nephew, George.) Paramount and Universal released newsreels the next day, shot on location at the pier. But they weren't about Clooney's smashing debut. They were about a trained seal.

Jumbo Steals the Show (Paramount) began with a narrated close-up of the bewhiskered sea lion. "This is Jumbo, every ounce loaded with talent. Jumbo is currently wowing visitors to Atlantic City's Steel Pier." The camera panned to Lew, who tossed a weighted doll in the water. "The daring rescue. Help! Help! Save my chee-ild." Jumbo dove underwater and surfaced with the doll upright on his nose, then swam the doll to safety,

A Postwar America | 173

exited the pool with the doll still on his nose, and flipped it to Lew. A full house applauded. The narrator concluded, "Back from a watery grave, everything in perfect balance."[18]

Meet Jumbo! (Universal) included the talents of Ed Herlihy, a narrator with a resonant and upbeat style instantly recognizable to anyone from the era, dubbed "a voice of cheer" by the *New York Times*. The piece opened with the star seal poolside. "Four hundred pounds of sinuous grace, 20-year-old Jumbo, the world's largest trained seal, takes to the water at Atlantic City's Steel Pier. And if you don't think Old Whiskers earns his 140 pounds of finny fodder each week, give a look." Jumbo again did his doll rescue. "Of course, Jumbo doesn't get all the credit for his amiable antics," Herlihy continued. "His trainer, war vet Lew Bohan, made many a Nazi say uncle. Come on, say uncle, Jumbo." Jumbo sounded imitations of a motorboat, General MacArthur's bombers flying over Tokyo, and a tobacco auctioneer.[19]

Paramount and Universal each packaged their Jumbo newsreel segment for nationwide theater distribution. Along with Jumbo were the week's other

Lew and Jumbo performing at Steel Pier.

topical events: eccentric billionaire Howard Hughes's infamous Beverly Hills plane crash, the Pope's canonization of Mother Cabrini, and the Major League Baseball All-Star Game.

Seal College wrapped up at Steel Pier the weekend after Labor Day, coinciding with the Miss America Pageant and annual Boardwalk parade. Marching bands blared. Batonists twirled. Thousands upon thousands watched Miss America contestants ride in a convoy of festive floats. Four contestants rode on the Steel Pier float, each in a bathing suit and high heels, one contestant situated up high on a trapeze. Joining them, stationed in the center of the float, were two representatives from the pier: Lew Bohan and Jumbo.

Golden Years

Sharkey's popularity meanwhile skyrocketed. Articles like "Sharkey, Champ Seal" and "Clown of the Sea" ran nationwide in Sunday papers. Magazines did feature stories. Sharkey worked clubs, played theater palaces, and toured the heartland. While at a Chicago club, working with singers, dancers, and comedians, a *Tribune* critic wrote, "I don't want to hurt any feelings, but I think the star of the show is Sharkey the seal." Months later, an Iowa paper described him as "one of the greatest performers ever seen in Des Moines."[20]

Journalists wrote about Mark and Sharkey's backstage antics and mutual affection, like when Sharkey sprang to life anticipating Mark's backstage arrival even though Mark was outside his range of sight. (Sharkey knew his footsteps.) Another time, Mark snuck up and whispered a greeting to Sharkey, who "bounced around in joy like a spirited puppy." Another time, between shows, Mark put a dollar between Sharkey's lips and sent him on his way. Sharkey returned with a souvenir program. Asked by a reporter how much he'd take for Sharkey, Mark replied, "Why, I'd never part with him."[21]

They were the golden years. And with golden years came golden moments. Whenever the Seal College van was parked with Sharkey inside, it attracted every kid in the neighborhood. Mark let them all have a good look, yielding delightful collections of excited youthful expressions that recall an earlier time, with nary a single smartphone distraction in sight. "When Sharkey decided they had looked long enough, he employed a most effective method of chasing them away," Mark said. "He squirted water at the surprised youngsters."[22]

Mark and Sharkey, cover of a promo booklet published during the "golden years." Press photo from the author's collection via Gary Bohan Sr.

In May 1947, Sharkey returned to Radio City Music Hall for another Leon Leonidoff production. The Music Hall Symphony Orchestra played Gershwin; the Corps de Ballet and Rockettes provided dance; and the two outside acts, Sharkey and the Wiere Brothers, provided comedy. We might excuse Leonidoff for having Sharkey open for the Wieres, established stage and film comedians who would last another twenty-three years, later appearing on shows like *Laugh In*. The result, however, should have surprised no one. *Variety* wrote, "Wiere-act with their customary zanyisms . . . unfortunately appears anti-climactic following the laughs garnered by Sharkey. Just a case of bad sequencing."[23]

Leonidoff at the time was also hiring entertainment for a ten-day fashion fair at Madison Square Garden. He booked acts for five stages. Among the acts was Sharkey. Aggregate performer fees (the industry-standard measure of a show's strength) ran $70,000. *Variety* reported the news on its front page: "This budget tops anything ever presented at a vaude house, even going higher than the recent Roxy show with Jack Benny." Leonidoff's Radio City Music Hall show, however, was held over, which excluded Sharkey from doing the fashion fair at Madison Square Garden. Off the bench came Jumbo. Sponsors billed the fair as the largest fashion show in history, where "America's foremost designers will present their latest creations." Fifty supermodels displayed lingerie, gowns, and everything else in the world of women's fashion. Cover girl Jinx Falkenburg paraded wearing a million dollars' worth of jewels. Tens of thousands came out daily: Hollywood agents, reporters, and clothes buyers from around the globe. On the main stage and four other stages were theater shows starring popular personages "whereon the actors act out clothes dramas and comedies." Jumbo starred in the main stage clothes drama. One is left to one's imagination what that may have looked like. United Press covered the fashion fair. Of all things, they wrote an article about Jumbo being jealous of the models. The story ran everywhere. "Sea lions are proud of their tricks and it burns Jumbo up when people turn from him and stare at the women."[24]

That summer, Sharkey worked at Cleveland Stadium, the largest baseball park in the country, where he did a ten-day show during an Indians road trip. Organizers built a 4,000 square-foot tank made of rubberized heavy canvas that covered an area around home plate, allowing Sharkey to do his wet act. Sharing the bill was Bobby Riggs, then the top-rated men's tennis player in the world, known today for his later match with

Billie Jean King, "The Battle of the Sexes." (King trounced him.) Riggs, a boastful sort, often challenged opponents while handicapping himself by doing things like using a frying pan as a racket. Whether he engaged Sharkey in a friendly game is unknown though quite possible. Mark had a routine during his Ringling Brothers days whereby seals played tennis with each other, using their flippers as rackets.[25]

Billy Roe assisted Mark during the Cleveland shows, much as he had since returning from serving overseas. He had worked with Mark going back to the start of Sharkey's career. Mark and Billy were a team: They traveled together; they dined together on the road; and they worked together at the college. Now in his sixties, Mark more than ever needed a right-hand-man. That man was Billy Roe.

Testament to their rapport, a satirist parodied them in a cartoon, set inside Seal College. Signs on the wall pointed to a classroom and a dormitory. One seal was in the pool, balancing a cylindrical canister. Another was relaxing in a tub, singing "Sea Food Mama."

Billy was in the kitchen, busy scaling a fish.

Mark approached the area. "Say Bill, we'll have to watch our language from now on. You know these seals are well educated and we can't get away with it like we used to."

"Okay, Mark, but if I cut my finger cleaning these fish, the bright students from the deep sea will have to wear ear muffs."

A seal chimed in. "Cut the chatter and serve us some fish."[26]

Two Babes

Sports shows introduced a feature that continued for years: having a star athlete in its variety act program. The athlete for 1948 was Mildred Didrikson Zaharias, who went by the name "Babe."

Babe started as a track and field competitor, winning two golds and a silver at the 1932 Summer Olympic Games. She was also an All-American basketball player and excelled in many other sports. She later became a golfer, for which she is best known today, racking up ten LPGA majors. The Associated Press named her Athlete of the Year a record six times. (Serena Williams is second with five; those named four times include Lance Armstrong, Chris Evert, LeBron James, and Tiger Woods. Babe is the only athlete honored in three different decades and in two different sports.)

Both ESPN and the Associated Press named Babe Didrikson Zaharias the top female athlete of the twentieth century. Babe was also gay and has recently been featured in articles that describe her as an LGBTQ icon. In 2021, President Donald Trump posthumously awarded her the Presidential Medal of Freedom.

Babe did trick golf shots at sports shows as part of a seventeen-act variety presentation. Babe and Sharkey headlined in Detroit and Boston before going to Manhattan for the National Sportsmen's Show. *Billboard* described the Manhattan event as "by far the best staged since the end of the war, both from the number and quality of exhibits and the entertainment offered."[27]

Babe, a chain-smoking, tough-talking Texan, hardly lacked in the ego department, once telling an opponent, "I'm going to whup you tomorrow, and whup you good!"[28]

Cool, cocky, and confident, the pairing of Babe and Sharkey for the opening day press conference was the obvious choice. The two prima donnas made their way onto a riser. Behind them was a canvass backdrop, depicting ocean waves crashing onto a rock outcropping.

Babe wore a women's suit jacket and skirt, accented with a flowing women's necktie. Sharkey came unadorned. Billy Roe stood nearby, dressed in a pinstripe suit and bow tie.

Sharkey pointed his nose upward.

Billy steadied a golf ball on the raised nose.

Babe pulled a golf glove tight over her left hand, grabbed a seven iron, and approached the distinctively teed ball with laser beam intensity. The nose-perched ball rested inches from her firmly gripped club. Billy watched with a bug-eyed look of peril.

Mark led a one-man cheering section, happily clapping away. Spectators gathered: men in suits and fedoras, smiling moms, and curious children. Press photographers dutifully assembled.

Babe joined her lips in determined formation. Sharkey kept the golf ball balanced on his nose as Babe prepared her swing.

Camera clicks resonated through the room like rain pelting on a tin roof. Pictures ended up in newspapers across the country.

Nat Fein of the *New York Herald Tribune* was among those who clicked away. But while others took shots of Sharkey and Babe predictably cropped in front of the backdrop, Fein expanded his shot to show a slice of the adjacent crowd. The effect, a picture within a picture, a story within a story, was compositionally compelling and a harbinger of his defining work, which would come four months later when he photographed another Babe: Babe Ruth. The occasion was the day Ruth's number was retired. While Ruth stood on the third base line, several photographers positioned for the obvious cropped, front-angle shot. Fein, however, took a rear-angle shot of a frail Ruth hunched over (Ruth died two months later) and expanded his shot to include ballplayers, photographers, and the crowd. The result, a picture within a picture, a story within a story, was a Pulitzer Prize–winning photograph.

Billy Roe watching Sharkey assist Babe Didrikson Zaharias. © The Estate of Nat Fein.

O Canada

Sharkey went from one national sports show to another, which is to say he went from the United States to Canada. Whereas the US had one such branded event, Canada opted for national sports shows in both Toronto and Ottawa, with that year, 1948, considered the first year of the Canadian National Sportsmen's Shows. A mission statement read as follows:

> We bring to the people of Ottawa and District a new departure in entertainment which will have great educational value and will appeal to every man, woman and child who enjoys the sports and pleasures of Outdoor Canada. We aim by means of this show to further promote the programme of conservation and development of our forest and lake resources sponsored by our Government.[29]

En route to Canada, the Seal College van stopped in Mark's hometown of Grand Island, New York, a town roughly five by seven miles, surrounded by the Niagara River, ten miles from both Niagara Falls and Buffalo, right on the way to Toronto. Although the island was rapidly developing—its population was 3,000, three times that of Mark's youth—it had retained its farmland charm.

Mark reminisced with family and friends about the days of old; one-room schoolhouses, corn-husking bees, and hayrides. Recollections of life on the family 300-acre farm included rehashing the mysterious "Case of the Butter Thieves," tried at town hall when Mark was manager of the Grand Island Creamery, a company his father had served as president. As a young man, Mark oversaw the production of 800 pounds of butter a week, before he set his sights on becoming on electrician.[30]

Electricity had come to the region during its earliest years. Wood-pole power lines went from hydroelectric generators at Niagara Falls to serve load in Buffalo. The lines were visible from the shores of Grand Island, of a size and voltage one might find today along a town road, then a groundbreaking feat of grand scale. An electric grid ran through Buffalo for lighting and street trolleys. Opportunities for Mark to apprentice as an electrician would be plentiful. But fate decided otherwise. Mark's trip to Buffalo to inquire about apprenticeship in his newly chosen field was the same trip during which he and his brothers visited their family acquaintance, Captain Webb—and his many trained seals.

Now, some forty years later, Mark visited Maple Grove Cemetery, located on former family farmland his parents had donated many years prior. He paid his respects to his parents and to his brother Frank—and to three siblings who had predeceased him, all dying of diphtheria as infants, the oldest markers in the cemetery. Water temperature permitting, Sharkey partook in his favorite Grand Island pastime, exercising in the open waters of the Niagara River.

From Grand Island, they headed to Toronto. Or so they tried.

Border authorities searched in vain for a suitable admittance form. They had paperwork for cattle, dogs, and other animals, but none for a seal. Officials summoned a veterinarian. The result was an overnight delay. "When the vet finally arrived," Billy Roe later recalled, "he asked how much Sharkey ate and what he weighed but admitted that he knew nothing about seals." Officials shrugged until at last an agent took a form, crossed out the word *dog*, wrote in the word *seal*, and sent them on their way. Not a bad call, given that sea lions belong to the species suborder *Caniformia*, literally, "doglike."[31]

Canada modeled its sports shows after the United States. Vendors displayed hunting and fishing gear, motor boats, and other outdoor recreation goods. Native Americans held skill workshops. A daily water and stage show featured archers, knife throwers, comedians, high divers, animal acts, and others, all accompanied by an emcee and orchestra. A Toronto critic wrote that Sharkey "brought down the house."[32]

Ottawa was two weeks later. In between, Sharkey headlined in Rochester, New York. His return to Canada left no room for another customs delay. Rochester ended with an evening show; Ottawa started the next afternoon. Billy revealed a strategy to help cut through red tape when Seal College hit a border checkpoint, one we may reasonably suppose accompanied this particular instance, given the circumstances and successful outcome. "Sharkey would set up a terrific clamor on cue so the authorities would just want to look and not go in and examine him."[33]

Opening day at the Ottawa Coliseum drew a modest 3,000. "The acts were excellent, but Sharkey the Seal was head and flippers above all the rest in crowd appeal," wrote the *Ottawa Journal*. "After seeing him perform, it would not have surprised anyone had he pulled out a pencil and started signing autographs." Word spread; turnout doubled, then tripled. Newspapers bloomed with headlines like "New Sportsmen's Show Limelights Sharkey" and "Sharkey Still Top Number at Sportsmen's Show."[34]

Governor General Viscount Alexander, Canada's commander in chief, was among Sharkey's most ardent new fans. Lord Alexander made a special morning visit, accompanied by military aides. Sharkey provided a private command performance. Newspapers splashed pictures of Sharkey performing for and greeting His Excellency.[35]

Toward the end of the run, the *Ottawa Journal* wrote of "the fabulous seal, whose personality has so impressed the people of Ottawa." The seal who also all but single-handedly thrust the startup Canada National Sportsmen's Shows organization into solvency. In 2022, the nonprofit will celebrate its seventy-fifth anniversary. To date, the organization has raised and awarded over 32 million dollars in grants "committed to conserving Canada's outdoors and instilling Canadian youth with an appreciation for nature and outdoor activity."[36]

Homecoming

A month after his Canadian tour, Sharkey returned home to Kingston, New York, rated the highest-paid single animal act in the world. After scores of requests for a local showing, Mark announced two free shows to be held in the parking lot of The Barn, his formerly owned nightclub next to Seal College.

Mark used the opportunity to debut his latest contraption, a portable pool-stage. The goal was to have wet-act capability at tour stops that lacked a pool or water tank. He fastened wooden side-panels using sheet metal fittings and brackets, then secured a liner to a twenty-by-forty-foot frame. A homebuilt stage attached to one of the short ends. Eighteen thousand gallons of water drawn from the adjacent Esopus Creek was used to fill the pool. Before long, the portable apparatus was set up for the upcoming shows. (With practice, setup and breakdown each took just a few hours. The collapsible frame, liner, and stage accessories fit snug into the back of a Seal College truck.)

The first free show was Sunday, May 9, at three o'clock. Westbound travelers heading over the Washington Avenue viaduct onto the steel truss bridge that spanned the Esopus Creek met with a mass of cars and people, as did those traveling eastbound into Kingston on Route 28. A thousand spectators packed their way into The Barn parking lot. Gatherers clumped around the novel pool-stage until there was room for no more.

Bob Teetsel, owner of The Barn, made introductory remarks. Sharkey stayed inside Seal College like a superstar poised backstage, ready to do a halftime show at the Super Bowl.

Pity Jimmy Leroy, for he had the unenviable task of warming up the crowd, there to see the world's greatest seal. The local entertainer sang numbers appropriate for Mother's Day. After Leroy finished, Teetsel approached the microphone and announced the main attraction.

Mark and Billy brought Sharkey out to a hero's welcome. Sharkey dove into the pool, zoomed around, and spurted onto the stage platform. He segued right into his shower routine. A parade of greatest hits followed, including his doll water rescue and bedtime snoring skit. Mark then brought out an eight-foot rubber life raft. Sharkey had balanced big objects before but this was his biggest attempt ever. Strong winds added to the difficulty factor. Mark placed the raft on Sharkey's nose. The long part of the raft stood straight up in the air. Sharkey contorted his neck in every direction as if guided by precision gyroscopes.

Sharkey went from the stage into the water; the raft still on his nose. He swam while keeping the eight-foot raft balanced upright, then exited the pool onto the stage, the raft still upright on his nose.

Mark said it was the heaviest object ever balanced by a seal. One reporter called the feat "a cuckoo."[37]

Fans formed a receiving line afterward to get an up-close glimpse at celebrity. Sharkey happily obliged, though he did scold a young boy who squeezed a little too hard on a flipper. Another full house appeared for a second showing at five o'clock.

Mark publicized three more free shows for the following weekend. He added two more the weekend after that and two more Memorial Day weekend. Demand was so high he added one last freebie, held after the Kingston Memorial Day Parade.

An exciting month it had been. But Sharkey's career was about to take another exciting twist, for on the horizon was a rapidly emerging entertainment medium, one that would shape popular culture and society for generations to come, in ways unimaginable. It would also provide Sharkey the opportunity to add to his résumé.

That medium was, of course, television.

Chapter 11

Sharkey Goes Television

Texaco Star Theater

A toilet. History remembers Sharkey's first television appearance all because of a toilet.

Television came of age in 1948. Regularly scheduled prime-time programming began, television ratings came into existence, and Hollywood conceived the Emmys. Two years prior, there were only six commercial television stations: three in New York City, and one in Chicago, Philadelphia, and Schenectady. But by mid-1948, over fifty commercial stations were broadcasting over four major networks: NBC, CBS, ABC, and a fourth mostly forgotten network that later dissolved, DuMont.

Variety eagerly covered the soon-to-be tidal wave of television popularity. A March 1948 front-page headline called television a "show-biz hero" ready to rescue the amusement industry as the "infant prodigy of show business." That same month, after years of covering film, stage, and radio, *Variety* introduced a new category on its front-page header, a term for television at the time: VIDEO. Television breathed new life into vaudeville, declared dead fifteen years earlier, following the demise of stage acts at the Palace. Vaudeville acts were visual, ready-made for TV, and available for stitching together a program with nominal production. *Variety* called the concept "television's hottest development" and came up with a buzzword for this new marriage of vaudeville and video: VAUDEO. "Vaudeville Is Back" professed *Variety* in a two-page spread announcing the debut of a vaudeo show called *Texaco Star Theater*.[1]

Texaco Star Theater premiered on Tuesday, June 8, 1948. Hosting was seasoned vaudevillian Milton Berle. The show triggered an unprecedented increase in the sale of television sets. So popular was the show, Berle was nicknamed "Mr. Television." Viewership topped at 83 percent of households with sets, a level unmatched since.

People wrote of *Texaco Star Theater* in a fifty-year retrospective: "Stores shut early. Restaurants emptied. Traffic vanished. Phone calls broke off. Dishes went unwashed. . . . Millions of people who for six days and 23 hours every week seemed perfectly rational went berserk on Tuesday night and, like ants on a triple-chocolate blackout cake, swarmed around tiny, blurry, 10-inch television screens."[2]

Mark and Sharkey appeared on the seventh episode of *Texaco Star Theater*. Guest hosting was Berle's good friend Henny Youngman. (Sharkey had an elevator encounter with Berle, recalled by Billy Roe's grandson Dave Fletcher: "Berle wanted to get in on the act with Sharkey and my grandfather told him that he worked alone. Berle made a move toward Sharkey and got bit in the elevator. Needless to say, Milton decided to not join Sharkey on stage that night."[3])

Youngman led an all-star lineup, including comedians Jack Carter and pioneer female stand-up Jean Carroll, both household names then, both all but forgotten today. *Variety* called the episode a "surefire vaudeo formula . . . a prime example of the formula's success," underscoring Youngman's "fast chatter and smart pace," Carter's "brash and likable zany," and Carroll's "top display of japeries," adding, "Sharkey the Seal's antics are as effective in this medium as they've always been in theaters."[4]

There was just one snag.

Unintended circumstances during live broadcasts often wreaked havoc with schedule, as was the case that night.

The culprit? A toilet.

Sharkey was to balance a toilet, but NBC nixed it. Milton Berle recalled the incident in his autobiography: "Nobody told Sharkey that NBC had cut the potty bit—too offensive in those days—from his act. Everything went great in Sharkey's act until it was time for him to balance the potty on the tip of his nose. No potty. The poor seal kept wandering around the stage looking for his potty. He wouldn't get off. The audience howled, and the show ran overtime again."[5]

Robert Pandillo writes in his 2010 book, *America's First Network TV Censor*, "Images of lavatory vessels, even one a sea mammal could counterpoise on his snout, would simply not be sanctioned for television viewing."[6] Such were the days of early television. Although much more television lay ahead for Sharkey, TV viewers for the rest of his career would never get the chance to see him balance a toilet.

Admiral Broadway Revue

Sharkey appeared months later on a new television variety show called *Admiral Broadway Revue*. It aired Friday nights on both DuMont and NBC, a rarity—that a prime-time program would air simultaneously on two major networks. It was a top-ten show in the national Hooper ratings; Claude Hooper had devised a system for measuring television audiences, an operation he sold a year later to Arthur Nielson.

Admiral Broadway Revue featured original entertainment and vaudeville-type guests and led the way in the burgeoning arena of television sketch comedy. Writers included twenty-two-year-old Mel Brooks and Mel Tolkin (future story editor for the 1970s sitcom, *All in the Family*). Hosting was up-and-coming funnyman Sid Caesar.

Admiral Broadway Revue had a single sponsor, as did all TV programs, in this case, Admiral, makers of Magic Mirror Televisions. Its product line went from a seven-inch, base-model screen to a deluxe wood console with a sixteen-inch screen and an integrated radio and phonograph. The deluxe model listed for $695 ($7,000 in today's dollars). Interwoven during the show were live advertising skits for Magic Mirror Televisions.

Billy Roe and Sharkey waited backstage at the NBC International Theater, located at Columbus Circle, near the southwest corner of Central Park. At eight o'clock, the house orchestra played a short overture before a live theater audience. Viewers at home watched opening credits scroll down their TV screens: the stars, cast members, orchestra leader, writers, choreographer, setting designer, costume designer, vocal arranger, producer, director, and special guest—Sharkey the Seal.

Three women and two men appeared onstage, each wearing a sailor uniform and admiral hat, each in military salutation. They broke into a choreographed routine and opening jingle, warbling in advertising verse.

In lighthearted fashion, they pantomimed the operation of several Admiral products: radios, phonographs, electric ranges, refrigerators, and most importantly, Magic Mirror Televisions.

The orchestra shifted into a fanfare. An offstage announcer delivered a grandiose introduction. "This week, the *Admiral Broadway Revue*, a happy blend of song, dance, and comedy, invites you to 'Sing in a New Day.' "[7] Seven cast members sang and danced an upbeat, five-minute, original routine on an outdoor-village set, as stylish a presentation as one could find anywhere on Broadway. No surprise given that Gower Champion was among those in the cast—Gower, just five days earlier, had won the Tony Award for Best Choreography. After the opening routine, the set morphed from an outdoor village to a greasy spoon, done with the speed of a tire change at a NASCAR pit stop. Sid Caesar did a comedy sketch, playing an ornery waiter serving a frustrated patron. (Think *Saturday Night Live*: cheeseburger, cheeseburger.)

After Caesar's skit, the curtain closed. Seconds later, without introduction, Sharkey and Billy emerged stage left, in front of the curtain. Giggles and a group "aw" effused from the crowd as Sharkey and Billy made their way center stage.

Billy placed a stack of items on his partner's nose. "Be careful now, Sharkey." Sharkey flipped the stack and caught it on his nose. After repeated flips, he thrust his nose and tossed the items back to Billy.

The curtain opened, revealing a lineup of Seal College props on a circus-themed set. Sharkey did more balancing stunts. He clapped for himself after the more difficult ones, drawing laughs on top of applause.

Then came the shtick.

Billy led Sharkey toward his custom seal bed. On the way over, Sharkey snuck up from behind and goosed him.

Billy jumped. The crowd laughed.

"Sharkey, don't do that to me. Now you be careful about that."

Billy again led him toward the bed. Sharkey again goosed him from behind. The crowd again laughed.

Billy pointed his finger. "Hey, you ought to be ashamed of yourself." Sharkey rolled to the floor and covered his eyes with his flippers. The audience let out another group "aw."

"I'll forgive you this time," Billy said with a grin. "Now pick up your pillow and put it down on your bed, sir."

Sharkey picked up his pillow, put it on his bed, and then crawled into bed. Billy draped a blanket over him. The audience let out yet another group "aw."

"Say, how 'bout that candle over there?" Billy asked.

Sharkey looked at the nearby candle and blew it out. After pretending to fall asleep, he belted out several loud, exaggerated snores, sending the audience into stitches. As the laughs died down, Sharkey "woke up," gave his blanket to Billy, and got out of bed.

"All right sir, come on over here now," Billy said.

Sharkey instead reached under his bed and used his mouth to pull out a bedpan. The crowd burst into hysterics. Sharkey ambled about the stage, bedpan in mouth. Bellyaching laughter filled the theater. Billy acted the stooge, shaking his head. "Oh no. Oh dear."

Sharkey did some more tricks and vocalizing imitations before Billy introduced the act finale: Sharkey's music feature. Billy held his baton and looked at Sharkey.

"Now get ready, sir. All right?"

Sharkey gabbled his displeasure.

"What's the trouble, sir?" Billy asked.

Sharkey gabbled some more.

"Oh, I see," Billy replied. "We'll have to take care of that."

Billy grabbed a handkerchief and placed it on his partner's nose.

"There you are, sir."

Sharkey snorted into the handkerchief. And snorted again. And again. Laughter once more filled the theater. Nasal passages cleared to his satisfaction, Sharkey nosed his way through his music number and exited to rounding applause.

∼

Admiral Broadway Revue would suffer a most unusual fate; it became a victim of its own success. So popular was the show, sales of Admiral Magic Mirror Televisions increased tenfold. Dealers sold out; backorders piled high. Five weeks after Sharkey's appearance, Admiral abruptly canceled its TV show in midseason, choosing instead to redirect resources toward bolstering manufacturing. Why spend money producing a show pitching Magic Mirror Televisions when there are no more Magic Mirror Televisions to sell?

Sid Caesar rebounded the next year with *Your Show of Shows*, using the same core team as *Admiral Broadway Revue*, powered by a dream team of writers, including Carl Reiner, Neil Simon, and Mel Brooks. It became the gold standard for television sketch comedy, paving the way for future creations like *Saturday Night Live*, which Caesar hosted.

Imogene Coca starred in both *Admiral Broadway Revue* and *Your Show of Shows*, becoming TV's first female comic celebrity, later influencing the likes of Carol Burnett, Lily Tomlin, and Whoopi Goldberg. The *New York Times* would write of Imogene, "To millions, that face—elfin, mischievous, wistful—was the funniest thing on television in television's golden age."[8] Imogene did a bit with Sharkey that night on *Admiral Broadway Revue*. Like many skits on the show, it was a Broadway takeoff, in this case, appropriately enough, a spoof on the haunted house scene in *Higher and Higher*. The skit opened on a scary-looking living room set. Heard in the background were cheesy ghost noises.

A pushy realtor was giving Imogene the hard sell. "I'm sure in this house you are going to find the answer to all your dreams."

"Well, I hear it's haunted," Imogene said.

"Rumors. Idle rumors."

Imogene sulked. "I know there's something else besides us in this house, and it's not human."

Ghost noises accompanied more banter.

The realtor continued insisting everything was fine, while Imogene became comically more and more unsettled. The realtor eventually decided to check on the basement furnace. "While I'm gone, why don't you stick around and look the place over."

"Stay up here alone in a haunted house?" she asked.

"You have nothing to worry about."

After he left, Imogene eyed a fruit bowl and stammered to herself, "I'll have this banana and just relax, because I know there aren't any . . . aren't any ghosts around here anyplace."

Imogene peeled the banana. As she did, ghost noises sounded stage right. Imogene peered right, holding the banana to her left.

Spot on cue, Sharkey entered stage left, dashed across the stage, ate the "banana" (a fish in a banana peel), and dashed offstage, looking more cheetah than seal. The crowd erupted with laughter.

Imogene turned and brought the empty banana peel to her mouth, stopping just short of a bite. Her mouth-open frozen gape broke up the crowd. She pondered the situation with comic perplexity. "That's the best banana I never ate."

The crowd laughed even harder.

Imogene peeled another banana. Ghost noises were again heard stage right. Again, she looked to her right. Again, Sharkey appeared stage left, darted over, ate the "banana," and darted off.

The audience burst into more laughter.

Imogene turned with another silent look; the empty banana peel just shy of her mouth. The crowd giggled awaiting her next punch line. "There's something fishy going on around here."

The audience laughed—and laughed, and laughed.

Imogene tossed the banana peel on the floor. "Oh, I shouldn't do that." She bent over to pick it up, leaving her in perfect position for the inevitable.

Sharkey crept onstage at just the right moment and glanced at the crowd with a smirk, as if asking, "Should I?" knowing well the answer. Without delay, he barreled nose-long into her buttocks.

Imogene leapt in the air with cartoon-like slapstick. Sharkey raced offstage, undetected, leaving her dumbfounded. The audience went from laughter to hysterical laughter.

Just then, the realtor reappeared. "Did you have a pleasant time?" Imogene gave a dazed look and dropped to the floor, barking and clapping like a seal. The orchestra zipped into a tune as the curtain fell to a thunder of cheers.

At the end of the show, cast members returned for a final curtain. The camera panned across the entire lineup. Applause filled the theater. Then out came special guest, Sharkey.

Audience applause went into overdrive. Cast members joined in the clapping. Sharkey graciously accepted his ovation, then made his way center stage and extended his right flipper to Sid Caesar.

The ovation continued while Sharkey proudly waddled offstage. Back came the five Admiral chorus members—again in sailor uniforms and admiral hats—to sing a closing number. Once again, in lighthearted rhyme, they serenaded a lively jingle, hoping they had "made a little bit of Broadway zoom . . . right into your room."

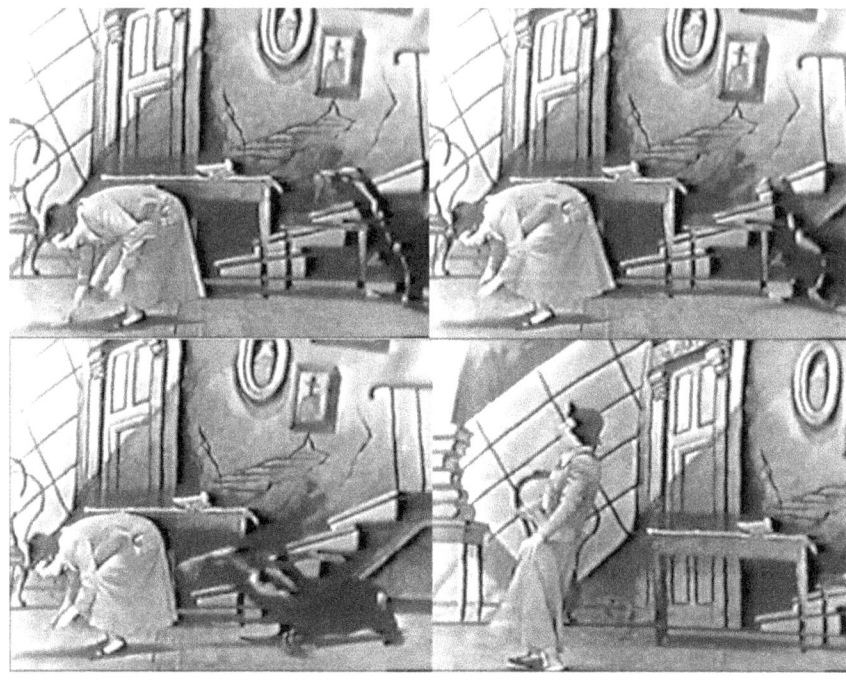

Sharkey makes his entrance, glances at the crowd, then gets nosy with Imogene and disappears offstage. Kinescope-stills, *Admiral Broadway Revue*.

The orchestra continued playing after the final verse. On screen was the applauding audience. The announcer ended the show: "Be with us again, same time, same channel, next Friday night, when your Admiral dealer, the man to see for . . . Magic Mirror Televisions, brings you another star-studded *Admiral Broadway Revue*."

Toast of the Town

Toast of the Town, later named *The Ed Sullivan Show*, was the most iconic of all the early television vaudeo shows. For twenty-three years, it was Sunday-night family TV for a generation of baby boomers. Guests included vaudeville-type acts and a wide variety of A-list entertainers. The show turned unknowns into stars and famously introduced television audiences to musicians like Elvis Presley and the Beatles.

Sullivan, a popular nationally syndicated columnist with the *Daily News*, was host from the start. The show premiered in 1948, placing second in the Hooper ratings, behind *Texaco Star Theater*.

Sullivan had long known Sharkey, having hired him several times while impresario at Loew's State Theater in Times Square. During the fall of 1949, he earmarked Sharkey to appear on his new TV show the Sunday after Thanksgiving. Sharkey's touring schedule, however, jeopardized the booking. Alas, when TV listings came out for the week of Thanksgiving, Sharkey was not among Sullivan's scheduled guests. That Sunday, at eight o'clock, a brass fanfare greeted CBS television viewers. Dreamy harpsichord sounds cued an off-camera announcer, who made his deeply resonating opening remarks.

"Good evening ladies and gentlemen. Your Lincoln-Mercury dealer presents *Toast of the Town*, starring the nationally syndicated newspaper columnist, Ed Sullivan."[9]

Joyous music filled the air.

Six dancing girls, affectionately known as the Toastettes, rollicked their way through a short routine on a cityscape set and arranged themselves on both sides of the steps leading to Sullivan's entrance platform, flanking them like choreographed runway lights, ready to guide the emcee to center stage. Singers joined the orchestra and concluded the opening jingle. On behalf of Lincoln-Mercury, the commercially upbeat choral ensemble prepared the crowd for the show's start by declaring its most important part: the revered host, the dapper toast . . . of the town.

Applause swelled.

Television cameras focused on the entrance platform. Out came not Sullivan, but rather, impromptu guest, Sharkey.

The slippery mammal slithered past the surprised Toastettes, who looked at each other, unable to keep a straight face. The audience cracked up as Sharkey took center stage, yapping up a storm.

Amid the chaos, Sullivan entered stage left and joined his animal guest. The curtain closed, removing the Toastettes from view, leaving Sharkey and Sullivan front and center.

"Hello, Sharkey. How are you?" Sullivan asked.

The host quickly impersonated Sharkey's presumed droll response. "This is Sullivan, huh?"

Sharkey kept happily barking away. Sullivan bent down. "Sharkey, give me a fin." They greeted hand and flipper.

Mark stood off to the side. "I'm over here, Sharkey." Mark's tone was reassuring, though his partner hardly needed consoling. Sharkey was getting along just fine with the host.

Sullivan motioned. "Mark, come over here a moment. How has Sharkey been? Has he been behaving himself for the holidays?"

"Fine," Mark replied, as he joined Sullivan. "We just came off a nice tour down south, on fairs."

"Uh-huh. Well, when did he come into New York? I didn't expect him here tonight . . . much." The audience chuckled at the host's stiff, deadpan delivery.

"Well, he just got in this morning about ten o'clock."

"Is he prepared to do an act?" asked Sullivan.

"Oh, surely. We're getting everything ready right now."

"Okay, suppose we go right into Sharkey's act. Open right up."

Sharkey slithers past the Toastettes, greets Ed Sullivan, and is joined by Mark Huling. Kinescope-stills, *Toast of the Town*.

The orchestra played. The curtain opened. Into view came a lineup of Seal College props. Mark tossed a softball-sized rubber ball to Sharkey, which he caught with his nose. Mark grabbed another. The two of them simultaneously and repeatedly zipped the balls back and forth to each other with synchrony and surprising speed.

Sharkey nose-caught each toss and whipped it back to Mark with one sweeping motion. A drum rim-shot accompanied each catch. Mark gave his animated approval. "*That's* the way to do it."

A bigger seal cheerleader there has never been. You would have thought Mark was presenting the act for the first time, so unbridled his enthusiasm. As he readied another trick, Sharkey gave himself an unplanned round of applause. Mark softly chuckled, "Whoa, wait a minute. Take it easy there, Sharkey." Mark knew better than to laugh too loud, lest the sea lion clap unabated to please the boss.

Mark placed a leather mouthpiece in Sharkey's mouth. Attached was a short, protruding steel prong. Sharkey displayed it to the crowd, like a magician informing of an ordinary item with no gimmicks. Mark grabbed a wooden disc about the size of a dinner plate. The disc had a one-inch hole in the center. "Now, do you see that little hole there, young man?" he asked Sharkey. "I want to see if you can catch it. Here we go."

Sharkey went to his pedestal stand and positioned his mouthpiece. Mark took several steps back and then threw the wooden disc across the stage like a Frisbee. Sharkey zeroed in and caught the disc; its center-hole encircled by the mouth-held prong.

Sharkey next balanced a volleyball on a pole. The pole had an apparatus of spinning cups on top. Sharkey climbed onto his pedestal stand, tossed the pole and spinning cups to Mark, caught the falling ball with his nose, and tossed the ball to Mark.

Sharkey instantly applauded himself, slapping his side, pumping up the crowd as if singing out, "I can't *hear* you." The audience howled watching the showoff in action.

Sharkey struggled with one of his next bits. He balanced a teddy bear on a pole balanced on his nose. But after taking the bear across the stage and back, he returned out of position, unable to maneuver the pole and return the bear to its chair, perched high above. Mark looked on with concern. "Closer," he whispered. Sharkey inched forward and completed the task. The crowd appreciated the extra effort.

Imitations followed, first Leo the MGM Lion, then a B-29 bomber. Mark set up another. "And now we'll have an imitation of one of your good ol' New York politicians. Just before election time of course." Sharkey blurted a flurry of nonsensical gabbles.

The crowd let out a torrent of laughs.

The act was five minutes and running, just enough time for a finale. Mark moved his homemade instrument into position. "Now for a little music." Sharkey again clapped for himself ahead of his routine, sending the audience into more laughter.

"Hey, wait a minute here," Mark protested. Mark acquiesced and offered up a fish, at once realizing Sharkey had just hoodwinked him into an extra treat on network television.

Mark took out a hankie and wiped down Sharkey's face. When he got to his nose, Sharkey sounded several loud snorts. The audience burst into another round of laughter.

Mark grinned at Sharkey. "That's enough of that, young fellow. We've got to get down to business here now."

Mark picked up his baton.

Sharkey swiftly moved into position.

Baton moved up and down, and nose moved side to side—simpatico. The camera zoomed in on Sharkey, who played the instrument with the intensity of a concert pianist. Out came a flawless rendition of "Where the River Shannon Flows." The orchestra punctuated his final note with a triumphant major chord.

Sullivan returned, smiling, and held out his left arm. "Little Sharkey." Applause continued over the peppy sounds of exit music. Mark was all pride as Sharkey gulped a fish and the curtain closed.

In 1984, the Academy of Television Arts & Sciences founded the Television Academy Hall of Fame. To this day, about a half dozen inductees are announced every year or so. Milton Berle was one of seven inaugural inductees. Sid Caesar and Ed Sullivan were inductees the next year. Sharkey holds the rare distinction of having performed on all three of their shows during the 1940s.

The Colgate Comedy Hour

The Colgate Comedy Hour premiered in 1950. The NBC variety show aired opposite CBS's *Toast of the Town*, competing in the coveted Sunday 8:00 p.m. slot, making for an early television ratings duel. The show soared in the ratings that year, handily beating its competition. Sharkey appeared on the twelfth episode of *The Comedy Hour*, which was sponsored by Frigidaire, one of a handful of episodes not sponsored by Colgate.

Bob Hope hosted, that year being his first of forty-seven with NBC-TV. A vaudevillian in early career, he joked, "When vaudeville died, television was the box they put it in."[10] His many TV specials along with his radio and film career and USO tours represents a body of work unrivaled—a recent biographer referred to him as "Entertainer of the Century."[11] The studio audience that night was all military; the Korean War was five months old and Hope was fresh off a USO tour of Korea. Among his writers at the time was twenty-two-year-old Larry Gelbart, who had traveled with Hope in Korea and whose experiences there would later inform his creation of the 1970s sitcom, *M*A*S*H*.

Sharkey's skit took place in a desolate cabin. Hope and two other men brooded, trapped for months in the tundra. Hope broke up the crowd with one-liners: "I don't mind the tundra, but I'm afraid of the lightning." "No dames. Long time, no she."[12]

Hope then segued into an exchange that would no doubt raise some eyebrows in today's world. An Alaskan Native visitor entered the cabin, bundled head to toe.

"You man or woman?" Hope asked.

The visitor replied, "Too many clothes. Never find out."

The audience roared for so long, the skit paused.

The overclad visitor then gave Hope an envelope with seven cents postage due. Hope handed over a large fish and received three small fish in return. Inside the envelope was a gift certificate for a home tango lesson. Someone in a bear costume suddenly appeared and danced with Hope in a comical big-band number, backed onstage by Les Brown and His Band of Renown.

After the music stopped and the bear exited, Hope kept dancing, amusedly, by himself, sans music.

Enter Sharkey, who shuffled over to his tapestry-decorated stand and positioned himself upright. After Hope finished dancing, a camera close-up showed Sharkey applauding.

The camera returned full-stage. Hope turned and froze, startled to see his sea lion admirer. Sharkey kept clapping, which kept the audience laughing. "How do you like that," Hope said, with a smirk. "Thank you very much, Sharkey."[13]

Sharkey was to exit, but he stayed onstage; the best seat in the house. Someone from the wings tossed him a fish, which he caught in his mouth and gulped. He was then coaxed off the set. But seconds later, the little rascal scooted back on his stand, in the middle of the action, on live television. The actors had no choice but to keep going. Moments later in the skit, a gunshot chased Sharkey into the wings like a frightened jackrabbit.

One Yuletide Square

Three days later, Sharkey appeared on CBS on another variety show, *Arthur Godfrey and His Friends*.[14] Godfrey emceed and often played ukulele on the show, sparking a nationwide ukulele craze. Sharkey appeared with eight-year-old Hawaiian ukulele prodigy Larry Ramos, future member of the pop group, the Association. Sharkey may have even played some ukulele himself that night. Mark had formerly trained seals to play the similarly plucked tenor banjo.[15]

Sharkey later appeared with Godfrey in a nationally televised special called *One Yuletide Square*, broadcast Christmas Day, based on an abridged version of *Coppélia*, a French comic ballet about a doll that comes to life in a toy store. Godfrey narrated. (At the time, his weekly talent show and variety show were the second- and third-highest rated shows on television, exceeded only by *I Love Lucy*.) George Balanchine, founder and director of the New York Ballet, staged the ballet sequences. Future Kennedy Center Honor recipient Jacques d'Amboise danced solo ballet. Harpo Marx played a toy store doll.[16] Thomas Mitchell, an Oscar, Emmy, and Tony winner, remembered by many today as Uncle Billy in *It's a Wonderful Life*, was lead actor. And Sharkey headlined a studio parade through Yuletide Square in the Town of Anywhere, joined by a drum major and majorette, the intriguing inhabitants of the Papa Klaus toy store, and one-legged tap dancer extraordinaire, Peg Leg Bates.[17]

Peabody Award–winning journalist Jack Gould of the *New York Times* wrote of "the wonderful tricks of Sharkey." *Variety* said, "Whenever the continuity proper seemed on the verge of sagging, [the producer] congested the screen with such sturdy act specials as Sharkey the Seal." *Variety* praised the special as "a Yule romp that elevated TV's stature."[18]

One Yuletide Square not only elevated TV's stature, it elevated Sharkey's stature, placing him among other showbiz greats as one of the premier stars of early television, cementing his legacy in the annals of performing sea lions as the GOAT: The Greatest of All-Time.

Chapter 12

Vaudeville Revival

A Key to the City

Thanks to television, vaudeville was back in style.

During TV's breakout year of 1948, Sharkey did a summer gala vaudeville show billed as "the largest and most complete outdoor revue ever to go on tour."[1] First up was a city centennial gala in Fredericton, New Brunswick. Next was the Central Canada Exhibition in Ottawa, the largest fair in Canada. Advance sales were so high, sponsors erected extra bleachers. A record-breaking crowd of 11,154 packed the opening-night grandstands in what was Sharkey's first return to Ottawa following his success there that spring. "Once more Sharkey was the main attraction," wrote the *Ottawa Journal*. "Fears expressed that the talented mammal would go 'stale' from overwork can be dispelled. After stealing the show at the afternoon performance Sharkey came right back with a few added tricks, to do it again last night."[2]

Sharkey made news that fall, aided by a Ringling Brothers gorilla named Gargantua, "the most ferocious, most terrifying and most dangerous of all living creatures."[3] Thomas Dewey was challenging presidential incumbent Harry Truman. Every pundit predicted victory for Dewey, but in a stunning upset, Dewey lost. A syndicated columnist wrote, "After what happened in this election, we wouldn't be surprised to hear the Phillies had won the last World Series, and that Sharkey the Seal had chased Gargantua right out of the circus."⁴ Sharkey was an ingrained part of pop culture. If you were hip, you knew about Sharkey.

Mark's wife, Lillian, died the week of the election. She had been without her faculties for years, living in an institution. Mark interred her at Maple Grove Cemetery in his hometown of Grand Island, New York.

Weeks later, Sharkey led an eight-act vaudeville troupe on a children's fund-raising tour. Tampa Bay was first—a five-day stadium stand. Sharkey met with the mayor at city hall and held a press conference; thousands of disadvantaged children attended a special opening matinee. Stadium stints followed in Miami and West Palm Beach, again with opening-day matinees for disadvantaged children. While in West Palm Beach, Sharkey met with the mayor and performed some tricks in his office. The mayor extended his gratitude for all of Sharkey's fund-raising efforts and bequeathed him a key to the city.

With that ended a packed 1948.

Swim Races

Sports shows continued featuring marquee athletes in their variety-act presentations. For 1949, two Olympic champions competed in swim races. The first race was held in Boston. Swimmers made their way to the indoor pool area and prepared for the start.

In lane one: Adolph Kiefer, US Olympic gold medalist, record holder in the men's 100-meter backstroke, and chief swim instructor for the US Navy during World War II, where he taught his Victory Backstroke, an energy-saving technique that allowed a downed sailor to remain afloat, credited with saving thousands of lives.

In lane two: Ann Curtis, America's top female swimmer, winner of two golds and a silver in the prior year's London Olympics, holder of thirty-six US records, three world records, and the Olympic record in the women's 400-meter freestyle.

In lane three: Sharkey the Seal.

But before we get to the race, some background: The pairing of Huling-trained seals with human swimmers goes back to the days of Ray Huling and Charlie. In 1927, Charlie regularly worked out in the Hudson River, training to swim the English Channel. His exercise regimen coincided with a highly publicized stunt involving thirteen-year-old twin girls

"Say Cutie, tell me, is my name in that program?" asks Sharkey the Seal who will appear in the mammoth outdoor "All Star Variety Show" to presented on the nights of December 6-7-8-9 by the Greater Miami Lions Clubs in order to raise funds for their charitable work among the underprivileged and blind.

December 1948 press release. W. M. Shilling press photo, from the author's collection.

swimming the Hudson River from Albany to New York. Charlie joined them in Kingston. All went well until Charlie slipped his harness, freeing himself into the open waters of the Hudson. Ray chased after him in his motorboat like Wile E. Coyote trying to catch the Road Runner. The *New Yorker* wrote that Charlie "cavorted around for a couple of hours, swimming underwater for yards and yards and coming up far away from the pursuing boat, catching fish, having a swell time."[5]

Three years later, Charlie participated in a pool race with the Dancing Sunbeams, seven aspiring starlets from a stage and screen school in Beverly

Hills. The event took place at the Ambassador Hotel, a popular celebrity hangout in Los Angeles, now infamously remembered as the location of Robert Kennedy's assassination. Ray offered some heart-to-heart advice to his amphibian partner, with every expectation of receiving his cooperation. "If a seal beats a girl, there's no news in it. But if a girl beats a seal—well, figure it out, Charlie, for yourself."[6]

Now faced with the dilemma of either letting his trainer down or letting his species down, the California sea lion mulled his options. Photographers, reporters, and spectators lined around the expansive outdoor pool. Charlie and the Dancing Sunbeams plunged into the water and splashed for victory. "The girls were hardly started across the pool before he had reached the other side and returned," wrote the *Los Angeles Times*, in a story titled, "Charlie Proves He's No Gallant, Trained Seal Refuses to Lose Swimming Race to Girls."[7]

Charlie racing the Dancing Sunbeams. Library of Congress, Chronicling America: Historic American Newspapers.

Beating the Dancing Sunbeams was one thing, but beating an Olympic swimmer was another. Charlie got his chance three years later. Academy Award-winning actress Claudette Colbert threw a pool party at her home in Hollywood. Among those invited were Charlie and Olympic gold medalist swimmer turned actor Buster Crabbe, known today for his movie roles as Tarzan, Flash Gordon, and Buck Rogers. It so happened that Claudette, Buster, and Charlie were then all under contract with Paramount Pictures.

Paramount staged a race between Buster and Charlie. A publicity shot showed them side-by-side, poised to dive into a pool. The press release stated that Buster was "getting ready to take to the blue water in Claudette Colbert's pool with his sleek-skinned pal, Charlie, known as the smartest seal in the world."[8] The result of the matchup, however, remained a mystery. The *New Yorker* later gossiped that the contest never occurred: "After a couple of tremendously fast practice sessions of the pool, underwater, Charlie found some live frogs and became so interested in eating them he wouldn't race. Crabbe, who had watched his rival swim, admitted Charlie probably had it on him in speed."[9]

Which brings us sixteen years forward to Boston, February 5, 1949, and the initially mentioned race. Spectators assembled by the thousands in Mechanics Hall. Swimmers took their mark: Adolph Kiefer in lane one, Ann Curtis in lane two, and Sharkey in lane three. Once again, a Huling-trained seal had a chance to beat an Olympic gold medalist, in this case, not one, but two, something Charlie had come so close to doing, but had failed to achieve.

The race was over in a blink.

Kiefer and Curtis barely got going by the time Sharkey swam down and back. The two Olympians were still swimming their return lap as the crowd cheered for Sharkey, who was already out of the pool, clapping his flippers, bowing side to side. Sharkey triumphed race after race. The nine-day occasion drew over 180,000, including actress Doris Day and the governors of both Maine and Massachusetts.

The two Olympians went from Boston to Chicago. Races awaited them at the International Sports and Outdoor Exposition. Sharkey was unavailable; he had commitments in New York and Philadelphia. Promoters went with plan B. A press release stated, "Heading the spectacular thrill cast is Ann Curtis, America's premier woman swimmer who is teamed with Adolph Kiefer in races with Jumbo the Seal."[10] Jumbo may have been just what the

Olympians needed. At age twenty, he was a sea lion senior citizen unlike Sharkey, a prodigious athlete still in his prime. And it was no secret that Jumbo carried a few extra pounds around his midsection. Officials further leveled the playing field by allowing the Olympians to use swim fins. We now had a race on our hands. Maybe.

Controversy threatened to mar the event when incontrovertible photographic evidence proved Jumbo guilty of a false start. He responded by spotting his competitors half a pool length. It still wasn't enough. Jumbo beat them every time.

Life covered the races in a piece, "Maid against Mammal." The glossy picture magazine had a circulation well in the millions. Readers that week learned that Ann Curtis "never has a chance when she matches strokes with a trained seal." *Life* called the event "one of the most ludicrous contests in the history of sport."[11]

Curtis and Kiefer nonetheless enjoyed racing Sharkey and Jumbo. Smiles filled the pool area, both seal and human. The Olympians received

Ann Curtis, Jumbo, and Adolf Kiefer. *Chicago Tribune* Archive Photo/TCA.

good pay for twice-daily enduring the agony of defeat. Kiefer made $6,000 a week in today's dollars and credited the seal races with providing the money to develop products for his startup aquatic company, a company that invented the nylon swimsuit, the swim kickboard, and the foam-type swim goggle.[12] The company thrives to this day. Kiefer became a philanthropist who combined swimming and charity. In 2013, USA Swimming named him the father of American swimming.

This author had the honor of speaking with Mr. Kiefer, who at age ninety-eight was then the oldest living US Olympic gold medalist, having won in Berlin in 1936. He has since died. Asked his thoughts on the seal races, he gave an extended pause and spoke just two words: "Very unusual."[13]

We Take Broadway to the Farmers

Sweeping the nation was a novel entertainment medium that melded postwar baby-booming prosperity with the country's love affair with cars. Drive-in theaters were suddenly everywhere. The Kingston Sunset Drive-In Theater opened April 1949, just down the road from Seal College. "Sharkey to be 'Sunset' Attraction" read a local headline.[14] He was to appear, not live, but projected on a multistory outdoor screen. The drive-in's inaugural movie was *Pardon My Sarong*, which, of course, had several scenes with hometown hero Sharkey.

Sharkey returned to television a month later on *The Bigelow Show*. It ranked seventh nationwide and was NBC's second-highest-rated show, behind only *Texaco Star Theater*. The show starred ventriloquist Paul Winchell and his wooden sidekick, Jerry Mahoney. Mahoney and Sharkey were to do a call and response version of "I'm Popeye the Sailor Man," but problems arose once again between Sharkey and ASCAP.

ASCAP controlled the rights to "I'm Popeye the Sailor Man" and was in the midst of negotiating new terms with television executives. A licensing agreement was set to expire days after Sharkey's live broadcast and given that many stations were on a one- to two-week broadcast delay to allow for a kinescope (a filmed recording of the show) to arrive in the mail, NBC scrapped the tune. Sharkey instead faked his way through a public domain tune, "Jeanie with the Light Brown Hair."[15]

A few weeks later, Mark's brother Ray died suddenly of a cerebral hemorrhage. He was sixty-one. Forty-two years had elapsed since the Huling brothers—Frank, Mark, and Ray—had begun working with seals; Mark was now the lone survivor.

Sharkey worked that summer at Steel Pier. He was soon making news. Gossip columns everywhere ran headlines like "New Love Interest Grips Sharkey." The lucky lady was Marion Foster, an aerialist who did stunt work high in the air on a swaying pole. One day, while on break, she joined Sharkey in the pool. Steel Pier PR director Max Rosey noted that "Marion swam around with Sharkey and held her arms outstretched while Sharkey joyously leaped over the shapely barriers." But the next day, during a performance, the smitten sea lion refused to hurdle. Ms. Foster was called on to help, and according to Rosey, "Marion went into the tank with Sharkey and he never leaped so gaily before."[16]

Sharkey and Marion parted ways later that summer. The man behind their separation was George Hamid Sr., a Lebanese immigrant of humble beginnings who started as a child acrobat in *Buffalo Bill's Wild West* and who now owned Steel Pier and the country's largest agency for outdoor amusement. *Billboard* would honor Hamid, Walt Disney, Ringling Brothers, and seven others as "outstanding individuals who have made an undeniable and indelible impact on the live entertainment and amusement business. . . . people of insight, creativity, and dedication."[17] Hamid had been good to Seal College. He had featured Jumbo in his Hamid-Morton circus and Sharkey in his top grandstand show. And, of course, there was Steel Pier. He managed over 300 acts from his Manhattan office. Among the entries in his catalog was "Sharkey, the high-IQ sea lion [who] has astonished spectators with his ability to do almost anything but pilot a jet plane." Hamid famously supplied entertainment to fairs across the country. Hailed as the undisputed king of the midway, his creed was "We Take Broadway to the Farmers."[18] Hamid booked Sharkey for a string of fairs that season. Jumbo finished the summer at Steel Pier, allowing Sharkey to go on the road.

Sharkey played the New York State Fair in Syracuse, one of the oldest and largest state fairs in the country. World War II sidelined the event while the fairgrounds served as a military base, but the fair had returned in abbreviated form in 1948, making way for a grand revival of the event in 1949. "Sharkey the Seal Featured Star of State Fair Vaudeville Bill" was the headline in the *Syracuse Post-Standard*.[19] The fair opened on Labor Day; attendance was 103,650, a record that still stands as the fair's biggest opening day ever.

Gold Rush Revue was next. Hamid produced and directed the show, which was a flurry of comedy, music, and dance in centennial celebration of the California Gold Rush. Featured were extravagant sets, lighting effects, and elaborate costumes of Broadway caliber: a San Francisco street scene had life-sized trees, a desert scene had covered wagons that went aflame, and the finale featured an eighteen-strong chorus-girl number by the Roxyettes, all attired in glittering gold.

Gold Rush Revue went to Pennsylvania to perform at the Great Allentown Fair. Advance notices informed fairgoers that they would be "pleased to learn"[20] of special efforts to exterminate the annoying flies and insects that had beleaguered previous fairs, those special efforts being the spraying of DDT over the entire fairgrounds. Reports claimed the spraying had eliminated the pests and had "greatly improved sanitary conditions."[21] Hamid's grandstand revue played to overflow crowds. Latecomers paid for standing room and watched from the paddock area. An opening night review in the local paper reported that a thrilled crowd laughed and clapped its way through the entire two-hour show.

The paper added: "The opening night star? A seal, Sharkey. He was a B-29. He was an Allentown politician. He played music. He did high dives and he slept. He did, as his press agent said he would, everything but talk. He also brought down the house."[22]

The Palace

That same year, 1949, the television vaudeo craze led to the return of stage acts to vaudeville's former hallowed shrine, Manhattan's Palace Theater. The theater went from all film to vaude-film, four-a-day. Though it may not have been the two-a-day, all-stage, no-film format of the glory years, the Palace was once again presenting vaudeville.

Sharkey made his Palace debut that December. The Yuletide bill had eight vaude acts followed by a holiday movie. Sharkey again did his teddy bear balancing routine, the same bit that had given him trouble the previous month on Ed Sullivan's television variety show.

Mark addressed the crowd. "Well, what do we have here? An old dilapidated bear."[23]

Mark turned to Sharkey. "Now you go over and take him for a nice little ride." Sharkey nose-lifted the pole-mounted teddy bear off its chair, high above. Mark motioned across the stage: "Down this way, sir."

Sharkey focused upward, keeping the bear balanced on the pole. After traversing the stage, he turned around.

"Oh, he's going back," Mark said.

Upon coming back, as with the Sullivan show, Sharkey struggled to reseat the teddy bear on its highchair. The bear wobbled atop the pole balanced on his nose. Sharkey finessed in vain, the audience no doubt silently rooting for him to regain control.

Mark gave a look of suspense. "Take it easy now, Sharkey." Sharkey tried again. This time, he successfully reseated the bear.

Mark leg kicked and fist pumped. "By golly, look at that!"

Booming applause sounded from the crowd.

And now we can reveal to the reader one of Mark's seal-training secrets he once disclosed: "Veteran showmen know that a stunt will be more appreciated by an audience if it is made to appear very hard. A proficient student will go through a really difficult trick so fast it seems easy to the casual onlooker. And so he must be taught showmanship, and the knack of doing things more slowly."[24]

Sharkey not only learned to do tricks more slowly, he learned to playact, in this case, making an already-difficult routine look practically impossible. *Billboard* wrote of Sharkey's opening-night teddy bear bit: "His recovery was so good Huling should keep it in the act. It brought bigger hands than if it had been done perfectly."[25]

If they only knew.

Take Me Out to the Ballgame

Five weeks after his debut at the Palace Theater, Sharkey worked with Boston Red Sox slugger Ted Williams, the greatest hitter in the history of baseball. It was not the first time, however, the celebrity seal had shared the bill with a well-known baseball player.

Sharkey had worked during the prior off-season with Brooklyn Dodgers All-Star pitcher Ralph Branca, mostly remembered today for later infamously surrendering a historic walk-off homer to Bobby Thomson. But it was vaudeville, not baseball, that brought Branca and Sharkey together. Branca was also a crooner. The pair led a vaude lineup that toured the northeast and Midwest, including a stop in Sharkey's hometown of Kingston, New York. The *Daily Freeman* said that Sharkey "needs no introductions" and described Branca as "pitching star of the Brooklyn Dodgers who sings when he isn't slanting 'em off the mound."[26]

That same year, twelve-year-old Johnny Ross, an avid sports fan and honor student struck blind with glaucoma, said he would "rather score a baseball game than do almost anything except be present [with] Sharkey." Goodwill ambassadors granted him both wishes. He caught Sharkey in Minneapolis, where, as one journalist put it, "he laughed as hard as anybody." Next day he went to Wrigley Field for the Cubs opener. "As he boarded the Chicago bound train, he was still raving about the exploits of Sharkey."[27] (Johnny later invented beep baseball, enabling the visually impaired to play America's favorite pastime by using a sound-emitting ball. The National Beep Baseball Association now holds tournaments countrywide.)

In Boston, that same year, Ted Williams was in top form. He led the league in homers and RBIs and batted .343, one hit shy of notching his third Triple Crown. He reached base safely in eighty-four consecutive games, a record to this day. He also led the league in slugging and was the American League Most Valuable Player.

Sharkey and Ted Williams. Press photo, from the author's collection.

Sharkey worked with Williams the following off-season. But much like with Branca, baseball isn't what brought them together. They headlined a thirteen-act variety presentation in Boston at the New England Sportsmen's and Boat Show. Williams did a fly-fishing casting exhibition; Sharkey was the show's finale.

The pair posed for a press photo. Sharkey balanced a baseball on his nose. Williams stood nearby, wearing dress trousers, dress shoes, and a white button-down shirt. He grabbed a baseball bat and struck a hitting pose, flashing a huge smile. Sharkey kept the neighboring baseball balanced on his nose, ready to whip him a fastball.

Williams took fishing as seriously as baseball. His average fly-rod cast went ninety feet, compared to sixty feet for most decent fishermen. "Each one of his casts was perfectly made," a colleague said. "The fly rolled over the end of the line and dropped into the water perfectly." For the sportsmen's show, Williams cast a line across a pool and put the fly into the center of a floating ring. Fishing expert Jack Gartside recalled another routine: "They had this beautiful babe in a bikini at one end of the casting pool with a cigarette in her mouth and Ted would try to knock it out of her mouth. He always did it." Fishing remained a lifetime passion for Ted Williams. The International Game Fish Association inducted him into their Hall of Fame. *Boston Globe* emeritus sportswriter Bob Ryan recently said of Williams: "In the world of fishing, he's bigger, honest to god, than he is in the world of hitting."[28]

After nine days in Boston, another nine followed in Manhattan. "Williams, Sharkey on Display" was the headline in the *Brooklyn Daily Eagle*. "The big pool and arena are constantly kept busy with stellar attractions like Ted Williams of the Boston Red Sox, who has a swell casting act, and who coyly confided that he is going after Babe Ruth's record this season. Sharkey, the educated sea lion, can't operate a typewriter but does do most anything else."[29]

Athlete turned sportswriter Ted Reeve was another who took note of Sharkey and his new partner. Reeve dabbled in poetry. And though his work will never be confused with that of Robert Frost, he did compose an ode to baseball that spoke of the Red Sox having acquired Sharkey the Seal, who had learned to hit, but couldn't always steal. Reeve closed his homage to Sharkey: "He played first base with his flippers and his jaws / And led the crowd in his own applause."[30]

Interviews, Fast Cars, and Young Women

Mark Huling soon introduced what would become another comic trademark; having Seal College graduates do their own interviews.

Milwaukee Sentinel sportswriter and bowling champion Hank Sayrs took the bait. He sat down with Sharkey, who snorted, barked, and gabbled. Sayrs couldn't understand a word. He deferred to Mark, who, rather conveniently, was the only one able to translate.

Mark deciphered some of Sharkey's snorts: "What's the matter with this guy, boss, don't he know anything 'cept bowling? He should get smart like me."

"That's no way to treat a guest," Mark replied. "He wants to write about you."

They hit on a solution. Hank would interview. Sharkey would snort. Mark would translate.

Sharkey delivered an opening statement. "A lot of guys think I'm a seal. It ain't true. I'm a sea lion and plenty smart. Who has a better racket? All I do on the stage are things I enjoy."

Hank questioned Sharkey on a range of subjects. When the subject turned to music, Sharkey snorted an earful.

"You ought to hear me play 'Chattanoogie Shoe Shine Boy.' My boogie-woogie is out of this world, but the boss won't let me. You know, it ain't longhair enough. You got to be dignified." Asked if he knew any Spanish, Sharkey grunted, "*Sí, sí. Cómo está usted?*"

The outspoken seal also talked some baseball. "That's one game I'm not too good at. I can catch with the best of them but can't bat a lick. Ted Williams, grand guy that he is, tried to teach me not too long ago but my flippers flap when they should flip."

"What about bowling?" Hank asked.

"I'm never in town long enough to join a league," Sharkey replied. "But I can average 200 anytime I want to. I balance those rubber balls just to keep in trim for the heavier bowling balls."

Mark interrupted, "That's enough of your fish stories, Sharkey."

The discussion ran in the *Milwaukee Sentinel*, word for word, snort for snort, in an article, "An Interview with a Sea Lion, Even Sharkey Admits He's Good!"[31]

That same month, Lew Bohan and Jumbo starred in a Los Angeles variety show. Over 300,000 people passed through the turnstiles at Gilmore Stadium during its eleven-day run. "Jumbo Wows 'Em in Seal Routine" was a headline in the *Los Angeles Times*. "The seal did everything but usher the cheering spectators into their grandstand seats. . . . a seal so valuable that he is watched by 24-hour guards."[32]

CBS booked Jumbo for a TV spot. When the *LA Times* requested a preview interview, they got the new format. Sportswriter Al Wolf interviewed, Jumbo snorted, Lew translated. Here's some of what Jumbo had to say, all of which made the paper.

"I got tipped off that show business is the easy life, free room and board just for putting on a few corny stunts like we did for free in the ocean. Diving, leaping, balancing things and stuff like that there. So when this Lew Bohan came around talent hunting, why I jumped right in his boat, and he's been telling people ever since what a battle he had catching me, the dope. Really, a nice guy though."

Jumbo called Seal College "a joint in Kingston, N.Y. where mostly you learn the fine points of entertaining humans."

Jumbo also bragged about his diploma. "A sealskin we call it instead of a sheepskin. Then I was signed, sealed—are you getting all these nifties, Wolfie?"

Al Wolf suggested that returning to Los Angeles must be somewhat of a homecoming for the California sea lion. That's when Jumbo went environmental.

"Yeah, sort of. But it ain't like the old Southern California any more. Notice these eyes of mine? I look like a Main Street wino, yet I haven't touched a drop for years, not since somebody lost a bottle off a fishing boat right where I was swimming with my mouth open. Boy, what a hangover! No, sir. It's your confounded smog that's doing this to my peepers. It's even in the water nowadays."

Jumbo glanced at a clock. "Jeepers, I gotta be waddling along. I'm on television tonight . . . and want to get my coat pressed and moustache trimmed first. In case you get a chance to catch the show, I'll be the one wearing a big ruffled collar. *Ta-Ta*."[33]

Chrysler Corporation at the time was promoting their latest Dodge Route Van. The oversized vehicle had side doors as big as house doors and was drivable either sitting or standing. Mark teamed with the Kingston Chrysler dealership and designed a souped-up vehicle. Sharkey had traveled in vans with built-in tubs, viewports, and other amenities, but this topped them all, complete with air conditioning and a heated water tank that ran off bottled gas. Bigger, better, fancier, the new custom van was the lap of seal travel luxury. Mark's grandson Gary Bohan Sr., then ten years old, recalls the vehicle well. "My grandfather Mark loved that thing. It was huge. The exterior was a light olive green with Seal College lettering on the side. The inside had a big, shiny stainless-steel tub for Sharkey."[34]

Power Wagon: The Motor Truck Journal and *Trucking News*, both national trade journals, ran a photo of Mark next to his new vehicle, extending his hand to Sharkey, who stood upright inside the van, mugging it for the camera as usual. "Sharkey, famous trained seal, is making his first inspection of a truck that will be his new home on his cross-country tours. The new truck has a swimming tank for Sharkey to play in and the doorstep on the Dodge Route-Van is so low that, for the first time, Sharkey climbed into the truck all by himself."[35]

Chrysler created a full-page ad that had a lifelike drawing of Mark and Sharkey, a milkman, a fisherman, and others, all gazing at a Dodge Route Van. The pitch was: "How can you please trained seals—and trained salesmen?" Chrysler engineers did so by "discarding old ideas" and using "practical creative imagination." The result was "a new kind of vehicle" that culminated in Chrysler's self-proclaimed victory: "Then it happened! An animal trainer bought one for his seal."[36] The ad ran in *Forbes*, *U.S. News and World Report*, and *Financial Times*.

Sharkey toured in his new van, performing all summer with George Hamid's *Grandstand Follies of 1950*. The lineup had an aerialist, a contortionist, acrobats, a marimba player, and a bicycle act, all backed by the Madison Square Garden Band. One promoter said the aggregation was "one of the best to play this event in years," adding, "Mark Huling and Sharkey the Seal, used as a closer for the revue and as a special feature, proved a show-stopper."[37]

Sharkey went to Manhattan that fall, where he played the Palace in an eight-act vaudeville show. *Variety* wrote, "Best applause-getter is Sharkey the Seal. Mammal mops up."[38]

Mark was at the top of his profession. Magazines and newspapers wrote feature stories. Mark and Sharkey received mention in two college-level psychology textbooks. A New York educator presented a case study paper titled *Sharkey* that dealt with animal behavior and intelligence.[39] Mark and Sharkey sharpened their act to a T, save for the occasional gaff, like the time Mark was preparing for a stunt during a show and "his feet became entangled in the loose canvas alongside the pool and he pitched headlong into the brink."[40]

Mark did well financially. Sharkey alone commanded $3,000 a week, $25,000 in today's dollars. Mark nonetheless led a relatively modest lifestyle. He lived, as he had for years, in a small home in Kingston, New York, on a postage-stamp lot, on a main drag. He was low-key about his fame and never put on airs. Known for his generosity, he often donated to charity and helped those in need. Family recollection has it he was the type who opened his wallet in a heartbeat and gave money to those who asked. To be certain, Mark also had nonaltruistic pursuits; fast cars and young women, not necessarily in that order.

Mark loved his Hudsons. He raced one 100 mph during a family trip, even while handicapped with a carload of relatives screaming at him to slow down. And he approached his newfound bachelorhood with equal zeal, disclosing his philosophy to his male friends: "When I get old, I don't want to wake up next to an old woman."[41]

One young lady had big eyes for Mark. Their relationship soured however during a trip to Bangor, Maine. She had a few too many cocktails backstage and caused quite a stir. When Mark came off his act with Sharkey, he went to the green room and found her naked in a closet, her prior antics witnessed by his young grandson and others backstage. That was that. Mark settled down with a woman named Marian. She would eventually have a lot to say about Seal College. They married. Mark was in his sixties. Marian was twenty-nine.

Montreal and Sandy

Seal College produced one last graduate; one so talented, he hit the circuit billed as "Sharkey Junior." The moniker was a gimmick. Sharkey fathered no offspring. Seal College was an all-male campus. Mark's assistant, Billy Roe, then a devout bachelor, explained, "Just like anything else, have women around and you're bound to have trouble."[42]

At the time, the orthodoxy in the scientific community was that California sea lions would not breed in captivity. Current literature now notes three key factors required for captive breeding of any marine mammal: "appropriate habitat, adequate nutrition, and a social structure conducive toward successful reproduction."[43] Early animal managers had little idea. It took until the 1970s before experts more routinely studied captive sea lion breeding. Even then, only 3 percent of California sea lions on display in North American were captive-born.

None of these challenges had stopped Mark from trying to breed at his former Kingston quarters during the 1920s. He was well aware of the difficulty, then stating, "During all the years that my brothers and I have been training and performing with seals, we'd never so much as heard of seals breeding in such close quarters and so never gave the idea much thought. . . . From all we could learn by talking with others who had experience with show seals we got little encouragement. It seemed to be the general opinion that a baby seal among trouping water dogs was one of those things that happened every hundred years."[44]

Mark tried the long shot during the 1925–1926 off-season. Neptune courted Lady. Whatever Mark did (to foster appropriate habitat, adequate nutrition, and a social structure conducive toward successful reproduction) worked. Lady was soon expecting.

Mark resumed with Ringling Brothers the following spring. Along went expectant Lady. After five weeks at Madison Square Garden, the circus loaded their railcar convoy and embarked on their annual pilgrimage. Aboard stowed Lady.

"We kept close tab," Mark said. After six weeks on the road, he concluded, "the stork was liable to be perching 'most any day."

That day came on June 22, with the circus in Montreal.

Mark's helper shouted, "Blow me if I know whether it's a boy or a girl, but it's arrived."

Mark recalled the reaction of his circus comrades. "Excitement! Why there couldn't have been more over a baby at the White House. I suppose I was as bad as anybody else."

Mark named the pup Montreal; or Monty, for short. The newborn male weighed fifteen pounds and was within a fraction of twenty-six inches in length. "We took great pains to get an exact record of that," Mark said.

Mark regularly recorded Monty's weight and length, and fostered a nurturing environment—not so easy with sixteen other seals, traveling with the world's largest circus.

"I had hide nor hair of a rule to go by," he said.

Mark partitioned one of the seal wagons so the pup could bond in private with his mother. He ensured Monty was well hydrated and kept the nursery floor sloshed with water for Monty's comfort.

Lady nursed her newborn. Eating for two, she was kept plenty nourished. Mark fed her and the others cut up smelt and herring, a favorite delicacy. "Fresh of course," Mark said. "They're given only the best here."

Mark encouraged Monty to take a dip in the seal wagon tank, figuring "it would be safe enough to wait for the matinee when the mob would be out of the tank and inside the big top."

Monty declined at first. Then at age two-weeks he took his first swim—with the other seals in the tank! "Once he made the plunge," Mark said, "it would have given you a good laugh to see Lady trying to get him out again. Monty didn't want to go home but wanted to stay and play with the other seals."[45]

Monty's first photo session was two weeks later in Chicago. The cameraman was Harry Atwell, a publicity photographer and circus lover, considered "the greatest visual chronicler of the circus in the American 20th century."[46] Mark outfitted Monty with a large, decorative bow around his collar. He stepped back and admired the seal pup. "There! How's that for a fine big boy? Just a month old yesterday and growing every minute. But then he was a bouncer right from the start."

Monty posed outside, near the seal wagons. A seven-year-old boy in a sailor outfit (the son of the circus property boss) joined him. The boy crouched and patted the pup. Next, a young lady-performer stopped by, holding a parasol umbrella. She made herself comfortable sitting on the ground as Monty squirmed on her lap.

"Monty stood for a couple of snaps and then decided he better be getting back to his mother," Mark said. "Though he couldn't see the den, he pointed his nose straight for it."

Month after month, Monty thrived; the picture of health. Mark provided a one-year update:

"Monty began to bark at the age of six months. A bark similar to that of the adults, only of a lighter and higher pitched tone. At about that time we gave him small live baitfish. He would play with these fish for hours together in the tank and end by chewing them into bits. As far as we could tell, he did not swallow any of the fish until he was 11 months old. He is still nursing."

Monty trained for the show world, specializing in comedy. He quickly became a talent. In the words of one journalist, he had "as much promise as the great Charlie."[47]

At age two, he made his screen-acting debut in a Fox Movietone News newsreel, shot on location at the Huling seal quarters in Kingston. Mark mainly used his experienced seals for the occasion but tried a skit that had little Monty making a phone call.

The camera focused on Monty.

Mark provided the setup. "Now we're going to call up Nero and have him play a little ball with us."[48]

Mark held a candlestick phone toward Monty. Monty stood silent and disinterested, then left his stand. The camera crew snickered at the failed attempt. Mark snapped back, "We're just practicing."

Mark patiently waited for his young student to retake his stand. "All right, Monty. That's a boy. Now call up Nero."

Monty sang a sonorous long tone. The director was still unhappy. This time the slipup was on the trainer.

"The telephone was far away, was it?" Mark asked.

Mark and Monty retook their positions. The camera rolled.

This time the pair executed flawlessly. Monty was smug with self-satisfaction as Mark beamed with pride.

"That's it. That's a good boy. That's a good little boy."

Nine months later, Monty was among the seals trapped in the fire at the Huling quarters. Firemen pulled him from the building. He was one of the three seals resuscitated. Two, it may be recalled, survived. The third, the one who died later that evening, was Monty.

~

Mark did not attempt to breed when he reopened as Seal College, which brings us back to the matter of Sharkey Junior, who arrived in 1949, twenty years after the fire, and went by the name Sandy. Sandy was another source of pride for Mark, who boasted that Sandy had it all: youth, talent, and

Monty calling up Nero. Film-still, Fox Movietone News. Moving Image Research Collections, University of South Carolina.

ambition. "I have the greatest admiration for Sharkey, my first love, but Sandy, my youngest seal, is as smart as Sharkey and learns about one-fourth faster."[49]

Sandy sailed through the Seal College curriculum. Mark worked up special routines as he had for Sharkey. In one bit, Sandy played a private eye in a film noir sketch. In another bit, he sang opera. Seal College agent Bill Shilling issued the following press release:

> Sharkey will now have to watch his step. Mark Huling has come up with another amazing seal. His latest graduate—Sandy.
>
> Great notices have been written about Sharkey and there are few who have not witnessed his outstanding performances. And now Sandy is ready to take top billing and raves from the audiences. Those who have already watched his performances are astounded that there should be another seal as great an actor as Sharkey.[50]

Would Sandy live up to the hype?
The answer was a resounding yes.

Sandy in a film noir sketch. Photo by Mark Huling from the author's collection via Michael Reilly.

"Sandy the Seal Steals [the] Show, Rules as Star Performer" read a headline in his second year on the circuit. A month later, he appeared on Milton Berle's *Texaco Star Theater*, still the top-rated show on television. (Berle had just signed a thirty-year mega deal with NBC that was the talk of the nation.) Sandy played the Palace Theater a month later. *Billboard* reviewed his act, writing, "Trained by Mark Huling, Sandy is a credit to the American Guild of Variety Artists. No AGVA member was a greater hambone, and justly so. Sandy balances balls and plates. He juggles. He plays music. He milks the audience. His technique is flawless, and it's plain he loves his profession."[51]

Sandy soared to stardom, joining the ranks of Sharkey and Jumbo. It came as no surprise to Mark, who said, "I can take a seal out of the ocean and in two years have him making more money than any ordinary individual."[52]

Seal College had its third celebrity alumni. Mark, Billy, and Lew could barely keep up with the workload. Not a bad problem to have.

Chapter 13

The Show Must Go On

The Rainmaker

That a celebrity would shun the media is nothing new. Most famously, movie star Greta Garbo became a recluse; her most-remembered quote: "I want to be left alone." That a seal might do the same? Well, that's a different story. Yet, it was true. Sharkey had lost interest in doing press conferences. Outside of his act, he now preferred the solitude of his backstage private tank and spiffed-up luxury van. While in Milwaukee, local press sought another seal interview like the one Sharkey had done the year before, but they couldn't help but notice he was less accessible. Out came another madcap story from the *Milwaukee Sentinel*:

**SHARKEY PULLS A GARBO
WHEN OUT OF SPOTLIGHT**

There are artists of the stage who maintain their high output of charm even when they're not in the spotlight. There are others who lapse into a moody aloofness whenever they're not on stage. Sharkey the seal belongs to the latter category. Catch his act . . . and what do you see? A charming fellow, joyously knocking himself out for your pleasure with tricks on the land

and in the water. But Sharkey backstage is a very different bundle of fish. He just wants to be alone in his tank. Never mind any attempts at conversation unless you have a camera in your hand. (Sharkey is about as camera-shy as a movie starlet with her way to make in the world.) The trouble is that this dousing of personality off-stage isn't doing Sharkey's future any good. What he should remember is that there's always competition in this world—and his competition is another seal named Sandy.[1]

Sharkey played the Milwaukee Arena, future home of the NBA Hawks and Bucks. It had opened the year before, prompting a one-year birthday bash. The arena manager carried out a frosted cake, lettered "Happy Birthday." On top was a lit candle. The crowd watched as Sharkey "bustled onto the stage, blew out the candle with one well-aimed blow, and then extended a friendly flipper."[2] Private disposition aside, Sharkey was still Milwaukee's seal of choice. Over 100,000 attended the multiday sports show. Sharkey supplemented his stay by doing free performances at a nearby VA hospital and for local orphanages.

While Sharkey splashed in Milwaukee, New Yorkers splashed in a different sort of way. The story began the prior year when the region suffered the biggest dry spell since New York City had begun relying on Upstate reservoirs thirty-six years prior. As reservoirs depleted, shortages were severe. (Water officials denied the National Sportsmen's Show permission to use city water to fill their pool; the show instead obtained water from Brooklyn salt wells, allowing Sharkey to do his wet act.) Before long, the biggest city in the world verged on running out of water.

The New York Board of Water Supply hired Dr. Wallace Howell, a Harvard-educated climatologist who formulated a plan to seed clouds with a rainmaking agent in the hope that artificially induced rain would shore up low reservoir reserves, a plan later called "one of this world's great experiments with the vicissitudes of nature." The media rather unflatteringly dubbed Howell "The Rainmaker."[3]

Howell commissioned plane flyovers and routinely seeded clouds across the region with silver iodine. The additive supposedly altered microphysical cloud processes that, in turn, made it rain. Howell deftly made no assurances nor took credit for any results.

New York received rain just about every day that spring. Upstate farmers complained of destroyed crops. Upstate resort owners complained that the rain had chased away vacationers. Appeals to the governor went unheard. The US Weather Bureau steered clear. Said one of their meteorologists, "We just measure the stuff."

By summer, even New York City residents were begging for the experiment to end. Palisades Amusement Park, a popular attraction near Manhattan, offered to double Howell's salary if he stopped. He didn't. Palisades answered by hiring two anti-rainmakers (at five times Howell's rate) to counter seed clouds.

Aggrieved parties sued the Board of Water Supply. The Upstate Nevele Country Club filed a cloud-seeding injunction that failed in New York Supreme Court. A justice wrote, "Until New York's long-range program to solve the water shortage has been completed, such emergency measures as artificially-induced rain . . . are necessary."

Howell's cloud seeding finished that fall. Reservoir levels reached and, in some cases, exceeded rated capacity.

Howell was long gone by the next spring. Mother Nature, however, showed up in full force. Torrential rain met with snowmelt. Ten miles upstream of Seal College, the 255-square-mile, 120-billion-gallon Ashokan Reservoir was already at 104 percent capacity before the storm. During the deluge, water overflowed its spillway in biblical proportions. The downstream Esopus Creek flooded to levels unseen in thirty-five years. Two died. Firemen in rowboats rescued trapped homeowners; a sheriff engaged a local rod and gun club to provide round-the-clock rifle patrol to discourage looting.[4] Seal College and The Barn bore the brunt of the flood as did a nearby diner that was all but submerged. Surroundings looked more like a lake than a commercial strip. A flyover shot of Seal College and the vicinity ran in the centerfold of the *Daily News*.[5]

Mark and four neighbors filed a federal lawsuit against the City of New York, seeking $89,500 in damages, claiming the prior year's "rainmaking experiments" had overfilled the Ashokan Reservoir, further claiming that during the flood, "the gates of the dam were negligently and knowingly permitted to remain open."[6] The Associated Press and *New York Times* reported on the lawsuit, but the outcome was unspecified.[7] The plaintiffs were likely unsuccessful. Courts dismissed most rainmaker cases.

Huling Estate

That June, while Kingston was still mopping up, CBS broadcast the first commercial television show ever in color. Arthur Godfrey hosted; guests included Ed Sullivan. CBS transmitted the broadcast to New York, Boston, Philadelphia, Baltimore, and Washington, DC. Color viewing required a special set, leaving most everyone in the dark except for those who went to auditoriums set up for the occasion. Black-and-white home sets displayed a blank screen. The public was underwhelmed.

Sharkey wasn't on the show but indirectly received press from a syndicated columnist who mock-praised Godfrey's place in history among famous firsts. "He will be up there with . . . the first vaudeville seal to play 'Where the River Shannon Flows.' "[8]

Sharkey may have missed TV's first color broadcast, but his resume of TV appearances was impressive nonetheless; three times with Arthur Godfrey, twice with Ed Sullivan, twice with Ken Murray, and once with Milton Berle, Sid Caesar, and Bob Hope, among others. That July, he appeared on *Ford Festival*, a weekly variety show featuring A-list musicians and entertainers.

Sharkey made his daytime television debut the next month on *The Garry Moore Show*. The program catered to housewives and was the second largest revenue producer for CBS. Sharkey was Moore's only scheduled guest that day. No kinescopes survive, leaving one to wonder what it was, exactly, they talked about for an hour.

The Palace Theater made headlines the next day by announcing a vaudeville show to run for four weeks that fall, all stage, no film: "Palace Two-a-Day" starring Judy Garland. Big-time two-a-day was returning to the Palace; vaudeo ruled the television airwaves; everything was coming up roses for vaudeville.

Seal College meanwhile remained water damaged. The Barn next door closed indefinitely; the flood had destroyed the dance floor and rustic decor Mark had conceived and built when he opened the nightclub eighteen years earlier. But that all paled in comparison to what happened next.

Mark suffered a heart attack. Medics rushed him to Kingston Hospital, where he remained under observation. While hospitalized, The Barn reopened after having been closed for six months. Mark publicly extended the owner his well wishes. It was his last public statement.⁹ Mark died twelve days later; he was sixty-seven. Sharkey's reaction, tempting though it may be to speculate, is unrecorded. He happened to make a television appearance that same afternoon on *The Steve Allen Show*.

Obituaries ran in the *Daily Freeman*, the *New York Times*, *Variety*, and many other news outlets, including the Associated Press. One small town paper wrote, "Mark Huling was a showman of the highest type and his death leaves a gap in the entertainment ranks that will be hard to fill." Others referred to him as the world's foremost seal trainer.¹⁰ Following services in Kingston and Tonawanda, the family interred Mark at Maple Grove Cemetery in his hometown of Grand Island. His plot is on prior-owned Huling farmland, just down the road from where he had worked as a young butter maker.

Mark's second wife, Marian, took over of the business. It thereafter formally operated under the name Huling Estate, though everyone still called it Seal College. Billy Roe and Lew Bohan stayed on as employees; Bill Shilling remained the booking agent. Jumbo retired, his final whereabouts lost to history. Another Huling-trained seal, Sammy, retired shortly

Mark and Sharkey. Seal College Christmas card two months after Mark's death. From the author's collection.

after, his final whereabouts also lost to history. No new seals arrived. Sharkey and Sandy stayed on as the final remaining Huling-trained performers. At ages fourteen and four, respectively—given that California sea lions in captivity often live for twenty years, or more—Seal College seemed set for a while. Marian assigned Billy with Sharkey and Lew with Sandy. Billy had handled Sharkey for years as Mark's right-hand man. Lew had recently been handling Sandy, after having handled Jumbo for much of his career. And so began the post–Mark Huling era at Seal College.

Sharkey Goes to the Opera

Within two weeks, Lew and Sandy were in Philadelphia to do a children's TV show called *Big Top* sponsored by Sealtest; kids in the studio audience got free ice cream. Featured was strongman Dan Lurie in the role of Sealtest Dan the Muscle Man and future Johnny Carson sidekick Ed McMahon in the role of Ed the Clown.

Lew enjoying ice cream while watching his partner blow out birthday candles. Press photo from the author's collection via Gary Bohan Sr.

Billy and Sharkey were also road bound within two weeks. They started with two weeks at the Chicago Theater, doing a vaude-film presentation, one that came with a twist. Sharkey was to share the bill with opera tenor Lauritz Melchior, renowned for his tenure with both the Danish Royal Opera and the New York Metropolitan Opera. Melchior's specialty was Wagner. So revered was his interpretation of the character Tristan in Wagner's *Tristan und Isolde*, conductor Arturo Toscanini nicknamed him Tristanissimo, the most Tristan of Tristans.

For someone of Melchior's stature to do a vaude show was most unusual. "Opera stars and theater men are watching the experiment with bated breath," wrote the *Chicago Sun Times*. "Theater operators hit hard by TV will be pulling for Melchior to be a smash."[11]

Sharkey opened the show. Billy programmed a comedy bit that Mark had developed for Sharkey early in his career. Sharkey was the only seal ever entrusted to perform the routine.

Thousands came out opening night. Onstage, a spotlight shone on Sharkey's instrument. Behind that was his pedestal stand. As showtime neared, orchestra members played their perfunctory warm-up tuning notes. The haphazard consonance evaporated into nothingness as a tuxedoed conductor took to his podium.

Polite applause wafted through the theater. Sharkey shuffled onstage and stood upright on his pedestal stand. The conductor tapped his baton. The crowd hushed.

Sharkey threw his bodyweight back and forth. He and his pedestal took three short hops, stopping just shy of his instrument. The audience giggled at his parody of a soloist readying into position.

The conductor looked at Sharkey; Sharkey looked at the conductor. Up went the conductor's baton, stopping with a pregnant pause. Sharkey readied his nose. Musicians poised their instruments. A split second later, the conductor issued his downbeat.

Sharkey faultlessly pressed his nose into action. The orchestra, however, bungled a cacophony of squeaks, flubs, and sour notes, enough to make an elementary school band director cringe. The musical train wreck screeched to a grinding halt.

Down from his pedestal lumbered Sharkey. He waddled across the stage and went straight to the conductor, yapping and bawling him out.

The embarrassed conductor shrugged. Fits of laughter filled the theater; orchestra members struggled to keep a straight face.

Sharkey returned to his stand. Again, the conductor issued his downbeat. Again, Sharkey began playing his instrument. Again, the orchestra members flubbed their parts.

Sharkey scurried back to the baton-waver and gave him another bawling. This time, Sharkey demanded to see the score. The conductor leaned over and showed him. Sharkey kept scolding as the conductor shook his head in confusion. Sharkey pointed a flipper at the correct score, which was sheepishly retrieved by the conductor, the audience by this point in a state of bellyaching laughter.

The orchestra and soloist set up for another try. The conductor reissued his downbeat, and Sharkey played "Where the River Shannon Flows," this time without a hitch.[12]

Billboard wrote a favorable opening night review of Sharkey. As for Melchior, they thought it "a bit strange," but said his performance was "letter perfect," noting his closing-curtain standing ovation.[13]

Chicago Tribune critic Claudia Cassidy was also in the house on opening night. Over her long and distinguished career, she could heap praise if so moved, but had a controversial reputation for often ripping apart artists. So much so, her nickname was "Acidy Cassidy."

She opened her review: "No wonder they call Lauritz Melchior, heldentenor. In his time, the mighty Dane has coped with everything from prima donnas, Wagner size, to Sharkey the seal, who shares his Chicago Theater billing this week and has a privilege other soloists may envy, but seldom share, that of barking at the conductor."

Cassidy went on to call Melchior "the man who was the only great Tristan I ever heard," describing his performance that night as "something rich and rare."[14]

Sharkey and Melchior received more press when a wire service arranged for a posed shot. The two faced each other, inches apart. Both sang at the top of their lungs as Melchior waved a baton in front of a music score. Papers ran the picture captioned: "A seal named 'Sharkey' rasps a high note under the baton of operatic singing star Lauritz Melchior."[15]

Melchior biographer Shirlee Emmons later wrote: "To Wagner-lovers it was a disgrace that such a man should be reduced to performing in a vaudeville show. They were shocked that Lauritz Melchior, the internationally revered Tristan, should be billed together with Sharkey the Seal, and even worse, that a most undignified picture of Melchior and that seal should be reprinted nationwide."[16]

Melchior, however, was unapologetic and genuinely pleased to be reaching a more general audience, even if others saw him as selling out. At age sixty-one, with nothing left to prove, he was also having the time of his life. He enjoyed mixing opera with show tunes, and took pleasure in the camaraderie he shared with others on the bill, especially Sharkey. In a letter to a close friend, Melchior's wife wrote, "Lauritz and the seal love each other. Every morning such a greeting. He gives the seal fish and the seal is happy. Lauritz's full-dress suit stinks like a fish market. But he doesn't complain."[17]

Melchior's success in Chicago led to a booking at the Palace in Manhattan. He was to follow Judy Garland, whose scheduled four-week run had lasted a record-breaking nineteen weeks, earning her a Special

Lauritz Melchior and Sharkey. Press photo from the author's collection.

Tony Award for "an important contribution to the revival of vaudeville." A critic at the time called it "one of the greatest personal triumphs in show business history."[18]

Garland closed her last show by bringing Melchior onstage, a customary passing of the baton. Someone from the crowd requested she encore with "Auld Lang Syne." She suggested the audience sing it instead. Melchior promptly led the crowd in singing the song to her. During the final bars, everyone rose to their feet. The ovation lasted minutes. Roses filled the stage. Judy Garland looked on, touched and overwhelmed, tears rolling down her cheeks.

Melchior went on to work his two-a-day stint at the Palace. In the span of a few months, he had gone from topping the world of opera to headlining vaudeville's most fabled stage, fish-smelling clothes and all, with a little help from his friend Sharkey.

The One and Only

Sharkey stayed in Chicago for a TV appearance on *Super Circus*. Aided by clowns, contests, and variety acts, the program starred the affable and voluptuous Mary Hartline, admired across the country by boys and girls, and by more than a few dads. The show broadcast from the Chicago Civic Center. Live commercials for Peter Pan peanut butter were read by future *60 Minutes* icon Mike Wallace.

Sharkey closed 1951 at the Baltimore Hippodrome. The former vaude house retried vaudeville after having gone all-film, perhaps inspired by Judy Garland's success at the Palace. *Billboard* said the theater "will go back to flesh . . . on an experimental basis."[19] Flesh and sealskin to be exact. The program costarred Sharkey. Lower on the bill was Alan King, a young Borscht Belt comedian on the brink of fame.

Variety Club was next. Originally a small Pittsburgh showbiz social club, it took on the cause of providing living expenses for a baby abandoned at a local theater. It also raised money for other disadvantaged children, forming chapters worldwide, and had recently spawned the Boston-based Jimmy Fund. On January 20, 1952, Variety Club's founding Pittsburgh chapter held its annual fund-raising banquet. Keynote speakers included the governor of Pennsylvania, a justice from the US Supreme Court, and the vice president of the United States. Three orchestras provided continuous dinner music. After that was the "Big Show." Acts included comedian George Gobel, later a popular television host and Hollywood personality. Future fame of Gobel aside, he and the others all bowed to a seal that evening. Sharkey was the "Big Show" finale, listed in the program as "The One and Only."

Shock and Awe

Boston's annual sports show was two weeks later. Sharkey again worked with baseball slugger and fly-fishing expert Ted Williams.

Also headlining was Jim Thorpe—a Native American baseball player, football player, and Olympian, whom the Associated Press had recently named the greatest male athlete of the first half of the twentieth century. Native Americans played a key part in sports shows. Opening day began with a Native American call of the loon. A tribal chief emceed the multiday festivities in full headdress and regalia. That year featured Thorpe and Native Americans from eleven tribes doing traditional tribal dances. Having Thorpe onboard was a big deal. And a big draw. The show broke attendance records; some days exceeded 20,000 patrons. *Boston Globe* sportswriter Harold Kaese contrasted the show to the less-than-capacity crowds at local professional games: "The Garden would profit if it swapped the Bruins and Celtics for Ted Williams, Jim Thorpe and Sharkey the Seal."[20]

After Boston, Williams reported for baseball spring training; Sharkey and Thorpe went to Manhattan to do another show.

Sandy meanwhile reported for duty in Milwaukee. Sharkey had been a favorite there, so when Sandy showed up instead, rumors surfaced he wasn't getting the respect he deserved. Sportswriter Hank Sayrs had interviewed Sharkey in years past and thought it only fair if he did the same for Sandy. This time, he let the seal do all the talking. Sandy snorted, Lew translated, Hank transcribed. Here's some of what made the sports pages of the *Milwaukee Sentinel*.

SEAL GETS "FLIP" AT SPORTS SHOW

By Sandy (As told to Hank Sayrs)

Most Milwaukeeans know my pal Sharkey. He's in New York with trainer Billy Roe. Confidentially, my trainer, Lew Bohan, recognized the fact that Milwaukee always wants the best. That's why I'm here and not Sharkey. . . . Boy is that Sharkey getting out of condition. He weighs over 220 pounds. Maybe late hours agree with him too well. I'm a perfect 125 pounds, slick as a whistle and jet propulsion in the water. And are my eyes good. Did you see that blonde in the 13th row Wednesday night? Was she a corker! Think I'll ask Lew if I can hang around Milwaukee for a couple of extra weeks. Nice town you've got here. That blonde! . . . Poor Lew, I really got him one night, but good. He was trying to get me to sing a bit of grand opera but he wasn't giving me the right cue, so I bit him on the shoulder and tore his shirt. Boy, did I fix him! He sure behaves now. Yes sir, he's even going in for some bribery. Just to make sure I don't embarrass him in front of all you people, Lew feeds me a bit of caviar in addition to my usual ten pounds of fish. I'm just one of those uppity Kingston, New Yorkers. That's where our Seal College is located. A nice place, believe me.[21]

Sharkey meanwhile finished his gig in Manhattan and went straight to the Canadian National Sportsmen's Show. Their brochure guaranteed completely new acts; well, almost completely new. Included in their brochure was an extra-large, bold disclaimer: "No repeats except Sharkey the Seal. Public demand forces us to once more present that fabulous animal personality."[22]

With Sharkey in Canada, Sandy went to Detroit, joining several of the acts that had just appeared in Manhattan. The *Detroit Free Press* gave high scores to the others, but said, "They all have to yield the spotlight to a prodigious performing seal named Sandy. He winds up the show by leaping out of a tank of water to clear a four-and-a-half-foot hurdle as neatly as Jesse Owens ever did it."[23]

"Thorpe Eying Medals Even at Sports Show, but Seal's Still Star" was the article headline. The jab at Thorpe involved two 1912 Olympic gold medals stripped away from him when officials learned he had previously played semipro baseball. He had been the first Native American to have won a US Olympic gold medal. (The International Olympic Committee posthumously re-awarded Thorpe his medals.)

Seal College received a scare that spring at another show. A dampened mat was accidently electrified through contact with an exposed outlet. When Sharkey left his tank, his flippers hit the mat. "By the force of what apparently was a terrific electric shock, Sharkey was catapulted back into his tank," a reporter wrote. "He appeared badly frightened and went through a frantic aquatic demonstration of swift turns and rolls." Billy Roe added, "Sharkey was scared to death. It took me 10 or 15 minutes to get him settled down." Luckily, Sharkey was uninjured. He even did a performance that night, though he refused to return to the area where the mat had been. His act moved to the other side of the stage.[24]

∽

Vaudeville grandstand shows had long been a part of fairs, but conditions in 1952 were extra ripe. The postwar economy was booming, automobiles were all the rage (making travel to fairs more attainable), and Judy Garland had just given vaudeville a double shot in the arm. If attendance is any measure, that season of fairs rates tops in terms of the popularity of vaudeville grandstand shows.

The Western Canada "Class A" fair circuit had long been coveted by booking agencies. As one agent said, "To win . . . the 'A' meant a fine income. More than that, it meant instant prestige."[25] Five agencies sought the grandstand contract that year. "Competition was keen," a fair official said. Delegates from all the fairs deliberated in closed session for over ten hours before awarding the grandstand show to Chicago agent Ernie Young, who offered a ten-act revue that included acrobats, a juggler, a six-person teeterboard act, a dog act, a vocal quintet, sixteen chorus girls, a comedy troupe, and Sharkey. Officials immediately issued a press release: "Featured performer, and highest priced act on the bill, will be Sharkey the seal."[26]

Billy loaded the Seal College van with props and one of the large collapsible portable pools. Sharkey would work the fairs doing both his wet act and dry act. They drove to Chicago where Ernie Young assembled his revue. While there, Sharkey snuck in another national television spot as a special guest on *Super Circus*.

Much like its US counterparts, Canada's premiere fairs had agriculture exhibits, carnival rides, and a nightly grandstand show. The tour started at the Provincial Exhibition of Manitoba, held in Brandon. Attendance was the highest ever in the event's seventy-year history. "Seal Draws Much Attention as Big Grandstand Feature" was a headline in the *Brandon Daily Sun*. "Sharkey is one animal that has taken Brandon by storm."[27]

The Show Must Go On | 237

Sharkey not only took Brandon by storm; he took all of Western Canada by storm. Billy told a reporter, "Edmonton's reception is far better than anything in the US. Audiences south of the border have been spoiled by television and the availability of live talent."[28] Fairs in Calgary and Saskatoon produced similar results. Attendance records tumbled at each location, surpassing even the most optimistic of attendance predictions made by fair directors.

Sharkey held a press conference in Saskatoon. Officials, photographers, and reporters gathered as he greeted a mayor. Billy translated Sharkey's barks: "I'm glad to shake your flipper, your worship. What stories I could tell you politicians about the finer points of barnstorming, but my lips are sealed." After some chitchat, Sharkey closed by barking, "I'd like to chat another time—drop in when you'd like a kipper for tea."[29]

By the time Sharkey pulled into Regina, Saskatchewan, his fifth and final Canadian stop, he was dominating the fair's marketing campaign. Ads billed him "the greatest single trained animal on earth."[30] Promoters distributed 40,000 place mats to hotels and restaurants, depicting cartoon illustrations of Sharkey doing his act.

Merchandisers elbowed in on the action. A Canadian beach toy vendor whose product line included beach balls for $0.79 and floats for $1.69 introduced a deluxe inflatable, with side fins capable of supporting an adult. It retailed for $2.20, bearing the likeness and selling under the name of one Sharkey the Seal.

The tour moved to the States. "Seal Sharkey One of Best in Show Biz" was a headline at the South Dakota Sioux Empire Fair.[31] Next was the Illinois State Fair, which set attendance records four consecutive days. One newspaper wrote that Sharkey stole the show "from such personages as Milton Berle," who was still the highest-paid performer on television, though apparently not quite as popular on stage, at least not when Sharkey was around.[32]

Top attraction at the Kentucky State Fair was a show featuring a water ballet, international championship high divers, and Sharkey. "For some reason, the biggest applause is always for Sharkey the Seal," wrote the *Louisville Courier-Journal*. "He seems to add character to [his act] as well as comedy."[33] Kentucky's governor was to attend a show. His late arrival kept thousands waiting. During the delay, a discarded cigarette set the wooden bleachers on fire. The stands went up like a tinderbox. High winds spread the flames. People panicked and trampled over one another. Some jumped from the railings. Remarkably, nobody died or was seriously hurt. Billy and Sharkey escaped unscathed.

From Kentucky, Sharkey returned home. He had worked eight fairs and traveled 6,000 miles, the longest such tour of his career.

That fall started in Manhattan at the Palace. "Sharkey, the seal, of course can't miss," wrote *Billboard*. "He is so smart it often seems he is running his own show."[34]

Radio City Music Hall was next with another Leon Leonidoff revue. *Variety* said that Sharkey was "in the show's key slotting, and the mammal, as always, is a strong get-over."[35] Three weeks later, Sharkey worked again with Leonidoff, who was hired by NBC to produce a nationally televised Christmas special. It was the finish to yet another successful year for Seal College, the first full year without its founder and mastermind, Mark Huling.

To borrow an old circus phrase, "The show must go on."

Indeed, it had.

Chapter 14

The End of an Era

In All Shows, There Is a Star

Sports shows and fairs were now Seal College's bread and butter. Theater and television rounded out the calendar.

Seal College agent Bill Shilling booked entertainment for practically every sports show in North America. "They represent mighty big business," he said.[1] The hunting and fishing industries spent tens of millions of dollars on their expositions, which were at their peak of popularity. The postwar economy was booming, indoor shopping malls had yet to arrive, and television hadn't fully taken its grip on leisure time. It all added up to sports shows being an ideal shopping and family entertainment event—a perfect cure for the wintertime blues.

Shilling represented everyone from slingshot artists to professional athletes to judo champions. "Naturally, these shows also rely on animal acts and I daresay we've used every type, from performing bears to penguins," he noted.[2] (Though it seems somewhat odd that hunters were drawn to animal artistes.) Pictured prominently on his one-page flier, and listed in double-size lettering above his roster of other acts, was Sharkey.

In an interview with *Billboard*, Shilling said, "Sharkey the Seal is one of the greatest attractions I've ever had. This amazing animal is in such demand that he is already booked thru the 1953–54 seasons. Few other seals can make that statement."[3]

Perhaps so. But Sandy ran a close second. Sandy began 1953 with a nine-day show in Manhattan, where he starred with Florence Chadwick, the first woman to swim the English Channel. Joining them was former world heavyweight boxing champion Jack Sharkey and twenty-one-year-old Mickey Mantle, hero of the prior fall's World Series. (Noticeably absent was Red Sox slugger and perennial fly-fishing favorite, Ted Williams, who was serving overseas as a fighter pilot in the Korean War.) Sandy followed with a packed itinerary. On his schedule was a command performance before newly elected President Dwight D. Eisenhower.[4]

Sharkey meanwhile was ubiquitous. He headlined sports shows and grandstand shows. He did a week at the Palace in the spring and again in the fall, where *Variety* said he was "one of the more versatile performers in the vaude domain." He played stage-film bills at movie palaces such as the Chicago Theater, where *Billboard* said he "shows plenty of training when he actually clowns with the audience." *Popular Science* featured him in a piece, "How to Train a Seal." And he made national television appearances, including a return on *The Ed Sullivan Show*. All of the above within the span of one year, 1953.[5]

Sharkey plays the 3,800-seat Chicago Theater. "New Star Shining on the Loop (1953)," licensed under Creative Commons, CC BY 3.0, cropped and retrieved from *Cinema Treasures*.

The next year was similar. Sharkey did a week in the spring at the Palace and returned for a week that fall in what would be the last stage-film movie palace bill of his career.

Movie theaters were in stark decline. (Television had finally taken its toll.) Attendance was down 50 percent from World War II highs, based on the percentage of people who went to the movies at least once a week; a number that would continue its precipitous drop, from 63 percent during World War II to practically nil today. Virtually every motion-picture house eliminated stage shows ahead of the feature movie. Many closed. Opulent movie palaces that had sprouted with abundance during the 1920s came crumbling down. The lucky ones survived as performance halls. The era of the movie palace, when patrons filled giant-sized theaters multiple times a day to see A-list entertainers perform onstage ahead of a Hollywood film, had ended. Perchance for many in today's world of cinema multiplexes, with their small cookie-cutter theaters that always seem to have plenty of empty seats, the bigger surprise may be that movie palaces ever existed in the first place.

Fortunately for Seal College, sports shows were still popular. During one such tour, Sharkey went from Seattle on the Great Northern Railway, lounging aboard a modern streamliner, the *Western Star*, where he took up residence in a lower berth—a cordoned area in a mail baggage car equipped with a temporary water tank. Officials reported that, before departing, "Trainer Roe put Sharkey through some of his paces for the benefit of Western Star passengers."[6]

From Seattle, Sharkey toured Canada. The tour ended in Toronto, where sponsors produced a short film titled *The Story of America's Finest Springtime Exhibition*. Footage showed gun exhibits, boats, an international auto display, archery, fishing, square dancing, an all-breed dog competition, a lady's fashion show, and the variety show, which included Native American dancers, fencers, and a man-wrestling alligator. The film mentioned nobody by name until the last segment, which showed a performer in action, accompanied by the following voiceover: "In all shows there is a star, and in the stage and water revue of the Canadian National Sportsmen's Show it's the very famous Sharkey the Seal. . . . It is acts such as this that fill the 7,000-seat arena performance after performance, including afternoons, providing the exciting climax to a thrill-packed show. Sharkey is sure to be back next year."[7]

Billy and Sharkey performing at a sports show. Press photo from the author's collection.

There's No Money in Crows

Marian Huling was now a widow in her early thirties, the sole owner of Seal College. She left Kingston shortly after Mark died, returning to her home state of New Jersey. That left Billy Roe and Lew Bohan to run the day-to-day operation—daily tank cleanings, buying fresh fish, keeping the customized vans in working order, maintaining the Seal College building, making travel plans, dealing with clients—everything.

Billy and Lew disliked Marian. If you asked them, she retained more than her fair share of profit. She paid them a modest salary, inadequate compensation in their view, especially because they had helped train and were handling two of the highest-paid animal acts in show business. She also made them submit detailed expense reports, or as Billy and Lew called them, "swindle sheets."[8] The fair-minded will note that Marian is no longer here to defend herself, but the business ran differently under her control and was less favorable for Billy and Lew. That much is certain.

Seal College in many ways became a regular job for Billy and Lew. With Mark gone, the acts stayed the same. And there was no shortage of mundane tasks: long, weary van rides; setup and breakdown at each venue; and the act itself, which largely became a matter of routine. Billy and Lew nevertheless approached their work with propriety and professionalism. Even on the financial side, though they considered themselves slighted, they represented Seal College and their vocation with a certain badge of pride.

One such instance happened after Billy had driven 1,000 miles to Missouri, following New York television appearances with Sharkey on *The Garry Moore Show* and *Ed Sullivan Show*. The occasion was a new sports show presented by Nick Kahler, his first in Kansas City.

If ever a father of sports shows, it was Nick Kahler. In 1933, he founded a sports show in Minneapolis, to this day the longest continuously running annual sports show in the country. So popular were his expositions, they later took precedence over the Minneapolis Lakers, who played home games in the same arena. (Kahler once demanded that the Lakers schedule their playoff games elsewhere to avoid interfering with his show, even though the Lakers were reigning NBA champions.) Kahler branched out to Chicago in the late 1930s with another mega annual sports show that continues to this day. Other cities followed with similar results.

Kahler was a longtime fan of Seal College. "Here's a good one on me," he said. "When I put Sharkey in business, I paid Mark Huling, the owner of the act, $600 for one stand. Huling had two other seals then, too. Now I must pay $3,500 and there's only one seal."[9]

Kahler went big for Kansas City. Local outdoorsman Harold Ensley had a new television fishing show and offered to do a remote telecast, the first ever for Kansas City's startup KCMO-TV. Ensley would broadcast on location from the sports show, at no charge, under the stipulation he choose which acts aired.

The TV station brought over its gear. The house filled for the nine o'clock show. The crew took their positions; headphones on, cameras aimed, six men hovered over equipment. All was set except for one detail. No one had told the entertainers. When they found out minutes before the start, they refused to go on.

Kahler was livid. He called over to Ensley. "We have a problem. The acts you selected will not perform without double pay. Even the band wants extra money."

Kahler and Ensley summoned the leader of a European tumbling group and Billy Roe. The four argued. Billy led the charge.

"I didn't let Ed Sullivan or Garry Moore show the seal in the tank, so why should I let this guy?"

Kahler pointed to the packed stands. "Why do you think they are here? If you don't go on his show, I'll cancel your contract."

The tumbler asked Ensley, "What do you get out of this?"

"Nothing but a headache from you guys."

"Why didn't someone tell me?" the tumbler replied.

Realizing Ensley was working gratis, the tumbler and Billy reconsidered. "Sure, we will really put on a show for you."[10]

Ensley later admitted that the selected acts put on a great show. Lucky television viewers in Kansas City got to see Sharkey do his wet act. Such is a sense of Billy's pride.

As for Lew Bohan, he revealed his vocational pride after presenting a seal act on a Detroit radio show. Lew had subbed for Blackie the Talking Crow after fog had grounded Blackie in Chicago. Needled later as to whether he would ever consider handling a crow act, Lew scoffed. "There's no money in crows. Seals are where the money is."[11]

Two Places at Once

Following Kansas City, Sharkey went to Milwaukee. He had been absent for three years, during which Sandy had done the annual tour stop. *Milwaukee Sentinel* sportswriters wasted no time ribbing Billy with "ugly rumors whispered here and there in trained seal circles."[12] "Sandy was moving to the top," the rumor-mongers hinted, "ousting 16-year-old Sharkey by the force of youth and personality."[13]

"Nonsense," Billy replied, reasoning that although Sandy was ten years younger, he had ten years less experience. As for personality, Billy said, "I'll take Sharkey's every time. Sandy's a good seal, you understand, but he's a more serious type than Sharkey. Now when Sharkey wants something, he lets you know it, always with one of his tricks, too. You know his imitation of a politician's gabble? That's what we get when he wants fish. But Sandy is calm at all times. You can't tell what he's thinking."[14]

The discussion shifted to the prior year in Milwaukee. An amateur photographer's flash bulb had exploded near Sandy, petrifying him to the point where he refused to perform for days on end. Billy explained that you never know what will frighten a seal. Recently a butterfly had caught Sharkey off guard. "He was so alarmed that he took an unscheduled dive into the tank," Billy said. "Veteran that he is, he quickly pulled himself together and clambered out to resume the act. That's the type of recovery Sandy must be capable of before he can seriously challenge the old master." Fans of Sandy no doubt saw it as apples and oranges, but the *Sentinel* sided with Sharkey. That year's article on Seal College began: "Chalk up a victory for experience over youth—this time in the battle of the trained seals, Sharkey vs. Sandy."[15]

Sharkey's Milwaukee stay included a performance for William Randolph Hearst Jr., and a fund-raiser for a local children's orthopedic institute, led by off-duty firefighters, who escorted physically handicapped children and an orphanage group, free of charge. Sharkey provided a thrill by balancing a giant-sized Easter seal on his nose.

Sharkey did plenty of other gigs, including a private party for philanthropist Vincent Astor at the St. Regis hotel in Manhattan, and a summer at Ocean Beach Park in New London, Connecticut, doing his wet act in an Olympic-sized pool. Night shows had underwater lights. The glow surrounding his submerged body made for spectacular viewing. Mike Reilly, grandson to Mark Huling, remembers seeing Sharkey there. "He swam like a bullet through the water. It was incredible to watch."[16]

~

Elsewhere in showbiz television ruled, though vaudeo had mostly disappeared, save for *The Ed Sullivan Show*. Sitcoms, quiz shows, and Westerns were the new darlings of the small screen. Seal College still routinely did children's shows, a last television hurrah for many vaudeville sight-acts such as jugglers, acrobats, and animal acts.

Sharkey returned to *Big Top* to celebrate its fifth anniversary, where he balanced a beach ball labeled "Big Top 5 Years Old." He also went on rival program *Super Circus*, where he costarred in an episode with the second baseman for the Brooklyn Dodgers, a man bigger than baseball, the great number forty-two, Jackie Robinson.

Sharkey also went on *Westinghouse Studio One*. The CBS drama series featured leading playwrights, directors, and actors. Each week a different lineup presented a live teleplay, including original classics like *Twelve Angry Men*. Although the show often struck a serious tone, Sharkey did a lighthearted episode about a washed-up tap dancer frustrated by being billed lower than a seal act. Eddie Bracken played the destitute hoofer; Bracken years later playing the owner of Walley World in the movie *National Lampoon's Vacation*.

That same year, 1955, was a mediocre season of fairs. To compete with TV, just a flick of a knob away, many fairs offered free-admission grandstand shows with low-priced acts. The trend all but killed the marketability of established talent like Sharkey. George Hamid called it a "give up" and "panic" attitude by fair operators. "Successful operation can be continued and created in spite of television," he said, when asked about paid-admission grandstand shows.[17] The industry saw it differently. Broadway-style revues and gala vaudeville shows as major fair attractions both became an endangered species.

Sports shows stayed strong but presented problems of a different sort, as occurred in early 1956. Sharkey headlined in Kansas City, during which he was also supposed to be headlining in Cincinnati. The scheduling quandary occurred from time to time and Seal College solved the problem by discretely dispatching Sandy as Sharkey. Fans were supposedly unaware of the switch, although the practice was more widely known than Seal College may have wished.

For starters, Seal College got busted that year in Cincinnati. During opening day, an observant spectator cried out, "That's not Sharkey. They've got a ringer in there."[18]

A reporter pressed Lew on the matter. Lew did damage control by having the reporter talk directly to the seal (Sandy), whose barks Lew translated. "Now what does that guy know about it? It's me Sharkey. . . . I've been around the shows for a long while you know and I've never had to toss in a ringer yet."[19]

The story rather awkwardly made headlines in the *Dayton Daily News*. There had been other awkward moments.

Right after Mark died, a reporter wrote, "Now that Mark, greatest of all sea lion trainers, has gone, we can now probably safely reveal something.

Mark had several seals trained for the 'Sharkey' routine of tank performances. If one seal happened to be indisposed, another could be substituted. That way no one was disappointed."[20]

Animal trainer and author Daniel Mannix further exposed the practice years later in his Newbery-nominated children's novel, *Drifter*, a tale about a boy and his rescued seal pup. At one point, the boy found himself awestruck over a trained-seal act. He relayed his zeal to an old salt of a seal-trainer captain. "I'll bet Sharkey couldn't have done no better," the boy assured the captain. "You heard of Sharkey? I read a book that said he was the greatest performing seal that ever lived." "Yes, I saw Sharkey plenty of times," replied the captain. "Mark Huling trained him. Matter of fact, there were several Sharkeys. Each one had his own routine but the audiences couldn't tell 'em apart and thought it was one seal. Huling was a good trainer—a good trainer. Some thought I was better, but I wouldn't know about that. One thing Huling had I didn't—he was a great showman."[21]

Undisclosed Sharkey substitutions did occur, though not nearly as much as stories like these might suggest. And there certainly weren't a bunch of seals masquerading as Sharkey. Most of the time, the seals went out under their own names. Admittedly, clients and spectators may not have always known when Sandy was surreptitiously filling in for Sharkey, but one thing is certain: It sure got Seal College out of some jams.

Sharkey followed his 1956 Cincinnati double-booking with dates in Kentucky, billed "The Greatest Comedian of Them All." Local press peppered Billy with questions. "What is it like to travel with a seal?" "It's no problem," Billy replied. "Just think if you had to travel with a dog. You couldn't get into hotels or motels. A seal? They feel honored to have him."[22] Sharkey finished his tour in Pittsburgh at Kennywood, one of the country's oldest amusement parks. For years each spring, Sharkey was a two-week attraction on their Lagoon Stage—with one caveat: Sandy had performed there the year before, even though Sharkey was the advertised attraction. Indeed, Seal College had pulled the secret switcheroo.[23]

Hound Dog

That spring, Lew and Sandy appeared on a new CBS-TV children's program called *Captain Kangaroo*. The gentle-paced show was broadcast from Manhattan, recorded live without a studio audience. It had premiered the previous fall and would air for twenty-nine years, the longest running children's network show of its day. Sandy did his dry act that morning for young television viewers across the country.

Lew and Sandy worked that entire summer at Steel Pier. On July 27, 1956, Seal College agent Bill Shilling died at age seventy. Four days later, Lew received a telegram, hand-delivered while he was working on the pier, telegrams usually reserved for something urgent. Billy had sent a message from Kingston: "Bicycle arrived safely. Missing air pump." Lew chuckled and smiled. Recalling lingo from their World War II days, he knew what the message really meant: "It's a girl." Lew's second wife had been expecting and Billy had stylishly delivered the good news. Lew was a proud, new father.[24]

Sharkey spent much of that summer resting an ailing tooth. Sharkey's eyesight was also deteriorating, which is common for an older California sea lion. His standard eye-care regimen included a bucket of salt added to his daily-changed water tank, but at age twenty, he was nearing his life expectancy. It was showing. Sharkey still worked special events and toured a bit with Hamid's top grandstand show. Though he was having difficulty juggling and balancing due to declining eyesight, he still shined doing the thing he did best—comedy.

Sharkey did a free show that summer for a small group of wheelchair-bound elders, who semicircled around him. Sharkey stood on his stand and held court like a neighborhood teenage jokester under a streetlamp, telling gags to his posse. A photographer captured the moment. If only pictures could talk. Joyful grins radiated from all, including a woman who was laughing so hard, it may very well have been the heartiest laugh of her life.

For the grandstand shows, Sharkey did his shower routine. It was impressive enough that a seal opened a door, turned on a shower, showered, dried off, went back to the door, reopened it, and exited. But what really made the bit was his endless flair for humor: a comic expression here, an exaggerated gesture there, sideways glances, pauses, and smirks. He performed that summer in Ottawa, at Canada's largest fair. Opening night drew 9,000 in a show described as "brilliant and well-paced" by the *Ottawa Citizen*. The paper added: "The crowd laughed until it cried as Sharkey the wonder seal took a shower."[25]

Elvis Presley upended the showbiz world that same week when his version of "Hound Dog" hit number one on the charts. He and his provocative gyrating hips revolutionized pop culture norms, displacing the so-called polite and nonvulgar B. F. Keith approach that had dominated show business for over fifty years. With every shake of Elvis's hips, and with the wave of entertainment provocateurs who would follow (to this day), each more provocative than the next, vaudeville looked more and more old-fashioned—and became less and less in demand.

Sandy worked that fall in Memphis at the centennial celebration of the Mid-South Fair, though it was someone else who provided the fair's most

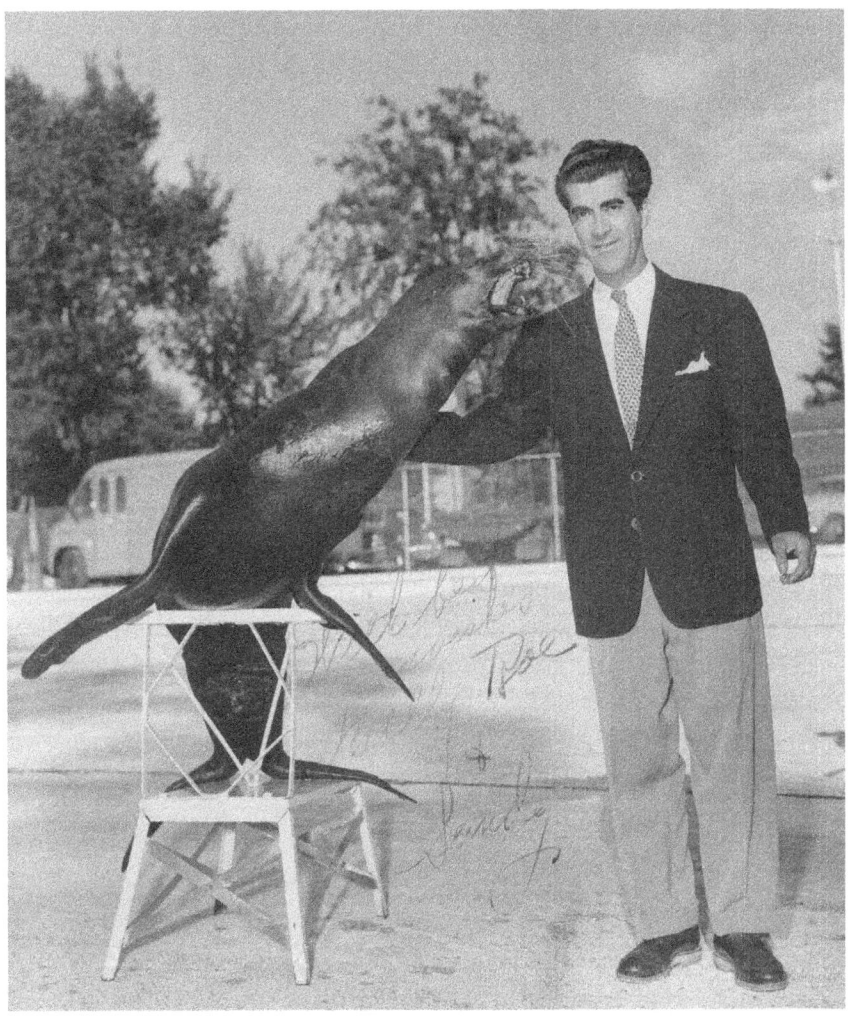

"With best wishes, Billy Roe & Sandy," Mid-South Fair, 1956. Photo by Robert W. Dye. Courtesy of Dye Photography.

memorable moment: Elvis Presley. Just three weeks after his historic first appearance on *The Ed Sullivan Show*, with "Hound Dog" still number one on the charts, Elvis returned to his hometown and made an unannounced visit to the fairgrounds, appearing onstage, much to the crowd's frenzied delight.[26]

Elvis impersonators have long been popular. Little known is among the first was a trained seal; Sandy was soon doing an Elvis impersonation. Sandy's gyrating hips provided the perfect parody, not that he needed to learn any new moves. His Elvis dance looked remarkably similar to the jitterbug that Mark Huling had taught him in the 1940s. A clever setup from the handler and a well-placed wardrobe prop was all it took to modernize an old routine.[27]

Final Curtain

That December, Billy wrote to Kennywood publicity director Carl Hughes to apprise him of how Sharkey was doing. "Last year he wasn't too well, but I had his tooth pulled since and now he is as good as ever." The *Pittsburgh Post-Gazette* reported that "Mr. Hughes doesn't know how many teeth a seal has but apparently Sharkey wants one for Christmas."[28]

Sharkey toured that winter of 1956–1957. Billy transported him in a cart from his private tank to the stage. The company line was that it avoided cuts to his flippers, but his declining vision was the real reason. Sharkey was rapidly going blind. He missed tosses during his juggling routines. Worse, he seemed to lose interest.

"He didn't flip his flippers with as much élan," a journalist observed. "Was at long last that human minus sign, boredom, getting through to Sharkey the Seal?"[29]

Billy shortened the act. Sharkey still did photo ops with children and mayors, but performances became a chore. By one account, "He gave the act the old school try, but there was sadness, not joy, in the failure."[30]

∽

Sandy also toured that winter during which the *Milwaukee Sentinel* conducted another whacky seal interview. No paper had more fun covering Seal College. Locals turned to the sports pages to read the latest.

"As the variety show opened, a famous star arrayed in sealskin lounged at the dressing room makeup table nibbling sea smelt as he conducted a press conference. Sandy the Seal is an old pro at interviews. His comments, which really need little interpretation, are translated by his devoted trainer, Lew Bohan."

The *Sentinel* published the interview translation, which ended when the stage manager rapped on the dressing room door.

"You're on in five minutes, sir."

"Barf," Sandy replied.[31]

~

George Hamid booked Sharkey to perform that summer of 1957 at an amphitheater on the former grounds of the New York World's Fair. The water show was to be one performance a night, reserved seating, from July 3 through Labor Day. An orchestra would provide dance music before and after the show. A stage with revolving units and a front pool area would feature diving acts, a water ballet, and Sharkey.

But Hamid ran into union trouble. The musicians' union demanded a twenty-five-piece orchestra; Hamid countered that fifteen pieces were sufficient. The press agents' union wanted two assigned agents; Hamid preferred his own agent. Electricians asked for a 20 percent pay raise; Hamid refused. The scenic-artists guild wanted scenery produced locally with performance royalties; Hamid wanted to employ a scenery shop from Atlantic City. Negotiations ensued. Unions hung tough, perhaps figuring the renowned presenter was bluffing. He wasn't. Days before the open, Hamid canceled the entire show.[32]

Next month, like another falling domino, the Palace gave up on its vaudeville stage shows; much like it had twenty-five years earlier. Once again, vaudeville died a symbolic death at the hands of the Palace, this time for good. The grim outlook only got grimmer.

Interviewed that fall after another drab season of fairs, George Hamid said, "The traditional grandstand revue has seen its day as a leading fair attraction. While variety and circus acts will survive on the fairgrounds as long as there are children, there must be a growing acceptance of television and a willingness to live with it."[33]

Future prospects were bleak. Sharkey was all but retired. Practically speaking, vaudeo, movie palace stage shows, and vaudeville grandstand shows were over. Even gala variety act presentations at sports shows, complete with an emcee and orchestra, entered a period of quiet decline on their way to oblivion.

Several factors converged to hurt Seal College's business model. Small family-run entertainment productions were no match for new corporate theme parks like Disneyland. Suburban shopping malls arrived, providing convenient alternatives to the big-city trade expositions frequented by Seal College. Baby boomers embraced the rock and roll cultural revolution and largely dismissed vaudeville-type entertainment as outdated. And TV became the leisure-time norm, leaving in-person live entertainment in the also-ran category.

Marian Huling—executor of Huling Estate and owner of Seal College—now held a losing hand. She wasted little time calling it quits. Beyond any outstanding commitments and taking incidental bookings to defray expenses, Seal College was finished.

Sharkey did a national telecast that November on *The Paul Winchell Show*. That same month, Sharkey (aided by Sandy) did shows in Texas.

Sharkey did his final turn a month later, in December 1957, on an NBC-TV Christmas special, broadcast out of Rockefeller Center. Details are few, other than it was definitely Sharkey, not Sandy, and it was definitely his last performance. How appropriate that Sharkey go out on top, just a few blocks from the Broadway theater where he had stormed onto the scene seventeen years prior, beheld by a critic who made his visionary opening night statement: "Sharkey? Do you know who Sharkey is? Well, at any rate he is well worth knowing."[34]

We'll Miss You Here

Sandy fulfilled Seal College's remaining obligations. He discretely covered for Sharkey in Boston and Philadelphia, and did shows under his own name in New York and North Carolina. His last known performance was in April 1958, back on *Captain Kangaroo*.[35]

So ended over fifty years of Huling-trained seals, an era that spanned the heyday of circuses and vaudeville, the rise and fall of movie palaces, the advent of talkies, the golden age of radio, two World Wars, the Great

Depression, and the recent meteoric rise of television. Sharkey retired to the halls of Seal College. Billy stayed by his side, comforting him in his final days. No one in the family knows what happened to Sandy.

Word of Sharkey's retirement spread. In some cities it was the first time in almost twenty years that he didn't make an annual tour stop. The omission particularly struck George Grim, a respected foreign correspondent and popular Minneapolis television, radio, and newspaper personality. "What had happened to Sharkey?" he asked.

Grim devoted fourteen paragraphs of his newspaper column to Sharkey's retirement, a poignant reminisce filled with praise. The type of sendoff typically reserved for a retiring sports hero or movie star. "There was no performer, in any medium, who was half the ham," he started. "Year after year, I'd go to the show and see Sharkey. Never bored, never upstaging anybody, always throwing every fiber of his blubber into the performance—he was a wow."

Grim closed with a remembrance and a personal message to the celebrity sea lion. "I'll keep seeing the old boy, toothless and going blind, trying to run through as much of the old act as he could, simulating glee, as life became darker and darker. Hope it's warm in Kingston, today, Sharkey. We'll miss you here."[36]

A month later, on May 14, 1958, Sharkey took his last breath.

Chapter 15

Bygone Days

Seal College for Sale

Sharkey received an obituary in the *Daily Freeman* the day after his death. The Associated Press and United Press released newswires.[1]

Billy buried Sharkey in his backyard and honored him with a memorial marker. A medical building now occupies the property, minus the marker. Billy kept the tooth from Sharkey's operation, since passed down as a Roe family keepsake. Huling Estate ran real estate ads: "A Seal College is now available (without the seals!)."[2] The building reopened as a display store for motor boats, touted as New York's only indoor marina. Many of Mark's props went to Steel Pier, used by others for their own seal acts. Lew salvaged one of Mark's portable water tanks and gave it to his brother in Schenectady to use as a backyard swimming pool, though its new function was short lived. On the evening of June 24, 1960, the Schenectady sky turned an unusual orange, accompanied by high winds. Moments later, a tornado touched down and destroyed the pool.

Lew bartended at The Barn and later at a small bar in Kingston, where he worked his remaining days. Billy acquired six performing Golden Retrievers. He premiered his dog show at The Barn, then took it on the road, if only briefly. Before long, both Billy and Lew were out of show business. The Barn and former Seal College building didn't last much longer. On August 28, 1962, an overweight cement truck collapsed the antiquated steel-truss bridge that spanned the adjacent Esopus Creek. The bridge tumbled thirty feet into the creek. Shortly after, the State of New York seized The Barn and former Seal College properties by eminent domain in order to accommodate a new bridge and area highway improvements. Wrecking crews descended on the area the next spring. Within forty-eight hours, the two buildings that had so uniquely defined Mark Huling's career vanished into a pile of rubble.

I Once Followed Sharkey

Sharkey posthumously endured his share of barbs. Pittsburgh pit musicians recalled him lounging backstage in the men's shower room. "For a fastidious man, this could be galling," a musician said. "Every time Sharkey was in town, one of the musicians purchased an atomizer, filled it with perfume, and fumigated the entire area. Pitmen referred to it as 'Allure, the cure for odeur.' "[3]

In 1962, on the fourteenth anniversary of *The Ed Sullivan Show*, the host received an on-air roasting from Bing Crosby, Lucille Ball, Jerry Lewis, and others. When George Gobel took his turn, he faked-sobbed and thanked Sullivan "for giving American viewers everything from Sharkey the Seal to Henny Youngman."[4]

That same year, NBC invited Soupy Sales to host *The Tonight Show*, following the departure of Jack Paar, who had hosted the show over the previous five years. Most remember Soupy for his children's TV shows that always ended with a pie in somebody's face. Skeptics doubted anyone could fill Paar's shoes, much less Soupy Sales. Soupy reassured the public, "Why should I be afraid to follow Jack Paar? I once followed Sharkey the Seal." One television critic condemned the comment, "a display of reckless bravado."[5] Sharkey and Paar got the last laugh. Soupy's stint as the show's host was a mere blip. After several interim hosts, NBC offered the job that fall to a thirty-six-year-old comedian named Johnny Carson, who hosted the show for the next thirty years.

In 1982, when Radio City Music Hall turned fifty, New York Metropolitan opera star Robert Merrill kicked off the evening's celebration by singing the national anthem, a role he also provided at important Yankee games. He spoke that night of having worked with Sharkey at Radio City Music Hall, a recollection that ended up in an Associated Press newswire and in the *New York Times*. "I followed him five shows a day for four weeks," Merrill said with a smile. "He got $1,200 a week and I got $400. I hated him."[6]

Kitty Carlisle was another who once followed Sharkey. Baby boomers best remember her as a panelist on *To Tell the Truth*, but she started as a singer. In her early career, a gossip columnist noticed her wearing a blemished evening gown. "The bottom of the gown became frayed from being dragged through so much water lately," Carlisle said. "In my last vaudeville appearances, I've followed Sharkey the Seal."[7] She wasn't kidding. She had played the Chicago Theater with Sharkey, Henny Youngman, bandleader Lou Breese, and others. "About the only act that got more applause than Breese was Sharkey the Seal," wrote *Billboard*.[8]

Some forty years later, Carlisle wrote about Sharkey in her autobiography. "I admired him, make no mistake. As a performer he was altogether delightful." She then spoke of his backstage pranks without a hint of jest. "He tried to splash water from his tank all over my evening dresses; and when I was going onstage as he was coming off, he deliberately barked at me and tried to step on my feet."[9] Sharkey apparently took no chances when it came to someone else trying to steal the show.

In the late 1980s, veteran slapstick performer Max Patkin, the Clown Prince of Baseball, enjoyed renewed popularity for having played "himself" in the movie classic, *Bull Durham*. He boasted having worked with personalities such as Jackie Robinson, Groucho Marx, Jack Benny, Pete Rose, Bruce Jenner, Roger Clemens, and Sharkey. "I've met them all," he told one reporter. Reflecting on his long and storied career, Patkin extended but one piece of advice: "If you ever work with a seal act, watch for seal droppings."[10]

Gone but Not Forgotten

A brief mention of those who are gone but not forgotten.

In 1970, Lew Bohan died at age fifty-eight. Personally speaking, I have fond and vivid memories as a young boy of my grandfather Lew coming over for dinner and me going over to his place to visit. Not once did he ever mention anything to me about seals.

In 1997, Billy Roe died at age eighty-two. He worked at Seal College from beginning until end, except for his overseas military service. His gravestone reads, "US Army World War II."

In 2000, Mark Huling's only child, Marjorie Reilly, died at age eighty-five. The only memory I have of my grandmother Marjorie mentioning her father was a comment she had made decades prior, during a rare, fleeting family discussion about his career. She reflectively said something to the effect, "He really did love those seals."

In 2001, one of Mark's great-grandchildren, my brother Darren, died on 9/11 in the terrorist attack on the World Trade Center. Coworkers informed the family that he stayed behind in the South Tower to assist with evacuation procedures. His remains were recovered six months later alongside another civilian and several firefighters.

Except for Marjorie and Darren, all of Mark's familial descendants—his three grandchildren, his three surviving great-grandchildren, and his six great-great grandchildren—are alive at the time of this writing.

∾

References to Sharkey and other Huling seals have occurred every so often in recent times, most notably in the 2015 podcast, "Why Won't They Let Sharkey on the Radio?" When Milton Berle died in 2002, *USA Today* printed his recollection of Sharkey censored from doing his toilet balancing routine. Two years later when Bob Keeshan (Captain Kangaroo) died, NBC aired a tribute that showed footage of Lew and Sandy. NPR later mentioned Sharkey in a piece about his former swim opponent, Olympian Adolph Kiefer. And a New Jersey blog wrote about Steel Pier, bemoaning its change from seaside icon to something less, calling it "the century-old pier where Frank Sinatra got his start, diving horses became stars, and Benny Goodman shared top billing with Sharkey the Seal."[11]

Days of yesteryear never to return, a fitting sentiment to close the story of Mark Huling and Sharkey. And so it goes, as it must, the vibrancy of an era and the best it had to offer, fading away, leaving in its wake the distant stories, images, and lore of days gone by.

Mark Huling and Sharkey. Press photo from the author's collection.

Epilogue

Mark once wrote, "If you have seen Sharkey but once, or countless times, as I have, you will at once understand and share with me my unbounded admiration for this little top-notcher of the show world."[1] And you can bet the feelings were mutual.

Mark and Sharkey were a special show business duo whose success resulted from their unique and deep bond, both on- and offstage. After Mark died, obituaries appeared around the country, including this from the editorial page of the *Herald Tribune*.

> Mark A. Huling was an upstate farm boy who went to the city to be an electrician. Then he met a man who owned some trained seals [and] became one of the nation's greatest trainers of so-called "seals" which are really a species of California sea lion, and the fun he must have had working all his life with these delightfully entertaining creatures was reflected in the perpetual look of abounding good cheer in his face. At his "seal college" at the edge of the Esopus Creek in Kingston, N.Y., Mr. Huling put his animals through basic training and graduate courses that must have entailed infinite patience on both sides and a whole lore of seal wisdom on the part of Mr. Huling. Sharkey was his greatest seal pupil—a natural born "ham" who learned to act, mimic, do acrobatics, juggle and balance, play music, "talk" and retrieve. An estimated 3,000,000 people have seen Sharkey . . . and most of them have had to hold on to their seats as they watched his Huling-taught antics. Sharkey thrived

on applause, and off-stage he demanded constant affection from his trainer. So we do not doubt that this actor-exile from the coastal waters of the Pacific will miss his trainer as much as audiences all over America will miss the genius that produced Sharkey and his animal colleagues and all the fun they were taught to bring to harried human folk.[2]

In the capable hands of Billy Roe, Sharkey lasted six more years, entertaining millions more. Shortly after his career ended, a reporter wrote, "Remember Sharkey the Seal? No single attraction has ever been more popular. Year after year, this sagacious water animal barked its joyous way into [our] hearts. When he appeared, cares were banished and life became a frolic. He gave the gift of laughter."[3] We should all be so lucky to be remembered so fondly.

Mark Huling and Sharkey, Mark's brothers Frank and Ray, Mark's assistants Billy Roe and Lew Bohan, and their many troupes of seals all leave behind a wonderful legacy. From free performances for orphaned children to command performances for British royalty, raising money for charities, selling war bonds, entertaining the president of the United States, countless stage, radio, and TV appearances, and everything in between, they brought laughs, fun, and wonderment to men, women, and children of all ages.

And for that, the world is a better place.

Acknowledgments

On a summer's day in 2015, I received a curious Facebook message from a journalist asking about a trained seal named Sharkey. The journalist turned out to be Matthew Billy, an award-winning podcaster. When his podcast about Sharkey came out, my jaw dropped. Here was this story about my relatives and their trained seals, based in my hometown of Kingston, New York, that I knew nothing about. A research frenzy followed. Within a month I decided to write a book. So it seems only fitting that the first big "thank you" goes to the person responsible for getting it all started: Matthew Billy.

A little more than a year later, I had completed a rough draft. Susan Mary Malone at Malone Editorial Services then helped me better shape the narrative and advised me on how to better convey the story. She also provided two rounds of editorial comments. This book would have never made it to fruition otherwise, and I am grateful to Susan. Thanks also to Jane Friedman, who reviewed my book proposal and offered expert commentary. Beta readers assisted at all stages of development. Of note: Allan and Cheryl Rice offered very useful feedback, as did Ellen Luksberg. Though I didn't join a writers group, I often spoke with Peter Thalmann, who took up writing about the same time I did. Our many discussions about honing our skills were a valuable part of the process.

I owe a huge debt of gratitude to my agent, Jennie Goloboy at Donald Maass Literary Agency. In seeking representation, I was hoping to find someone with an appreciation for historical research and with a sense of humor. Jennie is all that—and more. Her ideas on how to better organize some of the latter chapters were particularly helpful. She was also responsible for arranging the book deal with Excelsior Editions.

Richard Carlin, acquisitions editor at Excelsior Editions, is another to whom I offer my sincere thanks. In addition to being a Grammy-winning writer, a book author, and a seasoned editor, Richard's interest in vaudeville-era entertainment made for a perfect fit. Richard's efforts were key in helping me ready the book for publication, including providing a round of editorial review. Many thanks as well to the rest of the fabulous team at SUNY Press, especially senior marketing manager Kate R. Seburyamo, production editor Jenn Bennett-Genthner, and copyeditor Laura Glenn.

My biggest gratitude goes to my wife, Carol, and to my three daughters, Stephanie, Kimberly, and Nicole. Day after day, week after week, year after year, they patiently listened to my "Sharkey stories." I couldn't have written this book without their loving encouragement. Carol read many versions of draft chapters and developed a knack for pointing out deficiencies while still being supportive.

My father was an incredible resource and deserves a big thanks. Why he never told me any specifics about the seals for the first fifty-four years of my life has become a bit of a running family joke. But he more than made up for it these past five years. It seemed that the more nuanced my questions became, the more he was able to remember. Time and again, he provided vivid details that really brought the story to life. Several other relatives deserve my thanks. I was able to track down a distant cousin, John Huling, who I didn't even know existed prior to my research. John provided information about the Huling family history and shared old pictures and anecdotes about the seals. Two of my aunts—Kathy Setter and Noreen Kahlstorf—shared their memories and helped fill in certain details. One of my uncles, Michael Reilly, told me of his childhood recollections of Sharkey. He also found a treasure trove of pictures, articles, and promotional material left behind to him by his mother, Marjorie; Mark Huling's daughter. I'll never forget the phone call, during which he excitedly told me he had found pictures of Sharkey at Radio City Music Hall; with Lou Costello; and with the Three Stooges.

Last, I would like to acknowledge Mark Huling and Sharkey. Though both predeceased me, I have gotten to know them in ways deep and profound. It is every narrative nonfiction writer's dream to have a project like this fall into their lap. Mark and Sharkey provided a seemingly endless amount of riveting source material that kept me busy for years. I am honored to be the custodian of their story.

Notes and Sources

Researching this project required untold hours of digging. I am thankful to many, including the Town of Upton MA Library Director, Matthew Bachtold, who tracked down several obscure requests, including footage of Ray and Charlie performing their act. I am also grateful to the staff at the University of South Carolina Moving Image Research Collections, who digitized newsreels from their remote storage vault, one of which was suffering from "nitrocellulose decomposition." Luckily, the footage was mostly salvaged and I ended up with three newsreels of Mark Huling with his seals, including a 1920s talkie filmed shortly after that technology became available.

My research involved two trips to archive facilities in New York City. In both cases, the staff was very helpful. My first trip was to the Paley Center for Media, where I viewed television clips of Sharkey; the second was to the Billy Rose Theatre Division of the New York Public Library, where I examined the original *Higher and Higher* finalized manuscript. Many others helped with my research and are identified throughout these notes and in the photo credits and acknowledgments.

I acquired a stockpile of photos and films from various archivists and retailers. In some cases, film records were accessed and footage was digitized. In other cases, original photos had typewritten notes taped on the back with additional key information. Several of these pictures have been included throughout the book.

Sources are detailed herein. All dialogue throughout the book was taken verbatim from annotated sources. References for all quoted material may be found in the pages that follow.

Abbreviations

AP   The Associated Press
MIRC (SC)   Moving Image Research Collections, University of South Carolina
NYPL   The New York Public Library
UP   United Press

Notes to the Preface

1. John Mason Brown, "Sharkey and Jack Haley in 'Higher and Higher,'" *New York Post*, April 5, 1940.

2. Retrieved from *Between the Liner Notes*.

Notes to Chapter 1

1. Captain Webb was Mark's uncle's wife's brother. Webb knew the Huling family. A diary entry from Mark's first cousin Martha Kaiser indicates that Webb's mother had recently died. One may reasonably speculate that the Huling brothers ran into Webb at his mother's services, at which time they were invited to visit his seal-training facility.

2. Mark Huling, *Behind the Scenes with Sharkey, The World's Greatest Seal*, ca. 1945. This sixteen-page unpaginated booklet is hereafter referenced as *Behind the Scenes*. For clarity, Mark's third-person self-references have been adapted to read in the first person.

3. "Captain Huling Tells Story of Seal Training," *Referee* (Sydney, Australia), May 3, 1916, 15.

4. Frank's status as Webb's manager is documented in Tonawanda city directories.

5. "Vaudevilled in Venezuela and Gathered in All the Trouble There Was," *The Sun* (New York), July 14, 1909, 5. This source applies to all accounts and quotes associated with Ray's trip to Venezuela.

6. "Oil City Was Alarmed: Sea Lion Escaped and Finally Traced by a Bloodhound," *Times Herald* (Olean, NY), July 17, 1909, 3.

7. *The Evening News* (North Tonawanda, NY), August 29, 1910, 1.

8. Harpo Marx with Rowland Barber, *Harpo Speaks!* 20th Printing (New York: Limelight Editions, 2017), 100.

9. *Heart of the Tin Man: The Collected Writings of Jack Haley*, Jack Haley, 1978, 5.

10. Mark Huling, *Behind the Scenes*.

11. "Seals and How They Are Trained: 'Kindness Wins' Says Captain Huling," *Daily Herald* (Adelaide, Australia), July 11, 1916, 6.

12. "Kindness Wins," *Daily Herald*.

13. Additional sources for this paragraph include: "Captain Huling's Seals: Their Origin and Training," *Manawatu Times* (New Zealand), February 1, 1916, 8; "The Seal Act at Wirth's: Captain Huling Tells Story of Seal Training," *Referee* (Sydney, Australia), May 3, 1916, 15; "Wirth's Circus," *Independent* (Benalla, Australia), June 30, 1916, 3; "How They Trained California Sea Lions to Hunt U-Boats," *Oregon Sunday Journal* (London: Star Company), May 18, 1919.

14. Fred D. Pfening Jr., "The Final Years: Adam Forepaugh and Sells Bros. Big United Shows," *Bandwagon: The Journal of the Circus Historical Society*, July–August 1995, 5. The article misidentifies Frank Huling as "Fred Huling," a carryover from 1910 newspaper notices that similarly misidentify him, perhaps due to a typo in that year's circus program.

15. "Trained Seals with Circus," *Hopkinsville Kentuckian*, September 5, 1912, 3.

16. Wynn, "Ringling Brothers: Chicago, April 10," *Variety*, April 13, 1912, 22.

17. Harry F. Rose, "Big Ringling Circus Acclaimed in Chicago," *The Player: The Official Organ of the White Rats Actors' Union of America and the Associated Actresses of America*, April 11, 1913, 3–4.

18. The Huling seal training facility was on Plank Road, which is now Washington Avenue. The facility was actually in the Town of Ulster, not the City of Kingston. (The Esopus Creek demarcates the two municipalities.) Regardless, the Hulings, the press, and just about everyone other than the Town of Ulster tax assessor referred to the facility as being in Kingston.

19. "How They Trained California Sea Lions to Hunt U-Boats," *Oregon Sunday Journal* (London: Star Company), May 18, 1919.

20. "Entertainments," *Australasian* (Melbourne, Australia), November 13, 1915, 26; "Huling's Wonderful Seals," *Examiner* (Launceston, Tasmania), December 10, 1915, 3.

21. *New Zealand Herald*, March 22, 1916, 14; *Sydney Morning Herald*, April 25, 1916.

22. *Sydney Morning Herald*, May 16, 1916.

23. "A Circus Honeymoon," *Sydney Daily Telegraph*, April 24, 1917, 8; "Business as Usual," *The Bulletin: The National Australian Newspaper*, April 26, 1917, 8.

24. Mark Valentine St Leon, "Circus & Nation: A Critical Inquiry into Circus in Its Australian Setting, 1847–2006, from the Perspective of Society, Enterprise and Culture," (PhD doctorate thesis, University of Sydney, 2006), 128. I am grateful to Mark for providing me a picture of the bass drum used that year in Frank Huling's sea lion band.

25. Trav S.D. (Stewart Travis), *No Applause—Just Throw Money: The Book That Made Vaudeville Famous* (New York: Faber & Faber, 2005), 4.

26. "Present Bill Best So Far at Orpheum," *Altoona Tribune* (PA), September 14, 1916, 3.

27. "Palace," *Variety*, April 19, 1923, 22.

28. *Vitaphone Music Hall*, short film, Vitaphone Broadway Brevities, reel no. 1868, May 1935. This source contains Ray's setup dialogue and Charlie's hula dance.

29. Pat Dwyer, "Charlie the Seal Lends a Submarine Basso to a Grand Old Sea Ballad: Has a Tutor, but Tuning His Voice to the Scale Was His Own Idea," *Chicago Daily Tribune*, February 11, 1934, 61.

30. Dwyer, 61.

31. Dwyer, 61.

32. "Keaton in Knockabout Farce," *Buffalo Evening News*, April 7, 1931.

33. "Enormous Show at Hippodrome," *New York Times*, September 3, 1911.

34. Trav S.D., 202

35. *Pittsburgh Courier*, November 12, 1927, A8.

36. Trav S.D., 10.

37. "Ray Huling and his Dancing Seal: reviewed Monday matinee, October 26, at the Hippodrome," *Billboard*, November 7, 1925, 19.

38. "Florence Mills Dancing with Seal," October 28, 1925, retrieved from *Getty Images*. Florence Mills biographer Bill Egan notes that although Florence was associated with the Charleston, she did not credit herself with inventing the dance. Bill was kind enough to send me a copy of the Hippodrome program that featured Florence and Charlie, which was a thrill to examine and provided additional research possibilities.

39. *Billboard*, June 12, 1926, 112; "Doing Things Nature Never Imagined Man or Animal Could Do," *Pittsburgh Press* (American Weekly), April 11, 1926, 106; "The Circus Is Coming," *Pittsburgh Press*, May 16, 1926, 108.

40. Ibee, "Ringling-B. & B. Circus, *Variety*, April 23, 1927, 57.

41. Many thanks to London's Victoria and Albert Museum for unearthing and digitizing this poster as part of my research.

42. The souvenir program had Mark leading the performers' bios, declaring that his first animal act was with an elephant, a lion, and a dog, and that his father was "an elephant trainer descended from a famous 17th century magician" who died a tragic death when an elephant "threw him under the feet of the other elephants," none of which is even remotely true. Fake news, circus style, ca. 1927.

43. *Bertram Mills Circus: At Olympia, London, Recorded during Actual Performance*, Edison Bell Records, A.5639, 78-rpm recording. All associated dialogue was transcribed verbatim. The use of a music stand and glasses is documented in

a review of Mark's assistant in another performance: "The Seal Steals the Show," *St. Louis Post-Dispatch*, March 8, 1942, 37.

44. "College For Seals," *Popular Mechanics*, January 1940, 85.

45. Richard Thomas, *John Ringling: Circus Magnate and Art Patron* (New York: Pageant, 1960), 202.

46. Thomas, 202.

47. "Elephants Galore with Sells-Floto," *Waco News Tribune*, September 7, 1929, 14.

48. Fredrick Denver Pfening III, *The American Circus and the Great Depression: 1929–1939* (master's thesis, Ohio State University, 1976), 7.

49. "Valuable Seals Die from Smoke," *Saugerties Telegraph*, December 20, 1929, 3. The article refers to Mark by his less frequently used nickname, "Max." For clarity, I substituted the more familiar "Mark."

50. Interview with my aunt, Kathy Setter; Marjorie's daughter.

51. "13 Seals Owned by Huling Bros. Die in Fire," *Daily Freeman*, December 14, 1929, 1; "Valuable Seals Die from Smoke," *Saugerties Telegraph*, December 20, 1929, 3; "Hulings Lose Thirteen Seals," *Billboard*, December 21, 1929, 83.

52. Mark Huling, *Behind the Scenes*.

Notes to Chapter 2

1. John Margolies, Nina Garfinkel, Maria Reidelbach, *Miniature Golf* (New York: Abbeville Press, 1987).

2. Roland Gray, "Tom Thumb Golf," *Modern Mechanics and Inventions*, January 1931, 76.

3. *Daily Freeman*, August 8, 1930.

4. "Local Golf Champion Makes Record Score on New Golf Course," *New Paltz Independent and Times*, December 5, 1930, 1.

5. *Daily Freeman*, September 28, 1932, 8.

6. David Levine, "Legs Diamond: A History of Kingston, NY's Most Notorious Gangster," August 2011, retrieved from *Hudson Valley Magazine*.

7. Descriptions and accounts of the club were drawn from: " 'Huling's Barn' Will Be Opened July 4," *Daily Freeman*, July 1, 1933, 8; "Huling's Barn Opened to Capacity Crowd July 4," *Daily Freeman*, July 6, 1933; "Pabst Blue Ribbon beer now on draught at . . . Huling's Barn," *Daily Freeman*, August 16, 1933. Adding to the record is my father's recollection of the club, specifically, the red upright piano and the custom mahogany bar.

8. Arthur Unger, "Los Angeles," *Variety*, March 10, 1926, 52.

9. "Pantages," *Minneapolis Star*, October 29, 1927, 24.

10. "Trained Seal Owns Home of His Own with Tiled Bath," *Minneapolis Star Tribune*, January 3, 1932, 37.

11. Pat Dwyer, "Charlie the Seal Lends a Submarine Basso to a Grand Old Sea Ballad: Has a Tutor, but Tuning His Voice to the Scale Was His Own Idea," *Chicago Daily Tribune*, February 11, 1934, 61.

12. Sarah Addington, "Never Again Will the Two-a-Day Addict Witness Big-Time Vaudeville," *The Stage*, July 1932, 19.

13. "Hollywood Premiere of 'I'm No Angel,' 1933," retrieved from *USC Digital Libraries*.

14. Charles Beardsley, *Hollywood's Master Showman: The Legendary Sid Grauman* (New York: Cornwall Books, 1983), 123.

15. Taken from an original typewritten press release taped to the back of Ray and Charlie's "Sea Going Taxi" press photo.

16. George Ross, "Broadway: Piscatorial News," *Pittsburgh Press*, April 7, 1938.

17. Ross, "Piscatorial News."

18. "Ray G. Huling Dies at 62, Retired Seal Trainer," *Hartford Courant* (AP), June 7, 1949, 4.

19. "Huling Seal Dies in New York City," *Daily Freeman*, April 13, 1938, 2.

20. Mark Huling, *Behind the Scenes*.

21. "Lady in Ice Casket at Huling's Barn," *Daily Freeman*, October 22, 1938, 2. The *Freeman* ran stories practically every day for the duration of the stunt.

22. Frank J. Taylor, "Barker's Are Best," *Collier's Weekly*, July 19, 1941, 52–53.

23. "Starting a Seal Toward Stardom," *San Bernardino Sun*, January 22, 1939, 23.

24. "Barker's Are Best." Dialogue between Danny Pico, Al Newton, and George McGuire was taken verbatim from this article, which also mentions Mark Huling, Frank Buck, and the New York World's Fair.

25. A December 27, 1938, *Los Angeles Times* article titled "Santa Cruz Island Seals Sent by Train to New York" mentions seals tagged to Mark Huling and the upcoming New York World's Fair.

26. Mark Huling, *Behind the Scenes*.

27. Lon Kappill, "Seal Trainer's Iron Pants Discourage Biting Pupils," *Democrat and Chronicle* (Rochester, NY), August 11, 1940, 11.

28. John Webster, "Sportscope: Perennial Hit in Phila. Sportsmen's Show is Sharkey, Alumnus of Seal College," *Philadelphia Enquirer*, January 26, 1950, 26.

29. Mark Huling, *Behind the Scenes*.

30. "Sharkey, the Seal, Best in Business," *Daily Times* (Philadelphia, PA), (International News Service), February 11, 1944, 9.

Notes to Chapter 3

1. Prosper Buranelli, "Tour of the Oddest 'Hows' of a Circus: The Soul of a Seal," *Detroit Free Press*, June 8, 1919, 77. The interviewer refers to Mark as Professor Huling, which was his nickname with Ringling Brothers. He also went by Captain Huling, as did his brother Frank.

2. "Seal Act Is Special Attraction at Huling's," *Daily Freeman*, January 5, 1939, 9.

3. My father told me the story about the chair, which his father, Lew Bohan, had good-naturedly admitted to him many years ago.

4. "Trainer Tells How He Prepares Seals for Circus Acts," *Burlington Free Press* (VT), April 26, 1926, 5.

5. "Lure of Old Life Prompts Huling to Return Again: Former Owner of Dance Resort Joins with Walter Jennier; Will Train Sea Mammals for the Show World," *Daily Freeman*, March 4, 1939.

6. Edwin P. Norwood, *The Circus Menagerie* (New York: Doubleday, Doran & Company, 1929), 82–83.

7. Mark Huling, "Submarine Show-Offs Behave Like Children," *Baltimore Sun*, October 29, 1944, M1.

8. "Former Buffalonians Present Train Sea Lion Act at Circus: Mark and Frank Huling Visit Mother at Home in Tonawanda—Brothers Have Appeared All Over World With Animals," *Buffalo Evening News*, May 31, 1922; "Trainer Tells How He Prepares," *Burlington Free Press*; "Waterlooan Feeds Little Lions and Big Hippopotami in Ringling Circus Cages," *The Courier* (Waterloo, Iowa), May 7, 1927, 8.

9. Mark's typical seal greeting was taken from archival film footage.

10. "Lure of Old Life," *Daily Freeman*.

11. "Hotelmen Discuss Bringing Business Here During Fair," *Daily Freeman*, January 17, 1939, 1, 3.

12. My description of Seal College was drawn from several articles and pictures just before, during, and just after the grand opening, further benefiting from discussions with my father, who informed me of specifics regarding the building layout and little-known facts such as the location of the coal stove and pool pumps.

13. "Seal College Is Dedicated Sunday," *Daily Freeman*, March 6, 1939, 2.

14. "Children Enjoy Seals at Work: About 150 Children Watch Training of Animals," *Daily Freeman*, March 30, 1939, 2.

15. *Seals—Outtakes. Training*, Fox Movietone News, story 2-98, filmed on location at Kingston, New York, performed by Mark Huling and Major, March 11, 1929, MIRC (SC). Given that the April 1939 Fox Movietone News newsreel

is unavailable, the accounts and dialogue from this earlier shoot were substitued as a reasonable proxy.

16. Mark Huling, *Behind the Scenes*.

17. "Seals Will Appear in Sound Films," *Daily Freeman*, April 11, 1939, 6; "Star Seal of Circus Is a College Graduate," *Daily Mail* (MD), July 21, 1939, 2.

18. Alfred Eriss, "Trained Seals," *Life*, July 17, 1939, 74–75; *Popular Science*, "Education of a Trained Seal," August 1939, 98–99.

19. A July 14, 1939, *Daily Freeman* article titled "Kingston Hits Limelight Again" noted that "Jumbo [was] featured in both Popular Mechanics and Life."

20. Mark Huling, *Behind the Scenes*.

21. "Record Crowds at Library Fair," *Daily Freeman*, July 20, 1939, 18.

22. Famous Seal at Woodstock Fair: Sharkey, Barrymore of Seal to Return for Fair," *Daily Freeman*, July 17, 1940, 8. The article spoke of Sharkey as being at the Woodstock Library Fair the year before.

23. "Backstage Life of Sharkey, the Seal," *New York Herald Tribune*, June 9, 1940.

24. "Backstage Life," *Herald Tribune*.

25. Frederick Nolan, *Lorenz Hart: A Poet on Broadway* (New York: Oxford University Press, 1994), 269.

26. Trav S.D., 251.

27. Mack Nomburg, "Circus Animals 'On the Air,'" *New York Telegram and Evening Mail*, April 11, 1924, 11.

28. "Picturing Broadcast Activities," *Radio Digest*, September 1927, 6.

29. "Seal Tells of 'Hula' Over Microphone," *Democrat and Chronicle* (Rochester, NY), April 10, 1927, 78; "Not Music, but It Is a Novelty," *Corsicana Daily Sun* (TX), April 11, 1927.

30. "Gilda Gray and Seal Vie for Honors before Microphone," *Santa Anna Register*, April 4, 1929, 8.

31. "Seal Act Makes Excellent Number: Singing and Dancing Are Easy Work for Charlie," *Oregon Statesman*, June 8, 1930, 8.

32. "Trained Seal to Broadcast Tonight," *Evening Journal* (Wilmington, DE), March 5, 1929, 12.

33. "Gilda Gray and Seal," *Santa Anna Register*.

34. In a March 7, 1929, article titled "Huling and His Seal Heard over the Radio," the *Daily Freeman* reported that "Charlie's bass and tenor tones accompanied by music from an orchestra [were] coming in clear."

35. *New York Daily News*, March 6, 1929.

36. "Talk of Temperamental Artists! Charlie Beats Them All," *Public Opinion* (Newspaper Enterprise Association), March 22, 1929.

37. Darrel V. Martin, *Pittsburgh-Post Gazette*, August 29, 1939, 8.

38. "Huling's Seals Will Be Feature Fair Attraction," *Daily Freeman*, August 21, 1939, 12.

39. "Ulster County Fair Holds Its Own in Face of Modern Progress," *Daily Freeman*, August 26, 1939, 5.

40. *Daily Freeman* (AP), August 26, 1939, 1.

41. Mark Huling, "Submarine Show-Offs Behave Like Children," *Baltimore Sun*, October 29, 1944, M1.

42. Huling, "Submarine Show-Offs," *Baltimore Sun*.

43. Huling, "Submarine Show-Offs," *Baltimore Sun*.

44. *Brooklyn Daily Eagle*, September 19, 1939, 7.

Notes to Chapter 4

1. Frederick Nolan, *Lorenz Hart: A Poet on Broadway* (New York: Oxford University Press, 1994), 268.

2. Joshua Logan, *Josh: My Up and Down, In and Out Life* (New York: Delacorte Press, 1976), 146.

3. Meryle Secrest, *Somewhere for Me: A Biography of Richard Rodgers* (New York: Applause, 2001), 210.

4. Nolan, 269.

5. Elinor Hughes, "Dick Rodgers Reveals Secret of How to Write a Musical Comedy," *Boston Herald*, March 27, 1940.

6. Ken Bloom and Frank Vlastnik, *Broadway Musicals: The 101 Greatest Shows of All Time* (New York: Black Dog and Leventhal, 2004), 258.

7. Dorothy Kilgallen, "Backstage on Broadway," *Wilkes-Barre Record*, March 2, 1940, 4.

8. Dan Dietz, *The Complete Book of 1940s Broadway Musicals* (Lanham, MD: Rowman & Littlefield, 2015), 14.

9. Backstage Life of Sharkey, the Seal," *New York Herald Tribune*, June 9, 1940.

10. F. R. Johnson, "Last Night's Play: 'Higher and Higher' Hits High Mark," *New Haven Journal-Courier*, March 8, 1940.

11. J. A. Kneubuhl and H. M. Holtzmann, *Yale Daily News*, March 8, 1940.

12. John Chapman, "Mainly about Manhattan," *Daily News*, January 26, 1940, 26.

13. *New York Daily News*, January 3, 1940.

14. "Sallie the Seal," *Harper's Bazaar*, March 1, 1940, 72–73.

15. "Minnie the Seal Got Her Notice," *Brooklyn Daily Eagle*, March 10, 1940, 38. The headline even misnamed the already-misnamed seal. Minnie was the servant in *Higher and Higher*, played by Marta Eggerth. Also note: the more

accepted spelling of "Eggerth" includes the silent *h*, which I have included here and elsewhere for consistency. The press often omitted the *h* during this period.

16. "Higher and Higher," *Boston Variety*, March 13, 1940; Dorothy Kilgallen, "Finds Some Romance in Gotham Shows," *Miami News*, April 21, 1940, 15.

17. "The Stage: Shubert Theater: 'Higher and Higher,'" *Boston Daily Globe*, March 13, 1940, 13.

18. "As Lampy Sees Them: Theater: Higher and Higher," *Harvard Lampoon*, March 27, 1940, 58.

19. Elinor Hughes, "Dick Rodgers Reveals Secret of How to Write a Musical Comedy," *Boston Herald*, March 27, 1940.

20. "Sharkey, Shanghaied Seal, Found in Harvard Bathtub," *Boston Daily Globe*, March 18, 1940, 1.

21. Dorothy Kilgallen, "The 'Higher and Higher' Gazette," *News-Journal* (Mansfield Ohio), March 21, 1940, 20.

22. David Arnold, "Roots of a Quarrel: Vellucci, Lampoon Wage Feud over a Tree," *Boston Globe*, April 6, 1991.

23. "Sharkey, Shanghaied Seal," *Boston Globe*.

24. "Sharkey, Shanghaied Seal," *Boston Globe*.

25. Elinor Hughes, *Passing through to Broadway* (Boston: Waverly House, 1948), 76.

26. "Trained Seal Goes To Harvard," *Asbury Park Press* (NJ), (Central Press), March 19, 1940, 2; "Sharkey, Shanghaied Seal, Found in Harvard Bathtub," *Boston Daily Globe*, March 18, 1940, 1; "Seal Found in Harvard Bathtub," *New York Times* (UP), March 19, 1940; "Coppers Undercover Kidnapped Actress in Dorm Bathtub: Trick Seal, Star of Musical Show Disappears from Shubert in Publicity Stunt," *Harvard Crimson*, March 18, 1940.

27. "As Lampy Sees Them," the *Harvard Lampoon*, February 21, 1940, 30.

28. "University Authorities Balk at Oomph Girl Premiere at U.T.: Officers Afraid of Bad Publicity From Ann Sheridan–Lampoon Reconciliation," *Harvard Crimson*, March 18, 1940.

29. I am indebted to my father for bringing to my attention this little-known personality trait of Mark Huling.

30. Joshua Logan, *Josh: My Up and Down, In and Out Life* (New York: Delacorte Press, 1976), 146.

31. Burns Mantle, "'Higher and Higher' Adds a Trained Seal to the Ensemble," *New York Daily News*, April 5, 1940.

32. Logan, 147.

33. Richard Watts Jr., "Servants at Play," *New York Herald Tribune*, April 5, 1940; John Mason Brown, "Sharkey and Jack Haley in 'Higher and Higher,'" *New York Post*, April 5, 1940.

34. "The Theater: New Musical in Manhattan," *Time*, April 15, 1940, 76.

35. Gladys Hurlbut, *Higher and Higher* finalized manuscript, Performing Arts Research Collection, Billy Rose Theater Division, NYPL, call number NCOF+, 1940. All *Higher and Higher* stage dialogue presented herein was transcribed verbatim from this finalized manuscript.

36. John Chapman, "Mainly About Manhattan," *New York Daily News*, April 27, 1940.

37. Brooks Atkinson, "Jack Haley Renews Broadway Acquaintances In Rodgers and Hart's 'Higher and Higher'" *New York Times*, April 5, 1940; Backstage Life of Sharkey, the Seal," *New York Herald Tribune*, June 9, 1940; Walcott Gibbs, "A Seal, Miss Barrymore, and the Bard," *New Yorker*, April 13, 1940, 28; "Backstage Life," *Herald Tribune*.

38. John Franchey, "Hungarian Rhapsody," *Hollywood*, December 1942, 61.

39. Logan, 146–47.

40. Logan, 147.

41. Logan, 147.

Notes to Chapter 5

1. John Mason Brown, "Sharkey and Jack Haley in 'Higher and Higher,'" *New York Post*, April 5, 1940.

2. Richard Watts Jr., "Servants at Play," *New York Herald Tribune*, April 5, 1940; Sidney B. Whipple, "Higher and Higher Brings Bright New Personalities," *New York World–Telegram*, April 5, 1940; Richard Lockridge, Walter Winchell, "'Higher and Higher' Tops in Musical Joy," *Daily Mirror*, April 5, 1940, 28; "'Higher and Higher,' Rodgers and Hart Musical, Opens at the Shubert," *New York Sun*, April 5, 1940.

3. The "owlish and prickly" description of Gibbs is from Jon Michaud, "Q. & A.: Thomas Vinciguerra on Wolcott Gibbs," the *New Yorker*, October 10, 2011. The follow-up quote is from Walcott Gibbs, "A Seal, Miss Barrymore, and the Bard," the *New Yorker*, April 13, 1940, 28.

4. "Goings On about Town," the *New Yorker*, April 13, 1940; "Goings On about Town," the *New Yorker*, April 20, 1940.

5. "Theater Week," *Newsweek*, April 15, 1940, 33; "The Theater: New Musical in Manhattan," *Time*, April 15, 1940, 76; Jack Gaver, "Up and Down Broadway," *Bradford Evening Star* (UP), April 16, 1940, 3; Mark Barron, "Bergman, Hutton Win Praise for Season's Best Playing In Shows Along Broadway," *Akron Beacon Journal*, April 21, 1940, 51; Alice Hughes, "Seal Named 'Sharkey' Is Hit of New Comedy," *Akron Beacon Journal*, April 17, 1940, 10.

6. *The Brooklyn Citizen*, April 10, 1940, 14.

7. The *Higher and Higher* press agent recalled that *News of The Week* was at the luncheon in a November 11, 1951, *Boston Globe* article titled "Press Agent's Recollection: How Sharkey the Seal Inspired 'Never Say Never.'"

8. The quote is from the *Sand Springs Sun* (OK), May 23, 1940, 4. The description is based on a captioned photo of Sharkey (at the restaurant) that ran in the April 28, 1940, *Detroit Free Press*.

9. *Sand Springs Sun*, May 23, 1940; *Detroit Free Press*, April 28, 1940. The two Sardi's pictures are from an article "Seal Guest of Honor at Lunch," *Pix* (Associated Newspapers Limited, Sydney, N.S.W.), July 27, 1940, National Library of Australia, nla.obj-449711907.

10. George Ross, "Broadway," *Pittsburgh Press*, April 15, 1940, 13.

11. Vincent Sardi Jr., "The Voice of Broadway," *Lebanon Daily News*, August 8, 1970, 17.

12. Al Hirschfeld caricature caption, "Marta Eggert, Jack Haley and Sharkey," *New York Herald Tribune*, April 14, 1940.

13. Dorothy Kilgallen, "The Voice of Broadway," *News Journal*, April 18, 1940.

14. *The Era* (London), August 19, 1914, 12.

15. "Caught in Germany," *Sydney Times* (Australia), April 16, 1916, 9. Accounts and quotes associated with Frank's escape from Germany are all from this source.

16. Luree Miller's July 3, 1994, *Washington Post* review of *Like Hidden Fire*, a true story about a World War I secret plot, speaks of "a group of German agents, making their way from Berlin to Constantinople, posed as a traveling circus, hiding their wireless aerials in their tent poles."

17. Frank's departure from Manchester, England, was determined from the ship manifest, retrieved from *ancestry.com*.

18. "How They Trained California Sea Lions to Hunt U-Boats," *Oregon Sunday Journal* (London: Star Company), May 18, 1919. Accounts and quotes associated with training sea lions to hunt U-boats are from this source unless otherwise noted.

19. "How They Trained," (London: Star Company).

20. Admiral of the Fleet Viscount Jellicoe of Scapa, *The Crisis of the Naval War* (London: Cassell, 1920), note 14, vii, 1; Winston S. Churchill, *The World Crisis 1916–1918*, part II (London: Thornton Butterworth, 1927), 350–51.

21. "How They Trained" (London: Star Company).

22. Jay Pierrepont Moffat, diary entry, July 5, 1934.

23. The act description is based on two photos from State Archives: Freiburg, Germany: *Berlin: Scala—Ray Huling mit Seehund Charly*, picture #010171 and #010172. The archive incorrectly lists the date as January 1935. Ray and Charlie were in Boston during January 1935. A *Variety* January 1936 notice correctly lists their monthlong appearance at the Scala.

24. Maegie Koreen, *Claire Waldoff: Die Königin des Humors* (the Queen of Humor) (Gelsenkirchen, Germany: Chanson-Café, 2014), 210. The book mentions *Ray Huling mit der Robbe Charlie* as being at the January 8, 1936, show, when Goebbels stormed backstage.

25. The departure date and port, arrival date and port, and transport vessel were obtained from the ship manifest, retrieved from *ancestry.com*.

26. George Tucker, "Man about Manhattan," *Reno Gazette-Journal*, April 30, 1940, 4; Dorothy Kilgallen, "Backstage at Broadway: Highlights at 'Higher and Higher,'" *News-Journal* (OH), May 6, 1940, 4.

27. Kilgallen, "Backstage at Broadway," 4.

28. Kilgallen, "Backstage at Broadway," 4.

29. "Sharkey's Just a Sissy," *New York Daily News*, April 9, 1940. The article mistakenly identifies Sharkey's understudy as Freddy, not Teddy.

30. Samuel Marx and Jan Clayton, *Rodgers & Hart: Bewitched, Bothered, and Bedevilled* (London: W. H. Allen, 1977), 233–34.

31. Sharkey's Rockefeller Center antics were reported in an Associated Press article and photograph, "Sharkey Took a Dip," *Hartford Courant* (AP), May 26, 1940, 57.

32. Sharkey and Haley relaxing at the World's Fair is documented in two press photos: "Carrier Corp.—Jack Haley and son at thermometer, Higher and higher reaches Sharkey the Trained Seal at the Carrier Igloo at the World's Fair in New York"; "Carrier Corp.—Jack Haley and son with seal." Both photos can be found in the Manuscripts and Archives Division, NYPL Digital Collections.

33. Billy Spilo and Frank Jans, "New York: Night and Day," *Wakefield News* (MI), May 17, 1940, 8.

34. Robert Francis, "Candid Close-Ups," *Brooklyn Daily Eagle*, May 26, 1940, 48; "Dog's Will Do That," *Brooklyn Daily Eagle*, April 25, 1940, 6.

35. Billy Spilo and Frank Jans, "New York: Night and Day," *Wakefield News* (MI), May 31, 1940, 8.

36. "Well, Maybe," *New York Daily News*, May 16, 1940.

37. Mark Huling, *Behind the Scenes*.

38. *Tide of Advertising and Marketing*, 1940.

39. Lon Kapill, "Seal Trainer's Iron Pants Discourage Biting Pupils," *Democrat and Chronicle* (Rochester, NY), (AP), August 11, 1940, 11.

40. Kapill, 11.

41. *Journal Herald* (Dayton, OH), June 5, 1940, 10.

42. "Backstage Life of Sharkey, the Seal," *New York Herald Tribune*, June 9, 1940.

43. "The Theater: Annual Report," *Time*, June 10, 1940.

44. "Inside Stuff—Legit," *Variety*, July 3, 1940, 44.

45. Marjan Kiepura, email message to the author.

46. Alice Hughes, "Girl about Town," *Akron Beacon Journal*, June 23, 1940, 21.

47. Marguerite Hurter, "Woodstock," *Daily Freeman*, July 24, 1940, 11.

48. Mark Barron, "Sharkey the Seal Ready for Return to the Theater," *St. Louis Post Dispatch* (AP), July 28, 1940, 50.

49. Brooks Atkinson, "Broadway Is Preparing for Another Theater Season: Haley Is Back in Town," *New York Times*, August 11, 1940.

50. Meryle Secrest, *Somewhere for Me: A Biography of Richard Rodgers* (New York: Applause, 2001), 210.

51. Richard Rodgers, *Musical Stages: An Autobiography* (New York: Random House, 1975), 195.

Notes to Chapter 6

1. Gurney Williams, "Seals Go to College," *Scribner's Commentator*, December 1940, 65–68.

2. Lucius Beebe, "Uncouth Prospects Wished on Izzy and He Lands Commission," *Oakland Tribune*, September 1, 1941, 17; Dorothy Kilgallen, "The Voice of Broadway," *News-Journal* (Mansfield, OH), July 12, 1940, 11; Dorothy Kilgallen, "The Voice of Broadway," *Wilkes-Barre Record*, November 4, 1940, 9.

3. Lon Kapill, "Seal Trainer's Iron Pants Discourage Biting Pupils," *Democrat and Chronicle* (Rochester, NY), (AP), August 11, 1940, 11; Mark Huling, *Behind the Scenes*.

4. Acts Vie for Honors at Majestic Theater," *The Morning Call* (Allentown, PA), September 21, 1940, 6; Jiminy, "Checked and Double-Checked," *Courier-Post* (Camden, NJ), November 23, 1940, 24.

5. "Irving Stage Show Is Fast," the *Wilkes-Barre Record*, January 31, 1941, 13.

6. "Seals Will Appear in Sound Films," *Daily Freeman*, April 11, 1939, 6; Dale Harrison, "Dale Harrison's New York: Seals for Students," *Iowa City Press-Citizen*, February 5, 1940, 4; "Irving Stage Show Is Fast," the *Wilkes-Barre Record*, January 31, 1941, 13.

7. In 1884, Captain Adams taught a seal to balance a ball on his nose and presented the novelty at museums, the first of its kind in the US. He later befriended Captain Webb and gave him his first seals, putting Webb on the path of becoming a renowned seal trainer and eventual mentor of the Huling brothers. Though Webb is often credited as being the first US seal trainer, Adams made the first strides.

8. "Fair Diver's Manager Did Her Washing; Wife Burned It Up, She Says: Odiva Hales Mrs. Adams to Court, Exhibiting Charred Bathing Suits," *Evening

World (New York), August 29, 1912, 16. This reference also applies to the other quotes in this story.

9. Mark Huling, *Behind the Scenes*.

10. Mark Huling, *Behind the Scenes*.

11. Robert Morrison, "Sharkey, the Seal, Out to Steal Popularity from Sportsmen's Show Dogs," *St. Louis Post-Dispatch*, February 9, 1941, 35.

12. James Toomey, "Plaudits of Crowd at Sports Show Cause Sea Lions to Go 'High Hat,'" *St. Louis Star and Times*, February 10, 1941, 13.

13. John Bowman, "Chicago Sportsmen's Show Furnishes Tops in Amusement," *The Pantagraph* (Bloomington, IL), February 25, 1941, 10.

14. Mark Huling, *Behind the Scenes*.

15. "How They Trained California Sea Lions to Hunt U-Boats," *Oregon Sunday Journal* (London: Star Company), May 18, 1919.

16. "New Things at the Big Circus," *Pittsburgh Press* (American Weekly), April 19, 1925, 106.

17. Mark Huling, *Behind the Scenes*.

18. "Trained Seal Is Off the Air, His Sole Tune Is ASCAP," *New York Times* (AP), March 7, 1941, 11.

19. "Sharkey Is Out of Job," *Clarion-Ledger* (Jackson, MI), March 7, 1941, 13; "Woe Is Musical Seal; He's All-Out ASCAP," *Detroit Free Press*, March 7, 1941, 1; "Sharkey Stumped by ASCAP Tune," *Democrat and Chronicle* (Rochester, NY), March 7, 1941, 6; "ASCAP Puts End to Radio Career Of Trained Seal," *Kokomo Tribune* (IN), March 7, 1941, 13.

20. Mary E. Bostwick, "Last Page Lyric," *Indianapolis Star*, March 8, 1941, 26.

21. *Minneapolis Star*, April 14, 1941, 8; Virginia Safford, *Minneapolis Star*, April 11, 1941, 23.

22. "Wirth & Hamid, Inc., New York City, Presents Huling's Sea Lions," *Premium List, North Carolina State Fair, Raleigh, October 13th–18th 1930, Third Annual Exposition*, 46. Though Hamid had booked acts for Steel Pier and would later own Steel Pier, he operated the nearby Million Dollar Pier during the summer of 1941.

23. Nelson Johnson, *Boardwalk Empire: The Birth, High Times, and Corruption of Atlantic City*, 6th printing, paperback edition (Medford, NJ: Plexus, 2014), 90; Steve Liebowitz, *Steel Pier: Showplace of the Nation* (West Creek, NJ: Down the Shore, 2009), 76.

24. Steve Liebowitz, *Steel Pier* (Charleston: Arcadia, 2016), 78.

25. Mark's banter with his seals was transcribed verbatim from film footage, though not from Steel Pier. His banter was consistent over the years, making these quotes more than a reasonable proxy for his constant dialogue with the seals.

26. "He Flies through the Air," Newspaper Enterprise Association via the Steel Pier Publicity Department, August 7, 1941.

27. "AC Trade Best in 12 Seasons: Clean-Up Gets Part of Credit," *Billboard*, August 9, 1941, 50.

28. "Seals Perform Amazing Stunts, Atlantic City, N.J.," Universal Newsreels, Release 1, July 23, 1941. Archival records misidentify Sharkey as Sparky.

29. *Along Broadway*, Movietone News, reel #445; Herb, "Roxy, N.Y.," *Variety*, October 1, 1041, 28.

30. Dick Fortune, "'Thirteen' No Jinx to Variety Barkers Who Have Packed House for Banquet," *Pittsburgh Press*, November 3, 1941, 8.

31. Mark Huling, *Behind the Scenes*; Paul D. Greene, "Quiz Seal Kid," *Pageant*, June 1945, 57.

32. *Scribner's Commentator*, January 1942, 1.

Notes to Chapter 7

1. *Post-Crescent* (Appleton, WI), October 13, 1931, 6. Special thanks to Ms. Annichen Skaren—a Norwegian film restorer, historian, archivist, and leading authority on Al St. John—who further informed me of Al St. John's love of animals and that he got along well with Charlie.

2. "All Sealed Up," retrieved from *Park Circus Group Limited*.

3. Graham Webb, *Encyclopedia of American Short Films 1926–1959* (Jefferson, NC: McFarland, 2020), 36.

4. "Music Hall (Vitaphone)," *Motion Picture Daily*, August 9, 1935, 8.

5. "Shirley Wants Ray Huling and Charlie," *Daily Freeman*, July 11, 1935, 6.

6. "Sharkey Rival for Abbott, Costello," *Oakland Tribune*, November 22, 1942, 32; Irene Thirer, "Screen News and Views," *New York Post*, May 21, 1942, 45.

7. The January 24, 1942 issue of *Billboard* reported that "Sharkey the Seal has been set in the new Abbott and Costello film, *Pardon My Sarong* (Universal)."

8. "College for Seals," *Popular Mechanics*, January 1940, 142A.

9. John Franchey, "Hungarian Rhapsody," *Hollywood*, December 1942, 61.

10. *Pardon My Sarong*, film, Universal Studios, 1942. The movie dialogue presented herein was transcribed verbatim. Some modern sources inexplicably credit a "Charley the Seal" with having played the part of Sharkey, which is patently incorrect. Ray Huling's seal Charlie was dead, and the other famous "Charlie" of Tiebor-family seal-training fame had nothing to do with *Pardon My Sarong*, as may be readily determined from the article "Charlie the Seal," *Life*, July 27, 1942. Neither of those seals, by the way, was spelled "Charley." Most relevant to the movie-seal identity are the testaments from Mark Huling, who, of course, indicated the seal was Sharkey.

11. Bob Furmanek and Ron Palumbo, *Abbott and Costello in Hollywood* (New York: Perigee, 1991), 85; "Pardon My Sarong (1942)," reviewed June 30, 2018, retrieved from *Talk about Cinema*.

12. Scott Allen Nollen, *Abbott and Costello on the Home Front: A Critical Study of the Wartime Films* (Jefferson, NC: McFarland, 2009), 63.

13. Mark Huling, *Behind the Scenes*.

14. *Abbott & Costello: Bloopers and Outtakes*. All dialogue associated with the blooper story was transcribed verbatim from this source.

15. "Pardon My Sarong," *Motion Picture Reviews: September and October 1942*, The Women's University Club, Los Angeles Branch; American Association of University Women, 7.

16. "Movie Seal Is Scene-Stealer," *Havre Daily News* (MT), November 6, 1942, 3.

17. "Hollywood," *New York Daily News*, May 26, 1942.

18. *History of World War II, Volume 2: Global War* (New York: Marshall Cavendish, 2005), 590.

19. The accounts and descriptions of the Hartford bond rally were culled from several sources: "Seal to Purchase $500 Bond Today," *Hartford Courant*, September 4, 1942, 1; "Seal Holds Cash for $500 Bond," *Hartford Courant*, September 5, 1942, 4; "Den One Cub Scouts Do Good Turn Serving in Our Heroes Bond Drive," *Hartford Courant*, September 13, 1942, 68; Allen M. Widen, "Review: Hartford Conn. (reviewed Saturday evening, Sept. 5)," *Billboard*, September 14, 1942, 14. The *Courant* did not mention Sharkey by name but the *Billboard* article makes clear that it was indeed Sharkey at the bond rally.

20. "Acts Well-Arranged at K. of C. Ball," *Daily Freeman*, October 13, 1942, 9.

21. "Yule Prologue on Olympia Bill," *Miami News*, December 23, 1942, 9.

22. Les Simonds, "On the Night Side: It's Worth Going into Debt for a Gander at Sharkey, the Seal," *Miami News*, December 24, 1942, 7.

23. Simonds, 7; "Yule Prologue on Olympia Bill," *Miami News*, December 23, 1942, 9; "Movie Best Bets," *Miami News*, December 26, 1942, 7.

24. *Training of Performing Seals*, film, Fox Movietone News, shot on location, Kingston, New York, February 25, 1927, has Mark Huling and his seals frolicking in the snow. The family cat and an unidentified little girl on a sled, each makes a cameo. MIRC (SC). Though from an earlier time, this footage reasonably approximates Seal College.

Notes to Chapter 8

1. Michelle Pautz, *The Decline in Average Weekly Cinema Attendance: 1930–2000*, (2002), *Political Science Faculty Publications*, no. 25, retrieved from

eCommons, University of Dayton; "Frequency of going to the movies in the U.S. 2017," www.statista.com.

2. The description of Sharkey's B-29 imitation is based on footage of him doing the bit. Mark's dialogue was transcribed verbatim from footage and news accounts. The description of the Hitler and Tojo imitations are based on a compendium of news accounts.

3. "Return of an Old Grad," *Parade*, June 18, 1944, 22.

4. Joe Sommerlad, "Bugs Bunny at 80: How Warner Brothers' wisecracking 'wabbit' whipped Hermann Goring at the height of the Second World War," *The Independent*, April 30, 2018.

5. "Seal Act Steals Show at Keith's," *Indianapolis Star*, May 14, 1943, 8.

6. John DeRosier, "A Look Back at Atlantic City's Deep Ties to World War II," May 29, 2017, retrieved from *Press of Atlantic City*.

7. Morris Orodenker, "Personal Appearances: Promoting the Personal Appearance," *Billboard: Music Yearbook 1943*, 126.

8. Paul D. Greene, "Quiz Kid Seal," *Pageant*, June 1945, 56.

9. Based on footage from "'Sharkey the Seal' at the Steel Pier," newsreel, Fox Movietone News, story 49-960, shot on location, Atlantic City, New Jersey, performed by Sharkey and Mark Huling, August 15, 1943, MIRC (SC).

10. Bob Francis, "State, New York," *Billboard*, November 13, 1943, 22.

11. *New York Daily News*, November 25, 1943; "Follow-up Night Club Review," *Billboard*, December 25, 1943, 39.

12. Robert Sietsema, "10 Postcards of Long-Forgotten NYC Restaurants," the *Village Voice*, March 22, 2011.

13. Richard Rodgers, *Musical Stages: An Autobiography* (New York: Random House, 1975), 79.

14. Abel Green, "Billy Rose's Music Hall Is Another Phase of Show Biz," *Variety*, June 26, 1934; A. J. Liebling, "Master of His Own House," *New York World Telegram*, May 19, 1934.

15. Herbert G. Goldman, *Fanny Brice: The Original Funny Girl* (New York: Oxford University Press, 1993), 160.

16. Billy Rose's Music Hall Has Premiere Tonight," *Brooklyn Daily Eagle*, June 21, 1934, 21.

17. Art Arthur, "Reverting to Type: Roving Reporter Reviews Rumbles," *Brooklyn Daily Eagle*, June 25, 1934, 12.

18. Abel Green, "Billy Rose's Music Hall," *Variety*, June 26, 1934.

19. Burns Mantle, "Restaurant with Vaudeville Now the Rage in N.Y.," *Chicago Tribune*, July 1, 1934.

20. Abel Green, "Billy Rose's Music Hall," *Variety*, June 26, 1934.

21. My description of Ray and Charlie performing at Billy Rose's Music Hall relied on several sources, including a September 1934 press photo of them onstage at the hall during an actual performance. The picture showed Ray accompanied by Charlie on a ladder doing his double-stick balancing stunt; part of their "Sea Going Taxi" routine. Fortunately, Vitaphone documented "Sea Going Taxi" in their 1935 short film *Vitaphone Music Hall* from which the dialogue presented herein was transcribed verbatim. My description of Charlie's burlesque outfit was based on a press photo that had recently run in the *Chicago Tribune*. With regard to the Billy Rose's Music Hall naked lady wooden clackers, at last check, one is still available for purchase on eBay.

22. Abel Green, "Billy Rose's Music Hall," *Variety*, June 26, 1934.

23. Abel Green, "Billy Rose's Music Hall," *Variety*, June 26, 1934.

24. Abel Green, "Billy Rose's Music Hall," *Variety*, June 26, 1934.

25. Art Arthur, "Reverting to Type: Roving Reporter Reviews Rumbles," *Brooklyn Daily Eagle*, September 8, 1934, 4.

26. Radio interview with Billy Rose, "Long John Nebel Show," August 5, 1965.

27. James Aswell, "My New York," *Pottstown Mercury* (PA), June 28, 1934, 4; Lucius Beebe, "From Sticks to Broadway Riot," *Oakland Tribune*, July 29, 1934; Paul Harrison, "In New York," *Pittsburgh Press*, June 26, 1934, 16; Walter Winchell, "On Broadway," *Waco News-Tribune*, July 18, 1934, 4; Mark Barron, "A New Yorker at Large," *Wilkes-Barre Record*, August 1, 1934, 8.

28. Ross Firestone, *Swing, Swing, Swing: The Life and Times of Benny Goodman* (New York: W. W. Norton, 1994, paperback edition), 96–97.

29. "Benny Goodman and Orch. Big Success on Broadway," *DownBeat*, September 1934.

30. Firestone, 97.

31. The *New Yorker*, "The Great Seal," August 25, 1934.

32. Art Arthur, "Reverting to Type: Billy Rose—but with Thorns," *Brooklyn Daily Eagle*, September 5, 1934, 10.

33. *Downbeat*, June 1935, 4.

34. Leonard Feather, "Lionel Remembers Benny," *Los Angeles Times*, September 14, 1986.

35. "Apollo, N.Y." *Variety*, March 24, 1943, 24.

36. Some sources erroneously claim that Blakey joined Henderson's band prior to 1943, but Walter Allen's meticulously documented 650-page book *Hendersonia: The Music of Fletcher Henderson and His Musicians* has Blakey first appearing with the band at the Apollo, coinciding with Sharkey's appearance. Jazz discographers Steve Schwartz and Michael Fitzgerald further corroborate this on their website, *Art Blakey Chronology (and the Jazz Messengers)*.

37. "Sharkey, the Seal, Best in Business," *Philadelphia Daily Times* (International News Service), February 11, 1944, 9.

38. Robert Merrill with Sandford Dody, *Once More from the Beginning* (New York: Macmillan, 1965), 110.

39. Cosmos-Sileo Photography, picture S-260-19. My father explained to me how the cigarette apparatus worked. The dialogue beginning the story was taken verbatim from footage of Mark inserting an apparatus into Sharkey's mouth, though not the cigarette apparatus.

40. *New York Sun*, February 16, 1944, 31.

41. "Music Hall, N.Y.," *Variety*, February 9, 1944, 49; Paul Ross, "Music Hall," *Billboard*, February 12, 1944, 27.

42. "Charlie," *Art Digest*, April 15, 1932, 13.

Notes to Chapter 9

1. Retrieved from *Franklin D. Roosevelt: Day by Day*.

2. Donna L. Halper, PhD, email message to the author. Donna is the author of *Invisible Stars: A Social History of Women in American Broadcasting*.

3. Everett C. Watkins, "Hoosiers and Others on the Washington Front," *Indianapolis Star*, March 8, 1944, 5.

4. "Big Names Abound at Press Banquet," *Charlotte Observer* (AP), March 6, 1944.

5. *Wilkes-Barre Times Leader, the Evening News*, March 15, 1944, 11.

6. "Big Names Abound," AP.

7. Raymond Strait, *Bob Hope: A Tribute* (New York: Pinnacle Books, 2003), 229. Strait misstates the correspondents' dinner date as March 11, 1944, instead of the correct date, March 4, 1944.

8. Bill Henry, "By the Way," *Los Angeles Times*, March 8, 1944, 13; Everett C. Watkins, "Hoosiers and Others on the Washington Front," *Indianapolis Star*, March 8, 1944, 5.

9. *The Morning Call* (Allentown, PA), March 6, 1944, 11.

10. "The Talk of the Town: Parlor Animals," the *New Yorker*, December 31, 1932, 7.

11. Mark Huling, *Behind the Scenes*.

12. Sharkey Will Take Money for Red Cross," *Daily Freeman*, March 3, 1945, 1.

13. Mark Huling, *Behind the Scenes*.

14. The Leo the MGM Lion stage cue was transcribed from film footage of an actual performance. An April 14, 1946, article in the *Des Moines Register* documented Sharkey's practice of fending off "another driver (who) gives Huling

the squeeze." Sharkey's feature in *Parade* magazine pictured him in the front seat of a Seal College truck with his head out the window.

15. "Return of an Old Grad," *Parade*, June 18, 1944, 22–24.

16. My father recalls that Mark would occasionally take out a violin from its worn case and break into a tune.

17. *Nebraska State Journal*, September 26, 1944, 1; *Kane Republic* (PA), October 13, 1945, 5.

18. "Providence Shrine Has Large Crowds; Advance Sale Big," *Billboard*, July 8, 1944, 39.

19. Paul D. Greene, "Quiz Kid Seal," *Pageant*, June 1945, 57. The quote was in reference to Sharkey at Steel Pier during the prior summer.

20. Bill Smith, "Loew's State, New York (Reviewed Thursday Afternoon, September 14th)," *Billboard*, September 23, 1944, 33.

21. Ed Sullivan, "Little Old New York: 42nd Street," *New York Daily News*, September 21, 1944, 13.

22. Mark Huling, "Sea Lions—Show-Offs of the Animal World," *Reader's Digest*, December 1944, 71.

23. "Kahler Sportsmen Clicks Despite ODT," *Billboard*, March 31, 1945, 49.

24. "No Pink Lemonade, but Circus with Real Clowns at Keith's," *Indianapolis Star*, March 23, 1945, 15; "Keith's Indpls.," *Variety*, March 28, 1945, 28.

25. Bud Grant and Jim Burton, *I Did It My Way: A Remarkable Journey to the Hall of Fame* (Chicago: Triumph Books, 2013), 51.

26. Mark Huling, *Behind the Scenes*.

27. Stoney McGlynn, "Sharkey Chief Tonic on Sports Show Laugh Menu," *Milwaukee Sentinel*, April 16, 1945, 11.

28. "Caught Off Guard," *Milwaukee Sentinel*, April 23, 1945.

Notes to Chapter 10

1. "Circus Continued Until Saturday," Montclair Times (NJ), June 28, 1945, 7.

2. Walter Winchell, "Broadway and Elsewhere," *Indianapolis Star*, June 5, 1946, 15.

3. Three photos document Sharkey's appearance in Fort Worth: "Victory Bond Sale . . . Sharkey, trained seal, taking Victory Bond blanks from Red Cross Motor Corps girls. . . . at the Fort Worth National Bank," November 20, 1945; "Victory Loan Sales. . . . trained seal," November 21, 1945; and "Victory Loan Sales: 'Sharkey,' the trained seal delivering bond," November 21, 1945. University of Texas at Arlington Libraries Special Collections, *Fort Worth Star-Telegram* Collection.

In addition, several articles ran, including: "Sharkey the Seal Sells $11,000 in Victory Bonds," *Fort Worth Star-Telegram*, November 20, 1945, 9.

4. "Sharkey, Circus Seal, Out to Beat Bond Sales Record," *Fort Worth Star-Telegram*, November 21, 1945, 3; "Trained Seal Shows Off Some New Tricks to Increase His Bond Sales: Sharkey Struts His Stuff, *Fort Worth Star-Telegram*, November 21, 1945, 5.

5. "Sharkey to Resume His Bond Selling," *Fort Worth Star-Telegram*, November 23, 1945, 3.

6. "Radio City Music Hall, New York," *Billboard*, December 15, 1945, 33.

7. "Radio City Music Hall," *Billboard*, December 16, 1950, 42; "Music Hall, N.Y."

8. *Variety*, December 13, 1950, 71.

9. The September 8, 1943 article "Bath Fair" in the *Mansfield Advertiser* reported that "Jumbo, a trained seal . . . with the Ringling Spangles Show . . . recently closed a successful engagement at Madison Square Garden, New York."

10. As part of preparing this book, my father relayed to me recollections of my grandfather's sparse wartime talk over the years, including that my grandfather Lew had marched through Normandy and had fought in the Battle of the Bulge. It was the first time I had been told.

11. "24,854 See Sport Show Exhibit in Two Days," *Indianapolis News*, March 1, 1948, 40.

12. Lew was apparently not keen on paperwork. Some sixty years later, his son (my father) retired and contacted Social Security only to find a Bohunicki on file but no Bohan. With an administrative chuckle, the agency reconciled the issue noting it was a common occurrence of the era. The saga, however, continues; more recently, authorities informed my eighty-year-old father he would need to officially change his name from Bohunicki to Bohan in order to acquire the identification needed to board an airplane.

13. *Council Bluffs Nonpareil* (IA), April 20, 1946, 5.

14. Daniel Lionel, "New Equipment Galore at Sportsmen's Show, "*Brooklyn Daily Eagle*," February 18, 1946, 12.

15. "Sports Show to Provide Preview of Vacation Fun," *Des Moines Register*, April 7, 1946, 20.

16. "Jumbo, the Sea Lion, Gets Ulcers; Models to Blame," *Oelwein Register* (IA), (UP), July 4, 1947, 7.

17. "AC Roars thru Record Fourth," *Billboard*, July 20, 1946, 83.

18. *Jumbo Steals the Show*, film, Paramount News, no. 92, July 11, 1946.

19. *Meet Jumbo!*, film, Universal Newsreel, no. 519, July 11, 1946.

20. Will Davidson, "New Year to Bring New Talent," *Chicago Sunday Tribune*, December 29, 1946, 112; "Sharkey Eats a Few Words," *Des Moines Register*, March 23, 1947, 84.

21. "The Grapevine," *Star Tribune* (Minneapolis), March 22, 1951, 17; Gordon Gammack, "See Here!" *Des Moines Tribune*, April 16, 1946, 8.

22. Mark Huling, *Behind the Scenes*.

23. Rose, "Music Hall, N.Y." *Variety*, May 28, 1947, 19.

24. "Fashion Fair in 70G Talent Splurge," *Variety*, June 6, 1947, 1; Lois Fegan, "Dress Parade," *Harrisburg Telegraph*, June 12, 1947, 9; Arthur Pollock, "Playthings: Now Women's Clothes Are Dramatized," *Brooklyn Daily Eagle*, June 15, 1947, 27; Jumbo, the Sea Lion, Gets Ulcers; Models to Blame," *Oelwein Register* (IA), (UP), July 4, 1947, 7.

25. The *Pittsburgh Press* reported that "The seals play tennis, using their fins for racquets" in a May 5, 1912, articled titled "Wonderful Trained Seals: Capt. Huling Exhibits Two Troupes."

26. I am indebted to Billy Roe's grandson Dave Fletcher for providing the cartoon.

27. "Nat'l Sports Show Draws Huge Crowds," *Billboard*, February 28, 1948, 50.

28. Michael Beschloss, "A Maverick Golfer's Struggles in a More Conformist Time," *New York Times*, August 4, 2014.

29. *First Annual National Sportsmen's Show of Canada: Souvenir Program*, April 1947, 3. The program cites 1947 as the inaugural year of Canada's National Sportsmen's Show, but the generally accepted inaugural year is now considered to be 1948, the first year the show was held in Ottawa.

30. Martha Kaiser, a close first cousin of Mark, kept a diary that repeatedly references the Huling family, including Frank, Mark, and Ray. The reminisces described herein are drawn from her diary. The Huling 300-acre farm ran along Stony Point Road, from Staley Road to White Haven Road. The Huling's built the first log cabin on the island interior. The *State of New York, Department of Agriculture, Fourteenth Annual Report of the Commissioner of Agriculture, For the Year 1906* lists Mark as the manager of the Grand Island Creamery; the reported output of the creamery was 44,085 pounds of butter.

31. Lloyd Noteboom, "Fair Actor Paid Off in Fish: Sharkey the Seal Is Sea Lion," *Argus-Leader* (SD), August 20, 1952, 21.

32. "Varied Program," *Ottawa Journal*, April 5, 1948, 18.

33. Noteboom, 21.

34. "Ottawa Sports Show Attracts 3,000 Persons on Opening Day," *Ottawa Journal*, April 6, 1948, 3; "New Sportsmen's Show Limelights Sharkey," *Ottawa*

Citizen, April 6, 1948; "Sharkey Still Top Number at Sportsmen's Show," *Ottawa Citizen*, April 7, 1948.

35. "Governor General Shakes Hands with 'Sharkey,'" *Ottawa Citizen*, April 7, 1948. 30.

36. "Sportsmen's Show Attendance Reaches New High," *Ottawa Journal*, April 9, 1948, 21. The $32 million amount raised was retrieved from *Toronto Sportsmen's Show*.

37. *Journal News* (White Plains, NY), February 22, 1949, 6.

Notes to Chapter 11

1. "Television as Show-Biz Hero," *Variety*, March 3, 1948, 1; Joe Cohen, "Vaude's 'Comeback' Via Video," *Variety*, May 26, 1948, 43; "Vaudeville Is Back," *Variety*, May 19, 1948, 26–27.

2. "Milton Berle," *People*, May 5, 1989.

3. Dave Fletcher, retrieved from the Facebook page, "I'm From Kingston."

4. "Tele Follow-Up," *Variety*, July 28, 1948, 28.

5. Milton Berle, *Milton Berle, An Autobiography with Haskel Frankel* (New York: Delacorte Press, 1974), 280.

6. Robert Pandillo, *America's First Network TV Censor: The Work of NBC's Stockton Helffrich* (Carbondale, IL: Southern Illinois University Press, 2010), paperback edition, 172.

7. "Sing in a New Day," *The Admiral Broadway Revue*, April 29, 1949. All dialogue presented herein was transcribed verbatim from a digitized kinescope.

8. Robert D. McFadden, "Imogene Coca, 92, Is Dead; a Partner in One of TV's Most Successful Comedy Teams," *New York Times*, June 3, 2001.

9. *Toast of the Town*, November 27, 1949. All dialogue presented herein was transcribed verbatim from a digitized kinescope.

10. This circa 1950 quote is commonly attributed to Bob Hope, but is also sometimes attributed to Larry Gelbart.

11. Richard Zoglin, *Hope: Entertainer of the Century* (New York: Simon & Schuster, 2015).

12. *The Colgate Comedy Hour*, November 26, 1950. All dialogue presented herein was transcribed verbatim from a digitized kinescope

13. Hope's intended mention of Sharkey at the end of his line was cutoff and is difficult to decipher. He may have said *Charlie*, perhaps a slip in reference to Ray Huling's seal. It's hard to say. I stuck with *Sharkey* for narrative flow.

14. A November 25, 1950, article in the *Daily Freeman* noted that "Mark Huling's trained seal, Sharkey is scheduled on two television shows next week. He'll appear on Bob Hope's TV show Sunday at 8 p.m. over WNBT and again

next Wednesday 8 p.m. on Arthur Godfrey's video program over WCBS." A corresponding TV listing in the *St. Louis Post-Dispatch* read: "Arthur Godfrey; guests Larry Ramos and Sharkey the Seal (CBS)."

15. Luc Sante's book, *Folk Photography: The American Real-photo Postcard, 1905–1930*, has a postcard of Mark onstage with a seal band, circa 1910, the earliest-known picture of Mark working with seals, one of whom is playing a banjo.

16. In the book *I Remember Balanchine*, Jacques d'Amboise recalled Harpo appearing on this television Christmas special.

17. Peg Leg Bates and Sharkey routinely appeared on the same bill in theaters, at fairs, and on television, including on *The Ed Sullivan Show*. Peg Leg had coincidently just opened a country club just south of Seal College, the largest black-owned resort in the country. He ran the resort for thirty-five years, until 1987.

18. Jack Gould, "'No. 1 Yuletide Square' Houses Striking Christmas Production by Leonidoff—Bows on N.B.C.," *New York Times*, December 26, 1952; "No. 1 Yuletide Square," *Variety*, December 31, 1952, 25.

Notes to Chapter 12

1. "Mammoth Broadway Show at Reading," *Republican and Herald* (Pottsville, PA), September 3, 1948, 3.

2. "Record Crowd at Evening Grandstand Performance at 'Ex,'" *Ottawa Journal*, August 26, 1948, 17.

3. "Theater: Jungle to Garden," *Time*, April 18, 1938.

4. Dave Boone, "Dave Boone Says," *Post-Standard* (Syracuse, NY), November 5, 1948, 1. The Philadelphia Phillies that year finished 25½ games behind the first-place Boston Braves.

5. "The Great Seal," the *New Yorker*, August 25, 1934, 12.

6. "Charlie Proves He's No Gallant, Trained Seal Refuses to Lose Swimming Race to Girls," *Los Angeles Times*, June 28, 1930.

7. "Charlie Proves," *Los Angeles Times*.

8. "Two Champions" (Larry "Buster" Crabbe and Charlie), Paramount Pictures press release, 1932.

9. "The Great Seal," 12.

10. "Sports Show Continues Through This Weekend," *Arlington Heights Herald* (IL), February 25, 1949, 15.

11. "Maid against Mammal" *Life*, March 28, 1949, 139–40.

12. In an August 13, 2008, NPR piece titled "The Swimming Legend You Never Heard Of," Frank Deford noted that "The seal made $900 a week, Kiefer $600. But that was big money then. It allowed Kiefer, he says, to, No. 1: develop new products for his company."

13. Author interview with Adolph Kiefer, December 4, 2016.

14. "Sharkey to Be 'Sunset' Attraction," *Daily Freeman*, April 26, 1949, 5.

15. "Seal Level," *Variety*, May 25, 1949, 36.

16. "New Love Interest Grips Sharkey, Steel Pier's Trained Seal," *Morning News* (Wilmington, DE), July 22, 1949, 11.

17. "Amusement Business Hall of Fame, *Amusement Business* (*Billboard*), November 1994, 8.

18. Jean Libman Block, "He Takes Broadway to the Farmers," *Coronet*, February 1949, 130.

19. "Sharkey the Seal Featured Star of State Fair Vaudeville Bill," *Post-Standard* (Syracuse, NY), August 15, 1949, 8.

20. "95th Anniversary of the Great Allentown Fair Opens Monday Night," *Morning Call* (Allentown, PA), September 17, 1949, 13.

21. "95th Anniversary," 13.

22. "Gold Rush Revue of 1949 Combined with Vaudeville Thrill Fair First-Nighters," *Morning Call* (Allentown, PA), September 20, 1949, 5.

23. Dialogue for the teddy bear bit was transcribed verbatim from the Sullivan show a month before; a reasonable proxy given the consistency of the routine over the years and the fact that the Palace gig came shortly after the Sullivan show.

24. "College for Seals," *Popular Mechanics*, January 1940.

25. Bill Smith, "Vaudeville Reviews: Palace, New York," *Billboard*, December 31, 1949, 34.

26. "Star Show Slated for Dimes Ball: Social Event to Be Held Saturday Night in Port Ewen," *Daily Freeman*, January 28, 1949, 13.

27. Jack Conner, "Thrilled by Seal: Dog Owner Johnny 'Sees' Sports Show," *Minneapolis Star*, April 19, 1949, 27.

28. Martyn Vickers (as told to Bill Becher), "World's greatest flyfisher also played baseball," retrieved from *ESPN*; Jack Gartside (as told to Bill Becher), "World's greatest flyfisher also played baseball," retrieved from *ESPN*. The Bob Ryan quote is from a panel discussion on Ted Williams, "The Immortal Life of Ted Williams," Kennedy Center Library, December 8, 2013, retrieved from *John F. Kennedy Presidential Library and Museum*.

29. "Outdoors Show Four-Star Click: Williams, Sharkey on Display," *Brooklyn Daily Eagle*, February 19, 1950, 24.

30. Ted Reeve, "Sporting Extras," *Ottawa Citizen*, June 18, 1953, 27.

31. Hank Sayers, "An Interview with a Sea Lion: Even Sharkey Admits He's Good," *Milwaukee Sentinel*, April 26, 1950, 9.

32. Fred Young, "Sportsmen's Show Lures Thousands," *Los Angeles Times*, April 7, 1950, 57; "Jumbo Wows 'Em in Seal Routine," *Los Angeles Times*, April 9, 1950, 51.

33. Al Wolf, "Sportraits," *Los Angeles Times*, April 7, 1950.

34. Interview with my father.

35. "Wins Seal of Approval," *Power Wagon: The Motor Truck Journal*, April 1950, 27.

36. *U.S. News and World Report*, August 11, 1950, 57. Huling-trained seals had previously appeared in full-page magazine ads: A picture of Big Nep ran in the 1925 Ringling Brothers souvenir magazine opposite a page that had a penciled likeness of him balanced on a sphere that bore the insignia of a cosmetics company whose slogan was "Beauté Fraîcheur" (beauty freshness). Not the first thing that comes to mind when thinking of a sea lion, but there he was, Big Nep on a sphere, balancing an oversized jar of Crème Elcaya, an elixir that was "dainty exquisite nongreasy," guaranteed to make one's face "velvet fresh and glowing," it being "A Perfect Balance for a Perfect Complexion." Years later, New York's largest independent radio station used Sharkey in an ad titled "Balance Holds the Audience," comparing "Sharkey [who] holds his audience spellbound with his amazing balancing feats" to their skill at balancing "two great metropolitan New York markets": Italian-speaking programming listened to by 520,000 radio homes during the day, followed by mainstream programming at night.

37. "Dodds Sees Fast Finish in North N.Y.," *Billboard*, August 19, 1950, 68.

38. "Palace, N.Y." *Variety*, November 10, 1950, 54.

39. *Psychology in Action* author Joseph Clawson wrote of Mark's method of teaching a seal to balance a ball, describing Mark as "outstanding in the strange field of seal training." *The People's Psychology: Psychology's Path to Personality* author Fred M. Gregg, PhD, compared children's penchant for showing off to that of seals, Sharkey in particular, whose picture occupies a full page of his textbook. On January 25, 1951, Mrs. Alton U. Farnsworth presented her paper on animal intelligence, *Sharkey*, to a gathering in Upstate New York.

40. "Not on the Program," *Citizen Register* (Ossining, NY), March 28, 1950, 8.

41. My father told me about his being in a car (as a child) as Mark floored it down Route 9W on the way from Kingston to Schenectady, while others in the car yelled and screamed. My father also told me about the trip to Bangor, Maine, at which he was the grandson present. My uncle, Michael Reilly, filled me in on the "when I get old" quote, which he heard from his father, whom Mark had often told. Mark's proclivity for younger women ran in the family, at least among his sibling seal trainers. Frank's wife Rosie was eighteen years younger than Frank and Ray's wife Jane was sixteen years younger than Ray. Neither, of course, can hold a candle to Mark, whose second wife, Marian, was thirty-five years his junior.

42. Phil Willon, "Sharkey, a Sharp Seal, Balances Most Anything (He Should Try Budget), *Press and Sun-Bulletin* (Binghamton, NY), December 29, 1949, 3.

43. Todd R. Robeck, Justine K. O'Brien, Daniel K. Odell, *Encyclopedia of Marine Mammals: Captive Breeding*, 2nd ed. (Amsterdam: Academic Press, 2008), 178.

44. Edwin P. Norwood, *The Circus Menagerie* (New York: Doubleday, Doran & Company, 1929), 76.

45. Edwin P. Norwood, *The Circus Menagerie, Chapter VIII: The Baby Sea Lion* (New York: Doubleday, Doran & Company, 1929), 75–83. The book has an entire chapter on Mark Huling and Monty. All dialogue associated with the baby sea lion story was taken verbatim from this source. Monty was reportedly the first known celebrity sea lion to be born in captivity. Monty also provided the first known sea-lion paternity dispute. Exactly why this happened is unclear, other than to speculate that the brothers engaged in some playful opportunism with the press to promote the male star sea lion of the moment: Mark initially told the *Daily Freeman* that Major was the father, as did Frank in an interview with the *Montreal Gazette*. But shortly after, Ray told an Ohio reporter that Charlie was the father, adding that Charlie had never seen his son due to his touring schedule. Mark later told Edwin Norwood that Big Nep was the father, in what was, by far, the most detailed recounting of the story. And so, as best be told, Monty's father was neither Major nor Charlie, but rather, Big Nep.

46. Dr. David S. Shields, McClintock Professor, University of South Carolina, retrieved from *Broadway Photographs: Harry Alton Atwell*.

47. "13 Seals Owned by Huling Bros. Die in Fire," *Daily Freeman*, December 14, 1929, 1.

48. *Seals—Outtakes. Training*, film, Fox Movietone News, story 2-98, filmed on location at Kingston, New York, performed by Mark Huling and Monty, March 11, 1929, MIRC (SC). All dialogue from Monty's telephone routine was transcribed verbatim from this footage.

49. *Mark Huling Presents Stars of the Sea: Graduates From Seal College*, ca. 1949. This four-page brochure is hereafter referenced as *Stars of the Sea*. Captain McGuire, by then in his mid-90s, had supplied Sandy. McGuire deserves a special spot in the history of exhibited seals. He shipped over 3,000 during his career; some say 5,000. In 1946 alone, he sent 100 seals to Europe to help rebuild zoos decimated by World War II. He stayed in the business until his very last days. McGuire died in 1955 at age 102.

50. Mark Huling, *Stars of the Sea*.

51. Sandy the Seal Steals Akron Sportsmen's Show," *Akron Beacon Journal*, April 12, 1951, 44; Paul Ackerman, "Palace, New York," *Billboard*, June 16, 1951, 32.

52. Mark Huling, *Stars of the Sea*.

Notes to Chapter 13

1. "Sharkey Pulls a Garbo When Out of Spotlight," *Milwaukee Sentinel*, April 12, 1951, 21.
2. "Arena Gets Cake for First Birthday," *Milwaukee Sentinel*, April 10, 1951.
3. Charles R. Douglas, "$2,500,000 in Lawsuits Still Pending Decade after Seeding of Clouds in Area," *Daily Freeman*, March 19, 1960, 1. Douglas's retrospective thirteen-part series on the rainmaker ran in the *Daily Freeman* throughout March and April 1960. Unless otherwise noted, the quotes and accounts used in the rainmaker story have been taken from this series.
4. "Two Die in Flood, Hundreds Leave Ulster Homes; High Water Ravages National Area," *Daily Freeman*, March 31, 1951, 1. "Storm Damage in County Runs High, Streams Recede; Deaths Remain at Two," *Daily Freeman*, April 2, 1951, 1.
5. Charles Payne (photographer), Bill Warner (pilot), *New York Daily News*, April 1, 1951.
6. "Huling and Four Others Sue New York City," *Daily Freeman* (AP), June 29, 1951, 1. The reservoir had caused previous trouble, ironically, due to water deprivation. The Hulings filed for damages in 1920, shortly after construction of the reservoir, claiming that diversion of Esopus Creek waters was injurious because they had purchased the property to use those waters for their seals.
7. "Kingston Group Sues for Damages by Rains," *New York Times*, June 30, 1951; "Huling and Four Others Sue," *Daily Freeman* (AP), June 29, 1951.
8. H. I. Phillips, "Once Over: All Out with Your Adapters," *Evening Review* (Liverpool, OH), June 25, 1951, 20.
9. "Elaborate Show Set for Barn's Reopening Today," *Daily Freeman*, October 11, 1951, 31.
10. "Show Stars Mourn Death of Huling, Trainer of Seals," *Daily Freeman*, October 24, 1951, 1; "Mark Huling," *New York Times*, October 24, 1951; "Noted Seal Trainer Dies at Kingston," *Niagara Falls Gazette*, October 26, 1951; Mark A. Huling, *Variety*, October 31, 1951, 63; "'Seal College' Operator Dies," *Oneonta Star* (AP), October 24, 1951, 1; Mark Huling Gone," *Fitchburg Sentinel* (MA), November 6, 1951, 8.
11. Irv Kupcinet, *Chicago Sun-Times*, November 8, 1951.
12. Descriptions of Sharkey doing his arguing-with-the-orchestra-leader routine are based on a filmed snippet of the routine and a mass of newspaper articles.
13. Norman Weiser, "Chicago, Chicago," *Billboard*, November 17, 1951, 47.
14. Claudia Cassidy, "On the Aisle," *Chicago Tribune*, November 12, 1951.
15. "Fellow Singing Artists," *Indiana Gazette* (International Soundphoto), November 20, 1951, 14.

16. Shirlee Emmons, *Tristanissimo: The Authorized Biography of Heroic Tenor Lauritz Melchior* (New York: Schirmer Books, 1990), 279.

17. Betty Smith, *Journey to Valhalla: The Lauritz Melchior Story* (United States: Universal Sales & Marketing, 1993), 399.

18. Jack Garver, "Judy Garland Ends Triumphant Vaudeville Run: Leaves N.Y. for Hollywood," *The Independent* (Long Island), February 25, 1952, 24.

19. "Baltimore Hip: Back to Vaude," *Billboard*, December 15, 1951, 13.

20. Harold Kaese, "What's in a Name! Williams, Thorpe Play Sweeter Turnstile Turn than Celtics or Bruins," *Boston Globe*, January 25, 1952, 8.

21. Sandy (as told to Hank Sayrs), "Seal Gets 'Flip' at Sports Show," *Milwaukee Sentinel*, February 20, 1952, 14.

22. "Our Show Policy," Canadian National Sportsmen's Show promotional brochure, March 14–22, 1952.

23. "Thorpe Eying Medals Even at Sports Show: But Seal's Still Star," *Detroit Free Press*, March 16, 1952, 31.

24. "Electric Shock Moves Show Seal to Strange Antics," *St. Louis Post-Dispatch*, April 29, 1952, 11.

25. George A. Hamid and George A. Hamid, Jr., *The Acrobat* (Margate, NJ: ComteQ, 2004), 196.

26. "Two more vaudeville acts for grandstand," *Ledger-Post* (Saskatchewan, Canada), February 2, 1952, 23.

27. "Seal Draws Much Attention as Big Grandstand Feature: Animal Has High Degree of Intelligence Declares Owner," *Brandon Daily Sun*, July 4, 1952.

28. "Sharkey, the Seal, Eats 20 Pounds Fish Daily," *Edmonton Journal*, July 18, 1952, 15.

29. "Mayor Grant meets Sharkey, exhibition platform star: Trained seal flips pun as celebrities meet," *Ledger-Post* (Saskatchewan, Canada), July 26, 1952, 3.

30. *Ledger-Post* (Saskatchewan, Canada), July 26, 1952, 12.

31. "Seal Sharkey One of Best in Show Biz," *Argus-Ledger* (Sioux Falls, SD), August 15, 1952, 28.

32. "Massac Fair Opens Season," *Carbondale Southern Illinoisan*, June 30, 1953. The article referenced Sharkey and Berle as having performed at the previous year's fair.

33. Ben Reeves, "'Aqua Thrills' Packs 'Em in at Free Grandstand Show," *Courier-Journal* (Louisville, KY), September 11, 1952, 11.

34. Bob Francis, "Palace Theater, New York," *Billboard*, October 11, 1952, 17.

35. Kahn, "Music Hall, N.Y." *Variety*, November 19, 1952, 55.

Notes to Chapter 14

1. William Shilling, "Sportsmen's Shows: Surefire Box Office in Big, Little Towns," *Billboard*, August 9, 1952, 48.

2. Shilling, 48.

3. Shilling, 48.

4. The April 5, 1953, *Des Moines Register* reported that "Sandy the Seal is performing for his master, Lew Bohan . . . they will be in Washington, D.C. where they are scheduled to perform . . . for President Eisenhower."

5. "Palace N.Y.," *Variety*, September 23, 1953, 53; Steve Schieckel, "Chicago, Chicago," *Billboard*, October 10, 1953, 12; *Popular Science*, "How to Train a Seal," July 1953, 56–59.

6. *The Great Northern Goat*, volumes 22–24, (St. Paul, MI: Great Northern Railway).

7. *The Story of America's Finest Springtime Exhibition*, retrieved from *YouTube*, "Vintage Toronto Sportsmen's Show."

8. My father heard this phrase during his childhood, regularly spoken by his father (Lew Bohan) and Billy Roe. In recalling his childhood, my father also informed me, multiple times, unprompted, that "Billy was a real good guy."

9. "Sharkey's Price Up," *Minneapolis Star-Tribune*, April 1, 1949, 21.

10. Harold Ensley, *Winds of Chance* (Leawood, KS: Leathers, 2002), 11. All the dialogue associated with the Kansas City sports show story was taken verbatim from this source.

11. Lew often found himself on the same bill with Blackie. My father related to me the "crows" quote.

12. Helen Burrowes, "Sharkey the Seal Still the Old Master," *Milwaukee Sentinel*, April 1, 1955, 12.

13. Burrowes, 12.

14. Burrowes, 12.

15. Burrowes, 12.

16. Interview with my uncle, Michael Reilly.

17. "Hamid Claims Free Stands Are Road to Fair Deterioration," *Billboard*, October 29, 1955, 59.

18. "'I'm No Ringer,' Barks Sharkey," *Dayton Daily News*, January 29, 1956, 68.

19. "I'm No Ringer," *Dayton Daily News*.

20. "Mark Huling Gone," *Fitchburg Sentinel* (MA), November 6, 1951, 8.

21. Dennis P. Mannix, *Drifter* (New York: Reader's Digest Press, 1974), 178.

22. Bill Ladd, "Bill Ladd's Almanac." *Courier Journal* (Louisville, KY), April 26, 1956, 11.

23. When my father told me about going to Kennywood with his father (Lew Bohan) and Sandy, I told him my research indicated that Sharkey was the only seal ever advertised there. My father then educated me on the practice of double bookings. He had no recollection of any raised eyebrows that year with regard to Sandy secretly posing as Sharkey, though it is interesting what he *did* remember (some sixty years later) about his first big Seal College road trip as a fifteen-year-old. It had nothing to do with seals. Rather, it was the double wooden roller coasters and a park promo, allowing free use of AT&T's latest technology: direct-dial, long-distance calls without the need of a telephone operator. He called his grandmother in Schenectady.

24. The telegram story is another one from my father. During the summer of 1956, he worked at Steel Pier with his father and some of the other acts.

25. Tony King, "Not a Spot of Boredom for 9,000 at Big Show," *Ottawa Citizen*, August 21, 1956, 3.

26. Seal College likely pulled a secret double-swap. While Sandy was advertised at the Memphis Mid-South Fair, Sharkey was advertised at George Hamid's New Jersey State Fair with other Steel Pier acts. But there is every reason to suspect it was actually Sandy in Jersey given that he and Lew had just worked the summer at Steel Pier. That would put Sharkey in Memphis, which is very likely given that Billy, not Lew, was the presenter, further made interesting by a 1956 photo in the book *The Mid-South Fair: Celebrating 150 Years* that shows Billy and a seal. The photo was signed, "With best wishes, Billy Roe & Sandy."

27. A March 25, 1957, article in the *Milwaukee Sentinel* stated that Sandy's act included imitating Elvis Presley.

28. "Opening for Seal," *Pittsburgh-Post Gazette*, December 19, 1956, 31.

29. George Grim, "I Like It Here," *Minneapolis Star*, April 4, 1958, 13.

30. Grim, 13.

31. Joe Boyd, "Visiting Bowlers Throng Sports, Vacation Show," *Milwaukee Sentinel*, March 25, 1957, 15.

32. "Aquacircus: Union Talks Fail; Hamid Cancels Show," *Billboard*, July 8, 1957, 59. Hamid retried *Aquacircus* the next year and succeeded.

33. "Revue Fades: Hamid Labels TV Names as Antidote," *Billboard*, October 28, 1957, 74.

34. John Mason Brown, "Sharkey and Jack Haley in 'Higher and Higher,'" *New York Post*, April 5, 1940.

35. An April 16, 1958, listing in the *San Bernardino Sun* stated: "Capt. Kangaroo (Children)—Sandy the Seal brings his usual collection of exciting tricks to perform on today's show."

36. George Grim, "I Like It Here," *Minneapolis Star* April 4, 1958, 13.

Notes to Chapter 15

1. "Sharkey the Seal Dies; Thrilled Many World Over, *Daily Freeman*, May 15, 1958, 15; "Sharkey the Seal Dies in Kingston of Old Age," *Poughkeepsie Journal* (AP), May 15, 1958, 28; "Famous Seal Dies," *Republican and Herald* (Pottsville, PA), (UP), May 15, 1958, 3.

2. Real estate ad, *Daily Freeman*, April 17, 1959, 15.

3. Ann Zurosky, "Humor with a Perfect Pitch," *Pittsburgh Press*, June 28, 1964.

4. Harry Harris, "Sullivan 'Sits Out' Anniversary Show as 16 Stars Take Over," *Philadelphia Inquirer*, June 25, 1962, 20.

5. Hal Humphrey, "Viewing TV: Paar No Tougher to Follow Than Sharkey, Says Soupy," *Beckley Post-Herald* (WV), June 2, 1962, 17.

6. Judy Klemesrud, "A Gala for Radio City Music Hall's 50th," *New York Times*, January 20, 1982; "'Encore' Celebrates 50 Years of Radio City Music Hall," AP, March 27, 1982.

7. Leonard Lyons, "Revenue Agents and the Mob," *Honolulu Advertiser*, November 18, 1951, 6.

8. "Vaudeville Reviews: Chicago, Chicago," *Billboard*, January 27, 1945.

9. Kitty Carlisle Hart, *Kitty: An Autobiography* (New York: Doubleday, 1988), 95.

10. Glenn Miller, "Patkin's Life No Laughing Matter," *News-Press* (Fort Myers, FL), June 2, 1992, 27.

11. Ryan, J. "And so It Goes for Atlantic City's Steel Pier," June 2007, retrieved from *New Jersey Real-Time News*.

Notes to the Epilogue

1. Mark Huling, *Behind the Scenes*.

2. *New York Herald Tribune*, October 25, 1951.

3. "Remember Sharkey the Seal?" *Brandon Sun* (Manitoba, Canada), March 3, 1958, 32.

Index

References to illustrations appear in italic type

Abbott, Bud, 123–24. *See also* Abbott and Costello
Abbott and Costello, 115–16, 121–28
  Steel Pier, 112, 115–16, 122
  "Who's on First?," 123
  See also *Pardon My Sarong*
Academy of Music (Manhattan movie palace), 137
Adams, Captain C. F., 102, 280n7
Admiral Broadway Revue (TV show), 189–94
African Americans (billed with Huling-trained sea lions, partial list):
  Bates, Peg Leg, 200, 291n17
  Blakey, Art, 145, 285n36
  Fitzgerald, Ella, 145, *146*
  Henderson, Fletcher, 137, 144–45, 285n36
  Ink Spots, 112, 126
  Mills, Florence, 15–16, *17*
  Nicholas Brothers, 117
  Robinson, Bill "Bojangles," 16, 26
  Robinson, Jackie, 248
  Tip, Tap, and Toe, 126–27
  Three Chocolateers, 161
  Vodery, Will, 16
Alexander, Viscount Harold, 183
Allen, Gracie, 26
Allentown, Pennsylvania, 211
All Sealed Up (Paramount film), 119–20
All Sealed Up (Warner Brothers film), *120*, 121, 138
Allyson, June, 60
Alton, Robert, 60, 68, 98
Ambassador Hotel (Los Angeles), *206*
America First movement, 99–100, 118
"America (My Country, 'Tis of Thee)" (song), 18, 53
Andrews Sisters, 116
Apollo Theater, 145
Arthur Godfrey and His Friends (TV show), 200
ASCAP, x, 109–11, 209
Ashokan Reservoir, 227, 295n6
Astor, Vincent, 247
Atkinson, Brooks (*New York Times*), 73

Atlantic City:
  background, 111–12
  during World War II, 128, 136
  following World War II, 173
  Great Atlantic hurricane, 161
  See also Heinz Pier; Million Dollar Pier; Steel Pier
Atwell, Harry, 220
Australia, 8–10, 12, 32, 127

baby boomers, 194, 254, 259
Balanchine, George, 200
Ballard, Lucinda (costume designer), 59
Baltimore Hippodrome, 137, 234
Bargas, Pedro, 155
Barn, The, 172, 183–84, 257–58
Barnum & Bailey, 7, 9, 13, 21
baseball:
  beep baseball, 213
  Branca, Ralph, 212
  Mantle, Mickey, 242
  Patkin, Max, 259
  Robinson, Jackie, 248
  Ruth, Babe, 114, 180
  Thorpe, Jim, 235–36
  Williams, Ted, 212–15, *213*, 235, 242
Bates, Peg Leg, 200, 291n17
Bayes, Nora, 26
Beebe, Lucius, 101
beer, 24–25
  National Beer Day, 25
  "three-two beer," 25
Bells of St. Mary's, The (film), 170
Benny, Jack, 26, 177
Bergman, Ingrid, 170
Berle, Milton:
  Sharkey in autobiography, 188, 260

Texaco Star Theater, 187–89, 195, 209, 223
  TV Hall of Fame, 198
Berlin, Germany, 3, 83, 85, 87, 157
Berlin, Irving, 109, 138
Bertram Mills Circus (UK), 17
Bigelow Show, The (TV show), 209
Big Top (TV show), 230, 247
Billboard (magazine) reviews:
  Charlie, 16
  Sandy, 223
  Sharkey (Chicago), 232, 242, 259
  Sharkey (Loew's State), 137, 162
  Sharkey (nightclub), 137
  Sharkey (Palace), 212, 239
  Sharkey (Radio City), 149, 170
  Sharkey (sports show), 163
  Sharkey (Steel Pier), 136
Billy Rose's Music Hall, 138–144
Blackie the Talking Crow, 246
Blackpool Tower Circus (UK), 8
Blakey, Art, 145, 285n36
Blue, Ben, *120*, 122, 138, 142
Bohan, Lew, *172*
  background, 41
  Bohunicki surname, 41, 171
  Captain Kangaroo, 249
  death, 259
  military service, 130, 169, 171
  quotes, 216, 235–36, 246, 248
  sea lion handler (Jumbo), 171–75, 216
  sea lion handler (Sandy), 223, *230*, 235–36, 249–50, 253, 260
  Steel Pier, 173–75, *174*, 250
Boston:
  Globe, 63–64, 66, 214, 235
  Herald, 67
  Higher and Higher tryouts, 60, 63, 67–68

sports shows, 179, 204, 207, 235
WEEI, 49
Bostwick, Mary (*Indianapolis Star*), 110
Bracken, Eddie, 248
Branca, Ralph, 212
Brandon (Manitoba, Canada), 237
Breese, Lou, 259
Brice, Fanny, 138
Broadcast Music Incorporated (BMI), 109–11, 114, 116
Broadway Brevities (Vitaphone), 121
Brookgreen Gardens, *150*, 151
Brooks, Mel, 189, 192
Brown, Les (and His Band of Renown), 199
Brooklyn:
  Daily Eagle, 62–63, 214
  Dodgers, 212, 248
  Vitagraph Studios, 120
Buck, Frank, 31–32, 46
Buddy (sea lion), 44–46, 54, 122
Buffalo, New York, 2–3, 181
Burns, George, 26

Caesar, Sid, 189–190, 192–93, 198, 228
  TV Hall of fame, 198
Calgary (Alberta, Canada), 238
California sea lion. *See* sea lion
Canada:
  Central Canada Exhibition, 203
  crossing the border, 182
  National Sportsmen's Show, 181, 183, 236
  Western Canada "Class A" circuit, 237–38
  See also specific cities
canoe tilters, 105, 163
Captain Kangaroo (TV show), 249, 254, 260

Carlisle, Kitty, 259
Carroll, Jean, 188
Carter, Jack, 188
Cassidy, Claudia (*Chicago Tribune*), 232
CBS:
  Ed Sullivan Theater, 144
  Jumbo (radio), 56
  Jumbo (television), 216
  Sharkey (radio), 128
  Sharkey (television), 200, 228, 248
Celebrity Program (radio show), 53
Champion, Gower, 190
Chaplin, Charlie, 28
Charlie (sea lion):
  burlesque imitation, 141
  cellist tutor, 14–15
  dancing, 13–16, 49, 52, 86, 142
  death, 30
  how he got his name, 13
  motion pictures, 119–21, 138
  nightclub act, 138–42, 144
  private home, 26–27
  radio, 49–52
  singing, 13–16, 18, 20, 26
  statue, 149–51, *150*
  swim races, 204–7
Charlie (reviews):
  Motion Picture Daily, 121
  New Yorker, 144, 205, 207
  Variety, 13, 26, 142
Chicago:
  Civic Center, 234
  Coliseum, 7–8, 162
  Palace Theater, 26
  sports shows, 207–9, 162–63
  Stadium, 131
  Sun Times, 231
  Theater, 134, 144, 231–32, *242*, 259
  Tribune, 14, 156, 175, 232
  World's Fair, 144

Chrysler Corporation, 217
Circus Busch, 3
circuses:
  Barnum & Bailey, 7, 9, 13, 21
  Bertram Mills, 17
  Blackpool Tower, 8
  Cole Brothers, 31
  Circus Busch, 3
  Forepaugh & Sells Brothers, 7
  Hamid-Morton, 210
  Ringling Brothers (partial list), 7–8, 12
  Russell Brothers, 46, 54
  Sells-Floto, 21
  Shriners, 161
  Wirth Brothers, 8–9
Cleveland Stadium, 177
Clooney, Rosemary, 173
cloud-seeding, 226–27
Coca, Imogene, 192–93, *194*
Colbert, Claudette, 207
Cole Brothers Circus, 31
Colgate Comedy Hour, The (TV show), 199–200
Costello, Lou:
  blooper (with Sharkey), 126
  movie scenes (with Sharkey), 123–26
  Steel Pier (with Sharkey), 122
  See also Abbott and Costello
Crabbe, Buster, 207
Crosby, Bing, 108, 170
Crumit, Frank, 53
Cugat, Xavier, 117
Curtis, Ann, 204, 207–8, *208*

d'Amboise, Jacques, 200
Danish Royal Opera, 231
Des Moines, Iowa, 175
Dewey, Thomas, 203

dimouts (WWII), 128
Diving Horse, 113, 260
Drifter (children's novel), 249
drive-in theaters, 209
dry act (defined), 104
DuMont (TV network), 187, 189
Durante, Jimmy, 136

Edmonton (Alberta, Canada), 238
Ed Sullivan Show, The (TV show), 194–98, *196*, 243, 245
Ed Sullivan Theater, 144
Eggerth, Marta:
  background, 58, 60–61, 63
  Broadway (with Sharkey), 68–71, 73–76, 78, 94, 97
  dining (with Sharkey), *80*–81
  later career, 94
  photo shoot (with Sharkey), 61–62
  remembering Sharkey, 96
  World's Fair (with Sharkey), 91
Eisenhower, Dwight D., 242
Ellington, Duke, 110–11
Emery, "Big Brother" Bob, 49
Ensley, Harold, 245–26
Erickson, Leif, 122
Erie Canal, 5
Esopus Creek, 8, 43, 183–84, 227, 257, 263

fairs:
  Central Canada Exhibition, 203
  competition from TV, 248, 253
  Great Allentown Fair, 211
  Illinois State Fair, 238
  Kentucky State Fair, 238–39
  Mid-South Fair, 251–52
  New York State Fair, 210
  Provincial Exhibition of Manitoba, 237

South Dakota Sioux Empire Fair, 238
Western Canada "Class A" circuit, 237–38
Woodstock Library Fair, 47–48, 96
See also World's Fairs
Falkenburg, Jinx, 177
Fat Salvage Committee (WWII), 160–61
Fein, Nat, 179–*80*
Fields, Gracie, 28, 154
Fields, W. C., 28
Fish, Hamilton, 155
Fitzgerald, Ella, 145, *146*
fly-fishing, 214, 235, 242
football:
  Grant, Bud, 163
  Thorpe, Jim, 235–36
Ford Festival (TV show), 228
For Me and My Gal (film), 122
Forepaugh & Sells Brothers Circus, 7
Fort Worth, Texas, 168
Foster, Marion (aerialist), 210
Fox, Harry (foxtrot), 52
Fox Movietone News (newsreel), 44–45, 117, 136, 221
Fredericton (New Brunswick, Canada), 203
Freeman, Don (*Corduroy* author), 94, *95*
Fry's Harbor, 34

Garbo, Greta, 225
Gargantua (the gorilla), 203–4
Garland, Judy, 69, 122, 228, 233–34, 237
Garry Moore Show, The (TV show), 228, 245
Gelbart, Larry, 199

Gibbs, Wolcott (*New Yorker*), 78
Gobel, George, 234–35, 258
"God Save the Queen" (UK national anthem), 18, 20
Godfrey, Arthur, 200, 228. See also *Arthur Godfrey and His Friends*
Goebbels, Joseph, 85–86, 165
Gold Rush Revue (grandstand show), 210–11
Goodman, Al (conductor), 59, 68
Goodman, Benny, 138, 143–45, 173, 260
Gould, Jack (*New York Times*), 201
Grable, Betty, 101, 117
Grand Central Palace, 162
Grand Island, NY, 181–82, 204, 229
  Maple Grove Cemetery, 182, 204, 229
Grandstand Follies of 1950 (grandstand show), 217
Grant, Bud, 163
Grauman, Sid, 28
Grauman's Chinese Theater, 28
Gray, Gilda, 52
Great Allentown Fair, 211
Great Atlantic hurricane, 161–62
Great Depression, 29, 144
Great Lakes Exposition, 29
Great Northern Railway, 243
Grim, George (*Minneapolis Star*), 255

Haley, Jack:
  background, 58–59
  Broadway (with Sharkey), 60–61, 63, 68–75, 77–78
  dining (with Sharkey), 79–81, *79*, *80*, *82*
  World's Fair (with Sharkey), 91, *92*
Haley, Jack, Jr., 91

Index | 305

Hamid, George, Sr.:
  background, 210
  Gold Rush Revue, 210–11
  Grandstand Follies of 1950, 217
  grandstand shows, 210–11, 217, 248, 250, 253
  Steel Pier, 111–12, 210
Hamid-Morton Circus, 210
Hammerstein, Arthur, 138
Hammerstein, Oscar, II, 57, 138
Hammond, John, 144
Hampton, Lionel, 144–45
Hanyan the Hypnotist, 30–31
Harlem Renaissance, 15
Harper's Bazaar, 61–63
Hart, Lorenz, 48, 58–59, 68. *See also* Rodgers and Hart
Hartford, Connecticut, 129
Hartline, Mary, 234
Harvard University, 64
  Crimson, 66–67
  Lampoon club, 65, 67
Hearst, William Randolph, Jr., 247
Heinz Pier (Atlantic City), 161
Henderson, Fletcher, 137, 144–45, 285n36
Herlihy, Ed, 174
Higher and Higher (film), 98
  Broadway close, 96
  Broadway re-open, 97
  Higher and Higher (stage production, in chronological order):
  opening night, Broadway, 68–76
  preparation, 59–60, 62, 64
  reviews, 77–78, 81, 87, 94, 97
  tryouts (New Haven), 60
  tryouts (Boston), 60, 63, 67–68
Hippodrome:
  Baltimore, 137, 224
  New York, 15–16, 51
  Sydney, 9–10
Hirschfeld, Al, 81, *82*
Hitler, Adolph, 100, 134–36, 149, 155, 165
Holiday, Billie, 111
Hooper ratings, 189, 195
Hope, Bob, 156, 199–200, 228
Houdini, Harry, 3
Howell, Wallace ("The Rainmaker"), 226
Hudson River, 204–5
Hughes, Alice (journalist), 78, 96
Hughes, Carl, 252
Hughes, Elinor (*Boston Herald*), 67
Huling, Frank:
  Australian tour, 8–*10*, *11*
  background, 3
  death, 29
  Forepaugh & Sells Brothers Circus, 7
  Germany during World War I, 83
  military training of sea lions, 84–85
  musical training of sea lions, 107
  Ringling Brothers Circus, 7–8, 12
  training philosophy, 6
Huling, Lillian, 80, 159, 204
Huling, Marian, 218, 229–30, 244–45, 254
Huling, Marjorie. *See* Marjorie Rielly
Huling, Mark, *5*, *45*, *104*, *108*, *176*, *261*
  background, 1, 3
  butter maker, 181, 229
  Ed Sullivan Show, 194–98, *196*
  death, *229*
  Grand Island, NY, 181–82, 204, 229
  Herald Tribune tribute, 263–64
  London, 18–*19*

miniature golf course owner, 23–24
nightclub owner, 25, 29–30
Palace Theater, 211–12
Radio City Music Hall, 147–49
Ringling Brothers, 7–8, 12, 16–18, 20, 22, 40, 178, 219
sea lion breeding, 219–21, 294n43
Sells-Floto Circus, 21
Steel Pier, 111–13
training philosophy, 39–42, 44, 212
Huling, Ray:
background, 3
death, 209
Nazi Germany, 85–87, *86*
nightclub act, 139–41, 144
radio, 49–52, *50*
training philosophy, *27*
Venezuelan tour, 3–4
Huling Estate, 229–30
Huling's Barn, 25, 29–30, 172
Hurlbut, Gladys, 48, 56–58, 60, 68, 79, 96

Illinois State Fair, 238
I'm No Angel (film), 28
Infantile Paralysis. *See* polio
Ink Spots, The, 112, 126
In St. Louis This Week (radio show), 106
International News Service, 147
International Sports and Outdoor Exposition, 162, 207
interventionists/isolationists, 99–100, 118
Iowa, 175

Jane Eyre (film),149
Janis, Elsie, 155
"Jeanie with the Light Brown Hair" (song), 209

Jennier, Walter, 40–41, 44–45, 54, 56, 100, 122, 130
Jessel, George, 53, 138
Jimmy Fund, 234
Joy, Leatrice, 26
Jumbo (sea lion):
graduation from Seal College, 44
imitations, 174
interviewed by the *LA Times*, 216
Madison Square Garden, 177
newsreels, 173–74
radio, 49, 52–53, 56
retires, 229–30
Steel Pier, 167, 173–75, *174*, 210
swim races, 207–8
television, 216
Woodstock Library Fair, 47
world's largest trained seal, 47, 174

Kaese, Harold (*Boston Globe*), 235
Kahler, Nick, 245–46
Kansas City, Missouri, 111, 245–46, 248
Kaye, Sammy, 114, 136
Keeshan, Bob. See *Captain Kangaroo*
Keith, B. F., 12, 143, 251
Keith theater circuit, 12, 50, 157
Kelly, Gene, 98, 122
Kennedy, John F., 67
Kennywood, 249, 252
Kenton, Erle, 127
Kentucky State Fair, 238–39
Kiefer, Adolph, 204, 207–9, *208*, 260
Victory Backstroke, 204
Kiepura, Jan, 94
Kilgallen, Dorothy, 81, 87, 101
kinescope (defined), 209
King, Alan, 234
King, Frances Rockefeller, 157

Kingston, NY (references by decade):
 1910s, 8
 1920s, 20–22
 1930s, 23–24, 27, 29, 43–44, 56
 1940s (WWII), 129, 131, 159
 1940s (post WWII), 183–84, 209, 212
 1950s, 216, 218, 227–29, 255
 1960s, 257
Kingston, NY (selected topics):
 background, 8, 43
 Barn, The, 172, 183–84, 257–58
 bootlegging, 24
 Esopus Creek, 8, 43, 183-84, 227, 257, 263
 fire of 1929, 21–22
 flood of 1951, 227–28
 Huling's Barn, 25, 29–30, 172
 Sunset Drive-In Theater, 209
Korean War, 199, 242
Kreisler, Fritz, 154, 156

La Guardia, Fiorello, 91
Lambchops (short film), 26
Laurie, Joe, Jr., 52
Leonidoff, Leon, 147, 149, 170, 177, 239
"Liberty Bell, The" (march), 18
Life (magazine), 47, 208
Loew's State Theater, 133, 137, 195
Logan, Joshua, 48, 58–60, 67, 69–70, 76
log rollers, 105–6, 163
London Palladium, 28
Lorre, Peter, 53
Los Angeles, California:
 Ambassador Hotel, 206
 Orpheum Theater, 12, 26, 29
 Times, 206, 216

magazine articles:
 Life, 47, 208
 New Yorker, 78, 144, 205, 207
 Parade, 159
 Popular Mechanics, 56
 Popular Science, 47, 242
 Reader's Digest, 162
 Scribner's Commentator, 99–100, 118
 See also *Billboard*; *Variety*
Madison Square Garden, 217
 fashion fair, 177
 National Sportsmen's Show, 162, 179
 Ringling Brothers, 12, 17, 20, 49, 171
Magic Mirror Televisions, 189–91, 194
Mahoney, Jerry, 209
Major (sea lion), 17, 21, 294n45
Mannix, Daniel, 249
Mantle, Burns (*Daily News*), 68–69
Mantle, Mickey, 242
Marine Mammal Protection Act, 32
Marx, Harpo, 5, 200
McCormick, Robert (*Chicago Tribune*), 156
McGlynn, Stoney (*Milwaukee Sentinel*), 163
McGuire, Captain George, 32–36, *33*, 38, 294n49
McMahon, Ed, 230
McNamee, Graham, 114
Melbourne, Australia, 9
Melchior, Lauritz, 231–34, *233*
Merrill, Robert, 149, 155, 258–59
Metropolitan Opera, 149, 231
Miami, 129–30, 204
Mid-South Fair, 251–52

Mielziner, Jo (set designer), 59
Million Dollar Pier (Atlantic City), 8
Mills, Bertram, 18
Mills, Florence, 15–16, *17*
Milwaukee, WI, 163, 215, 226, 235–36, 246–47, 252
  Sentinel, 163, 165, 215, 225–26
miniature golf craze, 23–24
Minneapolis, MN, 111, 163, 213, 245
Miss America Pageant, 117, 175
Mitchell, Thomas, 200
Mix, Tom, 21
Montez, Jack, 113
Monty (baby sea lion), 219–21, *222*
Moore, Garry, 228, 246
Motion Picture Daily (daily magazine), 121
movie palaces:
  decline, 243
  description, 133
  during World War II, 133
  record weekly attendance, 173
movie palaces (venues):
  Academy of Music (Manhattan), 137
  Capitol Theater (DC), 133
  Chicago Theater, 134, 144, 231–32, *242*, 259
  Grauman's Chinese Theater, 28
  Loew's State Theater, 133, 137, 195
  Radio City Music Hall, 147–51, 177, 239, 258–59, 266
  Roxy (Manhattan), 28, 117, 177
movie palaces (movie premieres):
  Bells of St. Mary's, The, 170
  I'm No Angel, 28
  Jane Eyre, 149
  Yank in the RAF, A, 117

Munkácsi, Martin, 62
Murray, Ken, 228

Narragansett Park (Rhode Island), 161
National Sportsmen's Show (Manhattan), 162, 179
Native Americans, 182, 235–36, 243
Nazi Germany, 85–87, *86*, 135, 169, 171
NBC:
  censorship of Sharkey, 188–89
  formation of, 49
  International Theater, 189
  Orchestra, 149, 155
  radio, 49–52, 144
  television, 157, 187, 189, 199, 209, 223, 239, 254, 258, 260
Neptune (sea lion, a.k.a. Big Nep, 1920s), 16, 219, 293n36, 294n45
Neptune (sea lion, 1940s), 44, 54–55
New England Sportsmen's and Boat Show, 214
New Orleans, Louisiana, 107–10
New Paltz, New York, 23–24
Newsweek (magazine), 78
News of the Week (newsreel), 80
newsreels:
  Huling seals, 80, 221
  Jumbo, 173–74
  Seal College, 44–45
  Sharkey, 80, 122, 136
  Sharkey and Teddy, 114
New Haven, Connecticut, 60–62
New York:
  Aquarium, 29–30
  Board of Water Supply, 226–27
  Daily Mirror, 68, 78
  Daily News, 52, 68–69, 93–94, 162, 195, 227, 248

New York
  New Yorker, 78, 144, 205, 207
  Herald Tribune, 48, 68, 70, 74, 78, 81, 94, 179, 263–64
  Metropolitan Opera, 149, 231
  Post, 68, 70, 77–78, 81, 121–22
  State Fair, 210
  Supreme Court, 227
  Times, 15, 66, 68, 73, 97, 109, 174, 192, 201, 227, 229, 258
  World's Fair, 31–32, 46–47, 54, 91, 253
  World-Telegram, 68, 78
  Yankees, 147
New Zealand, 9
Niagara River, 2, 181–82
Nicholas Brothers, The, 117
Nielson, Arthur (Nielson ratings), 189
North Carolina, 162, 254

Ocean Beach Park, 247
Odiva the Samoan Nymph, 102
Office of Defense Transportation, 162
Olive and George, 142
One Yuletide Square (TV show), 200–201
opera, 14–15, 73, 94, 138, 149, 222, 230–34, 236
Orpheum Theater circuit, 12
Ottawa (Ontario, Canada), 181–83, 203, 250

Paar, Jack, 258
Palace Theater (Chicago), 26
Palace Theater (New York):
  Charlie, 13
  death of vaudeville, 27–28, 253
  revival of vaudeville, 211, 228
  Sandy, 223

Sharkey, 211–12, 239, 242–43
  significance, 13
Palisades Amusement Park, 227
Parade (magazine), 159
Paradise Theater (Detroit), 145
Paramount Pictures, 119, 121, 135, 173–74, 207
Pardon My Sarong (film):
  background, 122–23
  Charley the Seal, 282n10
  music features, 126–27
  reviews, 127–28
  Sharkey (blooper), 126
  Sharkey (movie scenes), 123–26
Parsons, Louella, 28
Pastor, Tony (bandleader), 173
Patkin, Max, 259
Paul Winchell Show, The (TV show), 254
Pearl Harbor, 117–18, 121, 155, 171
Philadelphia:
  Big Top, 230, 247
  World's Fair, 16
  Phillies, 203
photographers:
  Atwell, Harry, 220
  Fein, Nat, 179–80
  Munkácsi, Martin, 62
  Sileo, Jimmy, 147–49
polio, 154
Popular Mechanics (magazine), 56
Popular Science (magazine), 47, 242
Porter, Cole, 94
Presley, Elvis, 252
Previn, Charles, 126
Prohibition, 24–25, 138–39
Providence, Rhode Island, 137
Provincial Exhibition of Manitoba, 237

Punch and Judy, 8

radio:
  emergence, 49–52
  licensing dispute (ASCAP), x, 109–11
radio (sea lion performances):
  Charlie, 49–52
  Jumbo, 49, 52–53, 56
  Sharkey, 93, 106, 108–11, 128, 158, 165, 260
radio (personalities):
  Emery, "Big Brother" Bob, 49
  McNamee, Graham, 114
radio (stations):
  WABC (later WJZ), 49, 93
  WEAF (later WNBC), 51–52
  WEEI, 49
Radio City, 53
Radio City Music Hall, 147–51, 177, 239, 258–59, 266
  Christmas Spectacular, 169–70
Radio Corporation of America (RCA), 49–50, 52
"Rainmaker, The" (moniker), 226. *See* Howell, Wallace
Ramos, Larry, 200
Rapée, Ernö, 147, 149
Reader's Digest (magazine) 162
Red Cross, 131, 161, 167–68
Reeve, Ted, 214
Regina (Saskatchewan, Canada), 238
Reilly, Marjorie (Mark Huling's daughter), 22, 41, 80, 131, 260
Riggs, Bobby, 177–78
Ringling, Al, 8
Ringling, Charles, 13
Ringling, John, 20–21
Ringling Brothers, 27, 31–32, 178, 210
  1910s, 7–8, 12–13

1920s, 13, 16–18, 20–22, 40, 49, 219
1940s, 171, 203
Ringling Brothers and Barnum & Bailey Circus, 13
RKO (Radio-Keith-Orpheum), 50
Radio-Keith-Orpheum Hour, 50–51
RKO Pictures, 170
Robinson, Bill "Bojangles," 16, 26
Robinson, Jackie, 248
Rockefeller Center, 53, 89–90, 97, 254
  Prometheus statue, 90
Rockettes, 117, 147, 149, 170, 177
Rodgers, Richard, 58–59, 60, 63, 67, 69
  Irrefutable Rule, 97
Rodgers and Hart, 48, 56–58, 60, 63–64, 69, 71, 77, 97–98
Rodgers and Hart (*Higher and Higher* songs)
  "Disgustingly Rich," 69, 98
  "Ev'ry Sunday Afternoon," 75
  "I'm Afraid," 64, 74–75
  "It Never Entered My Mind," 97–98
  "Life! Liberty!," 63
Roe, Billy, *244*, 251
  background, 40
  dog act, 257
  death, 259
  Mark Huling's assistant, 178–80
  military service, 130, 169
  quotes, 182, 218, 237–38, 246–47, 249
  seal trainer beginnings, 40–41
  TV skit with Sharkey, 189–91
Roosevelt, Franklin D., 24–25, 121, 153–157, 165

Roosevelt, Mrs. Theodore, Jr., 53
Rose, Billy, 137–39, 142–44
Rosendale, New York, 96
Ross, Johnny (beep baseball), 213
Ross, Shirley:
    background, 58–61
    Broadway (with Sharkey), 68, 71, 74–75, 78, 88, 92, 97
    dining (with Sharkey), *80*–81
    photo shoots (with Sharkey), 62, 88–89, *89*
    World's Fair (with Sharkey), 91
Rothafel, Samuel "Roxy," 117
Roxyettes, 117, 211
Roxy Theater (New York), 28, 117, 177
Royal, John (NBC), 157
Russell Brothers Circus, 46, 54
Ruth, Babe, 114, 180

Saks Fifth Avenue, 96
Sales, Soupy, 258
Sandy (sea lion):
    Big Top, 230
    Captain Kangaroo, 249–50, 254
    comparisons to Sharkey, 218, 221–23, 226, 235–36, 246–47
    imitations, 252
    personality, 246–47
    press release, 222
    standing in for Sharkey, 248–49, 254, 298nn23 and 26
    Steel Pier, 250
Santa Barbara, California, 32, 34, 36
    Stearns Wharf, 36
Santa Cruz, California, 34
Sarasota, Florida, 20
Sardi's restaurant, *79, 80*, 81, 92
Saskatoon (Saskatchewan, Canada), 238

Sayrs, Hank (*Milwaukee Sentinel*), 215, 235–36
Scala Theater (Berlin, Germany), *85*–*86*
Schenectady, New York, 41, 257, 298n23
Scribner's Commentator (magazine), 99–100, 118
seal (versus a sea lion), ix, 3
Seal College:
    agent (*see* Shilling, Bill)
    business model, 46–47, 254
    decline, 254
    description, 42–43
    double bookings, 248–49
    enrollment size, 130
    flood, 227–28
    free shows, 44, 183–84, 250
    graduation ceremony, 43–46
    grand opening, 42–43
    post–Mark Huling era, 229–30, 239, 244–45, 254, 257–58
    vehicles, 122, *131*, 159, 175, 181–83, 217
sea lion:
    average speed, 84, 114
    breeding in captivity, 219, 294n43
    eyesight deterioration, 250
    life expectancy, 34, 230, 250
    military training, 84–85
    trapping, 34–36
    versus a seal, ix, 3
sea lion (interviews with):
    concept, 215
    Jumbo, 216
    Sandy, 235–36, 248, 253
    Sharkey, 215, 225–26, 238
sea lion (trainers):
    see Adams, Captain C. F.
    see Bohan, Lew

  see Huling, Frank
  see Huling, Mark
  see Huling, Ray
  see Jennier, Walter
  see Roe, Billy
  see Tiebors
  see Webb, Captain Thomas
  see Woodward, Joseph
sea lion (training and husbandry):
  balancing a ball, 39–40
  clapping, 40
  conversing with, 42, 113
  daily routine, 42, 93, 157
  dental care, 93, 252
  diet, 36–37, 220
  eye care, 250
  hurdling, 103–4
  jealousy, 54
  kindness, 6, 41, 44
  modernizing an old routine, 252
  musical instrument, 107–8
  retrieving, 103
  rewards, 41
  sea lion showmanship, 212
  singing, 14–15
  smoking, 54, 148–49
  taming, 37
Sealtest Dan the Muscle Man, 230
Sells-Floto Circus, 21
Sennett, Mack, 127
Sharkey, *176*, *261*
  autograph, 91
  balancing a heavy object, 184
  Broadway, 60–61, 63, 68–78, 94, 97
  censorship on television, 188–89
  death, 255
  graduation from Seal College, 44–45
  Hollywood, 121–26
  how he got his name, 38
  hurdling, 103–4, *104*, 111, 113–14, 210
  kidnapping, 64–67
  musician, 107–10, *108*, 128, 145, 149, 191, 211, 231–32
  painting of, 151
  poems about, 110, 214
  Steel Pier, 111–17, 135–37, 161
  swim races, 204, 207–8
  war bonds, 129, 158, 167–68, *169*
  World's Fair, 91–92
Sharkey (imitations):
  B-29 bomber, 134, 198, 211
  farting, 93
  Hitler, 134–36, 149, 155
  Leo the MGM Lion, 101, 159, 198
  nagging wife, 101–2
  politician, 198, 211, 247
  Tojo, Hideki, 134, 136, 149, 155
Sharkey (photo shoots):
  Broadway, 88–*89*
  Chrysler Corporation, 217
  Haley, Jack, 91–*92*
  Harper's Bazaar, 61–62
  Melchior, Lauritz, 232–33, *233*
  Rockefeller Center, *90*
  Williams, Ted, *213*–214
  Zaharias, Babe Didrikson, 179–*80*
Sharkey (TV appearances, partial list):
  Admiral Broadway Revue, 189–91, *194*
  Arthur Godfrey and His Friends, 200
  Bigelow Show, The, 209
  Big Top, 230, 247
  Colgate Comedy Hour, The, 199–200
  Ed Sullivan Show, The, 194–98, *196*
  Ford Festival, 228
  Garry Moore Show, The, 228, 245
  One Yuletide Square, 200–201

Sharkey (TV appearances, partial list) *(continued)*
   Paul Winchell Show, The, 254
   Steve Allen Show, The, 229
   Super Circus, 234, 237, 248
   Texaco Star Theater, 187–89
   Toast of the Town. See *Ed Sullivan Show*
   Westinghouse Studio One, 248
Sharkey, Jack, 242
Sheridan, Ann, 67
Shilling, Bill (Sharkey's agent):
   background, 105–6, 131
   Billboard interview, 241
   death, 250
   press release (Sandy), 222
Shriners, 56, 161
Shubert Theaters, 60
Sileo, Jimmy, 147–49
Sinatra, Frank, 98, 260
Smith, Kate, 109
Smith and Dale, 26
South Dakota Sioux Empire Fair, 238
South Pacific (Broadway show), 76
sportsmen's shows (a.k.a. sports shows):
   Boston, 179, 204, 207, 235
   Chicago, 162–63, 207–9
   Cincinnati, 248
   description, 105–6
   Detroit, 179, 236
   Indianapolis, 172
   Kansas City, 245, 248
   Louisville, 172
   Milwaukee, 163, 226, 235, 246
   Minneapolis, 111, 163, 245
   New Orleans, 107–8
   New York City, 162, 179, 236
   Omaha, 172
   Ottawa, 181–83

Philadelphia, 172
Seattle, 243
St. Louis, 106
Toronto, 181–82, 243
SS *Bremen*, 86–87
SS *Normandie*, 28
Stark, Mabel, 18
St. Armand's Key, 20
"Star-Spangled Banner, The" (national anthem), 18
Stearns Wharf, 36
Steel Pier (Atlantic City):
   description, 112
   Marine Ballroom, 112, 115–16, 173
   Ocean Stadium, 112–13
   Water Circus, 113
Steel Pier (seasons):
   1941 (Sharkey and Teddy), 111–17
   1943 (Sharkey), 135–37
   1944 (Sharkey), 161
   1945 (Jumbo), 167
   1946 (Jumbo), 173–75
   1949 (Sharkey and Jumbo), 210
   1956 (Sandy), 250
Steve Allen Show, The (TV show), 229
St. John, Al, 199–20
St. Regis (hotel), 247
Sullivan, Ed:
   movie palace impresario, 133–34, 137, 161–62, 195
   newspaper columnist, 162, 195
   TV personality, 194–96, 198, 211–12, 228, 243, 245–47, 252, 258
   Theater, 144
Super Circus (TV show), 234, 237, 248
swimmers:
   Crabbe, Buster, 207
   Curtis, Ann, 204, 207–8, *208*
   Kiefer, Adolph, 204, 207–9, *208*, 260

Sydney, Australia, 9–10

Tasmania, 9
Teddy (sea lion)
   Sharkey II, 87–88
   Steel Pier, 111, 113–14
   retires, 131
   understudy/foil for Sharkey, 81, 106
Teetsel, Bob, 184
television:
   first commercial broadcast, 46
   first commercial broadcast (color), 228
   Hall of Fame, 198
   impact on live entertainment, 187, 248, 253–54
   rise in popularity, 187–88
Temple, Shirley, 121
tennis, 177–78
Texaco Star Theater (TV show), 187–89, 195, 209, 223
Thirer, Irene (*New York Post*), 121–22
Thorpe, Jim, 235–36
Three Chocolateers, The, 161
Three Stooges, The, 116
Tiebors (sea lion trainers), 31
Tip, Tap, and Toe, 126–27
Toastettes, 195–96
Toast of the Town (TV show). See *Ed Sullivan Show*
Tojo, Hideki, 134, 136, 149, 155
Tonawanda, NY, 3–4, 6, 8, 31, 229
Toronto (Ontario, Canada), 181–82, 243
Truman, Harry, 165

U-boats, 84–85, 128
ukulele craze, 200
United States:
   Army, 128, 130

Air Force, 157
Navy, 128, 154, 156, 161, 204
Supreme Court, 234
Weather Bureau, 227
Universal Newsreel, 114, 173–75
Universal Studios, 121–22, 126–27
USO, 156, 171, 199

Van and Schenck, 52
Varga Girls, 170
Vargas, Alberto, 170
Variety Club, 234–35
Variety (magazine) reviews:
   Charlie, 13, 26, 142
   Major, 17
   Sharkey (Apollo Theater), 145
   Sharkey (Indianapolis), 163
   Sharkey (Palace Theater), 217, 242
   Sharkey (Radio City Music Hall), 149, 171, 177, 239
   Sharkey (Roxy Theater), 117
   Sharkey (television), 188, 201
vaudeville:
   demise (first), 25–28
   demise (second), 248, 251, 253–54, 259
   description, 11, 187
   legacy, 15, 106
   most famous venue, 13
   revival, 133, 187, 211, 228, 234, 237
   two-a-day (defined), 12
   vaudeo (defined), 187
Venezuela, 3–4
Vera-Ellen, 60
Victory Bonds. See *war bonds*
Vitagraph Studios, 120–21
Vitaphone Music Hall (short film), 121
Vodery, Will, 16

Waldoff, Claire, 85–87
Waldorf Astoria, 157
Wallace, Mike, 234
war bonds, 128–29, 158, 167–69, *169*, 171
Warner Brothers, 67, 120–21, 135
Washington, DC, 60, 133, 153–57
Watson Sisters, 130
Webb, Thomas, 3–8, 40, 182
Welles, Orson, 101
West, Mae, 28
Western Canada "Class A" fair circuit, 237–38
Westinghouse Studio One (TV show), 248
West Palm Beach, Florida, 204
wet act (defined), 104
"Where the River Shannon Flows" (song), 108–10, 198, 228, 232
White House Correspondents' Dinner, 154–57
"Why Won't They Let Sharkey on the Radio?" (podcast), x, 260
Wiere Brothers, 177
William Penn Hotel, 117
Williams, Ted, 212–15, *213*, 235, 242
Williams, Wheeler (sculptor), 151
Willie, West, and McGinty, 113
Wilson, Teddy, 144
Wiman, Dwight Deere, 48, 59–60, 63, 78–79, 81, 94
Winchell, Paul, 209, 254
Winchell, Walter, 78, 168

Wirth, May, 9–10, 12
Wirth Brothers Circus, 8–9
Woodstock, New York, 47–48, 96
Woodward, Joseph, 84
World War I, 12, 83–85
World War II:
  begins, 53
  dimouts, 128
  ends, 165, 167
  Fat Salvage Committee, 160–61
  interventionists/isolationists, 99–100, 118
  Keep America Out of War Committee, 100
  movie theater attendance, 133, 173, 243
  Office of Defense Transportation, 162
  phony war, 82, 87
  rationing, 146, 167, 172
World's Fairs:
  1926 Philadelphia, 16
  1934 Chicago, 144
  1937 Great Lakes Exposition, 29
  1939–40 New York, 31–32, 46–47, 54, 91, 253

Yank in the RAF, A (film), 117
Youngman, Henny, 137, 188, 258, 529

Zaharias, Babe Didrikson, 178–80
Zorina, Vera, 48, 56, 58

www.ingramcontent.com/pod-product-compliance
Lightning Source LLC
Chambersburg PA
CBHW031428160426
43195CB00010BB/654